GCSE
ENGLISH

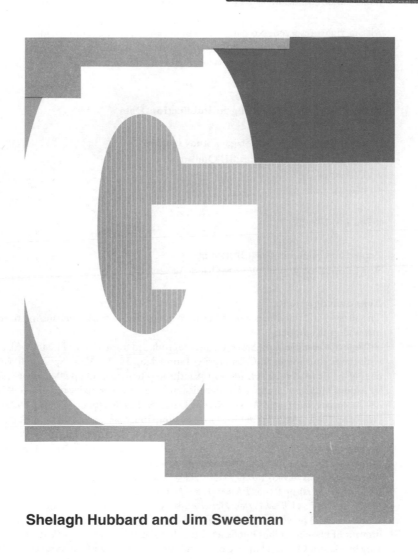

Shelagh Hubbard and Jim Sweetman

BPP Letts Educational Ltd

First published 1993
Reprinted 1994
BPP (Letts Educational) Ltd
Aldine House, Aldine Place, London W12 8AW

Text © Shelagh Hubbard and Jim Sweetman 1993

Typeset by Carla Mans, BPP (Letts Educational) Ltd

Editorial team Rachel Grant, Wayne Davies

Design Watermark Communications Ltd (cover), Carla Mans (text)

Illustrations Barbara Linton, Viv Quillan
Design and illustrations © BPP (Letts Educational Ltd)

British Library Cataloguing in Publication Data
   Hubbard, Shelagh
   English. – (GCSE/Key Stage 4 Study Guides)
   I. Title II. Sweetman, Jim III. Quillan, Viv
   IV. Series
   420.71

ISBN 1 85758 235 7

Printed and bound in Great Britain by
W M Print Ltd, Walsall, West Midlands WS2 9NE

Acknowledgements
The authors and publishers would like to thank the following for permission to reproduce material in this book:
A Cream Cracker Under the Settee, chapter reproduced from *Talking Heads* by Alan Bennett with the permission of BBC Enterprises Limited pp 35–37; MEG Specimen paper, p 45; *Song of the Battery Hen* by Heathhead Winthrop (Heinemann,) pp 50–1; *Brave New World* by Aldous Huxley reproduced by permission of Mrs Laura Huxley (Chatto & Windus) pp 68–70; *Second from Last in the Sack Race* by David Nobbs (Methuen London, 1983) © David Nobbs pp 70–2; *The Fifth Child* by Doris Lessing (Jonathan Cape, 1988) pp 72–3; *Girl* from *At the Bottom of the River* by Jamaica Kincaid (First Aventura Edition, 1985) pp 73–4; *Runaway Nurse* (Mills and Boon) pp 81–4; *Lily and Colin* by Elisabeth Bond (Hodder & Stoughton Limited, 1989) pp 87–88; *Lark Rise to Candleford* by Flora Thompson (Oxford University Press, 1945) pp 89–91; *A Ragged Schooling* by Robert Roberts (Manchester University Press) pp 91–3; *I Know Why the Caged Bird Sings* by Maya Angelou (Virago, 1984) pp 94–5; *A Traveller on Horseback* by Christina Dodwell (Hodder & Stoughton Limited, 1987) pp 96–7; *Arabia Through the Looking Glass* by Jonathan Raban (Collins, an imprint of Harper Collins Publishers Ltd, 1979) pp 97–8; *My Sister Betty* from *Song of the City* by Gareth Owen (Harper Collins Publishers); *Incendiary* from *New & Collected Poems* (Robson Books Ltd) by Vernon Scannell printed by permission of Vernon Scannell p 107; *The Choosing* by Liz Lochhead from *Dreaming Frankenstein and Other Poems* (Polygon) pp 111–12; 'A-Plant "puts children at risk" – report' from *Lancashire Evening Post* (18 November, 1991) p 117; 'Safe in our hands' from *Lancashire Evening Post* (19 November, 1991) p 118; 'A-plant fails test' from *Lancashire Evening Post* (20 November, 1991) p 118; 'Protecting the Public' from *Nuclear Waste, what's to be done about it?* (British Nuclear Fuels plc, 1991) p 121; extract from National Radiation Protection Board poster *Radiation Protection At-a-Glance*, 1989, pp 122–4; extract from *Physics Matters* by Nick England (Hodder & Stoughton Limited, 1989) pp 125–6; MEG English – Syllabus B, Paper 1, 9 November 1989, pp 136–8; MEG English, Paper 1: Literary and Media Texts – Reading and Writing (specimen paper) pp 165–7; MEG English, Paper 2: Reading and Writing Literature (specimen paper) pp 171–6.

Contents

Contents

Exam Boards and Addresses

MEG Midland Examining Group

1 Hills Road
Cambridge
CB1 2EU

Tel: 0223 61111

NEAB Northern Examinations and Assessment Board

Devas Street
Manchester
M15 6EX

Tel: 061 953 1180

NISEAC Northern Ireland Schools Examinations and Assessment Council

Beechill House
42 Beechill Road
Belfast
BT8 4RS

Tel: 0232 704666

SEB Scottish Examination Board

Ironmills Road
Dalkeith
Midlothian
EH22 1LE

Tel: 031 663 6601

SEG Southern Examining Group

Stag Hill House
Guildford
GU2 5XJ

Tel: 0483 506506

ULEAC University of London Examinations and Assessment Council

Stewart House
32 Russell Square
London
WC1B 5DN

Tel: 071 331 4000

WJEC Welsh Joint Education Committee

245 Western Avenue
Cardiff
CF5 2YX

Tel: 0222 561231

Chapter 1
About this book

Starting out

This book is full of information, exercises and advice designed to help you achieve the best results from your GCSE English and GCSE English Literature courses. There is advice on how to improve your coursework and on how to practise and revise effectively for examinations, in order to achieve higher National Curriculum Levels in both subjects.

To help you practise and improve, there are also exercises for you to do, and the chance to check your progress as you go along. Finally, there is up-to-date information on the examinations you will be sitting and the kinds of question you will have to face. Of course, some of the advice given here will echo what your teacher tells you already, though it has the great advantage of being written down, which might increase your chances of remembering it! Remember, too, that while reading this book may be useful, only constant practice – putting the advice to use when, and wherever, you are actually doing your work – will be the test of whether you have understood what you have read.

English in the National Curriculum

This book is designed for students who are working through Key Stage 4 and towards GCSE assessment at age 16. The period over which this course takes place – normally in Years 10 and 11 – is known as Key Stage 4. A detailed Programme of Study for Key Stage 4 sets out the kind of work you must be attempting at this level. If you are at school, you will already know something about Key Stage 3 tests.

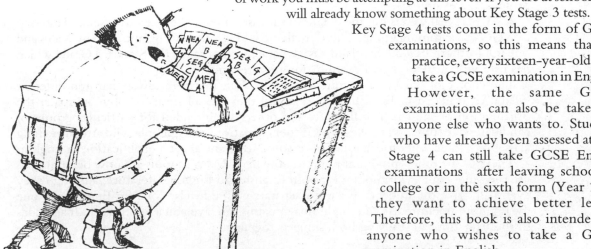

Key Stage 4 tests come in the form of GCSE examinations, so this means that, in practice, every sixteen-year-old must take a GCSE examination in English. However, the same GCSE examinations can also be taken by anyone else who wants to. Students who have already been assessed at Key Stage 4 can still take GCSE English examinations after leaving school, at college or in the sixth form (Year 12) if they want to achieve better levels. Therefore, this book is also intended for anyone who wishes to take a GCSE examination in English.

English Literature is another GCSE subject. It is not a compulsory subject in the National Curriculum, but many people choose to take it at the same time as English when they are at school. People who are taking an English GCSE after the age of 16 may choose to take English Literature as well because it gives them two chances of showing an improvement in their performance in English. This book is intended to help anyone who is taking GCSE English Literature.

GCSE/Key Stage 4

Relationship between grades and National Curriculum levels:

Up to and including 1993	From 1994 onwards
A*	10
A	9
B	8
C	7
D	6
E	
F	5
G	4
U	3
	2
	1

For everyone and for both subjects, the GCSE result comes in the form of a grade based on a scale from A–E. Grade A is the highest grade you can achieve. You will be graded for each of the different skills practised in English. In the National Curriculum, these skills are called Attainment Targets and for English there are five of them. This is less complicated than it sounds, because Spelling and Handwriting are grouped with Writing. Therefore, in practice, you can think of the Attainment Targets as being Speaking and Listening, Reading, and Writing (including Presentation). They are tested in a combination of coursework (work collected over the period of the course and marked by your teacher) and a terminal examination (usually made up of two timed papers and marked by a professional examiner).

A GCSE syllabus sets out the details of the assessment. The syllabus is set and assessed by a GCSE examining group. There are five GCSE groups in England, one in Wales and one in Northern Ireland. Scotland has a separate system called the Standard Grade which has its own coursework and examination requirements.

The choice of syllabuses is quite limited. In fact, there are fewer than ten different syllabuses available in English at present and they are all similar. Some approach the organisation of the papers differently and others are intended for particular groups of candidates like students at colleges of further education, older people who attend evening classes or people who, for all kinds of reasons, just want to get a qualification in English.

There is one other important point to note here. Many schools are now beginning to use the same coursework folder for both English and English Literature, although they eventually give the students two quite separate GCSE levels – one for English and one for English Literature. As you might imagine, this can save you a lot of work. It also adds to the attractions of studying both subjects together.

About GCSE English

In some ways, English is very different from your other GCSE subjects. For many of you it is the first language you learnt. You were listening to and speaking English for years before you learnt to read and write it. There can be very few of you who could say that everything you know about English has been taught to you in school. Your language abilities will have grown and developed in many ways because of the experiences you have had outside school, the way you talk to your family and friends and the way you read all sorts of written English, from signs in shop windows to newspapers and novels.

In other words, you are already a competent user of language. Imagine how odd life would be otherwise. You could be out with your friends and ask a question and they would all look at you strangely and ask you to say it again, or more slowly. Or, they might ask you to correct what you were saying and rephrase it! Luckily, people do communicate what they mean without any difficulty most of the time. But there are occasions when you have to write or say something which you find difficult or unfamiliar. Giving a talk to an audience, writing a letter to a boyfriend or girlfriend saying that you no longer want to see them, phoning up someone you don't know to ask for a job, making a complaint in a shop, summarising something you've read in school or following a difficult set of instructions to put together a kit are all occasions when your use of language can be stretched to the limits.

These are the kinds of situations where practice can help. You know that is true because the second time you do something it is always a little bit easier. It is also true that someone who practises a particular language skill outside school will be more competent at that use of English than other people of the same age, regardless of what school has taught him or her. For example, students whose parents are in the catering business are often skilled at making polite conversation with unfamiliar adults. So your command of English is a skill which will be improved by all your experiences throughout your life, not something which is confined to the years you spend at school.

About GCSE English Literature

This book is also intended to help you with English Literature examinations and coursework. Like English, English Literature builds on what you already know about reading and the reading you already do. So it isn't surprising that students who belong to libraries and read lots of fiction are often good story writers as well as skilled readers.

The study of English Literature is not expected to make you a faster reader or anything like that, but it does give you the chance to think more about the books you read and to write down and discuss your views of them. There are two good reasons for this. First, when you discuss the kind of music you like or talk about why you liked a particular film, you use the sorts of language skills that an English Literature course develops. But you may also use the same kind of vocabulary to discuss motorbikes, sport, food or politicians whenever you want to evaluate, make comparisons or judge what something is worth.

The second reason is more complicated. A course in English Literature will almost certainly require you to read books, poetry and plays which you would not otherwise read. Sometimes that can be off-putting but it can also introduce you to some of the novelists, poets and dramatists who make up our shared culture. If that sounds rather self-important and irrelevant, try thinking about it in this kind of way. Take a very well-known play of the kind you might be asked to study – like Shakespeare's *Romeo and Juliet*. First of all it has a story which you may well enjoy. The idea of two young lovers kept apart by the feuding between their families is a timeless one and you may well have come across the same plot in television soap operas, comics, other films and books. You may also have read real-life accounts of people trapped in this sort of situation or be able to relate it to events in the lives of people you know, or even to yourself. Shakespeare's play is part of all this – people faced the same problems when he wrote it, and that is how the play can come alive for a modern audience.

Over the course of hundreds of years, the play itself has become part of our culture so

that when we think of young lovers who are forced apart by circumstance, most people think of the story of *Romeo and Juliet*. Because of this, the story keeps cropping up in different ways, so that there are modern versions of the play like the musical *West Side Story* and rock songs like *Romeo and Juliet* by Dire Straits, while newspaper editors often talk about 'Fearless Romeos' or 'Modern-day Romeos and Juliets' in their headlines.

That is what it means to say that a play, a book or a poem is part of our culture. If you know about what Noah did in his spare time, what the Ancient Mariner shot, where Alice ended up after following a rabbit and who asked for more soup, then you are part of that culture. But, you are also part of it if you can name Bart Simpson's family, list most of the current top ten records or remember what is on television this evening. In other words, you can't help being part of the culture within which you live. One reason for the choice of the books, plays and poetry you have to read for English Literature is to introduce you to some of the best-known and most influential writers in our culture.

If you are at school, it is likely that you will be taking English and English Literature together. You will probably have one folder for your coursework and you will be studying the same books for each subject. In fact, sometimes it will be hard for you to tell whether a piece of coursework is for English or English Literature and, sometimes, it can count towards both subjects.

Of course, you will have to study set books and answer questions on them in the examination. This book offers help with that, too.

Something about you

Not all of the readers of this book will be between the ages of fourteen and sixteen. It will be clear that those of you who are undertaking GCSE at college or as mature students are likely to have certain advantages over the conventional GCSE age group, simply by having wider experience of language in the 'real' world.

It is also likely that those of you who speak another language as well as English will have the advantage of insight you may gain by comparing the way the two languages work. You may have grandparents who speak a different dialect of English from your own. You may have learnt French or German in school and begun to see how the grammar of languages differs. When you were little, you may have been told stories, in another language or in a dialect which is different from the standard English used in books.

Improving your English is not a matter of trying to learn another language for when you have to write. Being aware of and interested in all sorts of language in your own life: adverts, films, TV plays, poems, and so on, will also enrich your English. Reading a newspaper each day, or the occasional novel, will underline the fact that the more you bring to reading this book, the more you get out of it. This book does not set out to teach you English: it will help you to use the English you have acquired to the best advantage when tackling your GCSE work.

How to use this book

The sections in this book relate to the different skills you have to practise in English and the variety of written work you have to complete. Each section gives you an opportunity to practise what you have learned and offers you tips for success. That means you can go directly to a particular section to find immediate help in an area where you know your work is weak. There is advice to cover both the final examination and the coursework you have to do leading up to it.

Many of the sections contain boxes which summarise important information for you. You will find:

Tip Boxes These cover the little things which can help you get your work right, from remembering to check it for specific mistakes to including a title.

Workbench Assignments For the main sections of the book, these go over exactly what you should have learned from the section. If you are unsure about them, you know you need to work through that section again.

Revision Files You will find it useful to refer to these in the last few weeks or days before the examination, to make sure you have not missed anything vital.

Get used to flipping through this guide and reading these boxes regularly. They will help the information to stay in your mind – ready for when you need it most.

Chapter 2

The study of English

What is English?

The forms of the English language you have to study and the skills you must master are set out in your syllabus. Put at its simplest, what is required for any GCSE English course are linked opportunities for speaking and listening, reading and writing. For example, you could read a story, discuss it with your group and then write one of your own. Or you could watch a play, discuss it with your teacher and write about a character in it. In these examples you would be doing some reading, some writing, some talking and some listening.

On another occasion you might just do some writing, maybe after watching a film or perhaps after being given the title of a story. If you think about it for a moment, you will see that it is really only possible to tell how well you read by what you write afterwards. Reading aloud does not help you understand what you read. Only writing or talking about it will show that you have understood what you have read, and only writing is permanent enough to be looked at much later and to show how much you understand.

So you could think of the relationship between reading, writing and speaking and listening like this. The diagram shows how important your written work is:

Attainment Targets	AT1 Speaking and Listening 20%		AT3–5 Writing 40%
		AT2 Reading 40%	
Programmes of Study			
Assessment	Oral records 20%	Coursework 20%	Examination papers 60%

It is important not to forget how these aspects of English overlap, especially because when syllabuses talk about Attainment Targets they appear to treat Speaking and Listening, Reading and, lastly, Writing separately. Bearing this in mind, we can go on to look at the different National Curriculum requirements for each of these areas. Remember that, whatever syllabus you choose, it must cover these three areas.

The Attainment Targets explained

AT1 Speaking and Listening

The National Curriculum states that pupils should be able to:

4 **(a)** give a detailed oral account of an event, or something that has been learned in the classroom, or explain with reasons why a particular course of action has been taken.
   (b) ask and respond to questions in a range of situations with increased confidence.
   (c) take part as speakers and listeners in a group discussion or activity, commenting constructively on what is being discussed or experienced.
   (d) participate in a presentation.

5 **(a)** give a well-organised and sustained account of an event, a personal experience or an activity.
   (b) contribute to and respond constructively in discussion, including the development of ideas; advocate and justify a point of view.
   (c) use language to convey information and ideas effectively in a straightforward situation.
   (d) contribute to the planning of, and participate in, a group presentation.
   (e) recognise variations in vocabulary between different regional and social groups, and relate this knowledge, where appropriate, to personal experience.

6 **(a)** contribute, in group discussions, considered opinions or clear statements of personal feeling which are clearly responsive to the contribution of others.
   (b) use language to convey information and ideas effectively in a variety of situations where the subject is familiar to the pupils and the audience or other participants.
   (c) contribute to the planning and organisation of, and participate with fluency in, a group presentation or performance.
   (d) show, in discussion, an awareness of grammatical differences between spoken Standard English and a non-standard variety.

7 **(a)** express a point of view clearly and cogently to a range of audiences and interpret accurately a range of statements by others.
   (b) use and understand language which conveys information and ideas effectively on occasions where the situation or topic is less readily familiar to the pupils and/or their audience.
   (c) take an active part in group discussions, contributing constructively to the development of the argument.
   (d) show, in discussion, an awareness of the appropriate use of spoken language, according to purpose, topic and audience.

8 **(a)** express points of view on complex matters clearly and cogently and interpret points of view with accuracy and discrimination.
   (b) convey information and ideas in a variety of complex situations involving a range of audiences, and in language which is matched in context and purpose.
   (c) take an active part in group discussions, contributing constructively to the sustained development of the argument.
   (d) show, in discussion and in writing, an awareness of the contribution that facial expressions, gestures and tone of voice can make to a speaker's meaning.

9 **(a)** give a presentation expressing a personal point of view on a complex subject persuasively, cogently and clearly, integrating talk with writing and other media where appropriate, and respond to the presentations of others.
   (b) take an active part in group discussion, displaying sensitivity, listening critically and being self-critical.
   (c) show, in discussion and in writing, an awareness of the ways in which language varies between different types of spoken communication.

10**(a)** express a point of view on complex subjects persuasively, cogently and clearly, applying and interpreting a range of methods of presentation and assessing their own effectiveness accurately.
   (b) take a variety of leading roles in group discussion, including taking the chair, listening with concentration and understanding and noting down salient points.
   (c) show, in discussion and in writing, an awareness of some of the factors that influence people's attitudes to the way other people speak.

At first sight, what you have to do and the ways in which you have to perform seem very challenging and difficult. It is important to remember that these statements are written for teachers to use rather than pupils. They give more detail than you would usually require. In fact, they describe four main areas of activity:

1. describing and narrating;
2. explaining;
3. working together and discussing;
4. talking about language.

Finally, whatever syllabus you follow, there must be plenty of opportunities for speaking and listening. While there are slight variations between syllabuses concerning the number of occasions which have to be assessed and the kinds of activities which you have to undertake, it is important to remember that your assessment in speaking and listening contributes one-fifth of your final level for the subject as a whole.

Standard English

Languages vary all over the world and each single language also varies according to the particular area where it is spoken. A dialect is a version of a language which changes the words in the language, or their order. An accent is a version of the language which is pronounced slightly differently. In fact, the language of any area always features variations in both dialect and accent. It is not really correct, for example, to say that cockneys or Americans speak a different version of the English language because there is no single language to which they can be compared. However, in practice, people compare other dialects of English to what people agree is the correct form for writing – the dialect called Standard English.

Standard English differs from most regional dialects because it is used by, and can be understood by, English speakers all over the world. People from other countries who want to learn English are taught Standard English. Standard English can be spoken with any accent and should not be confused with 'talking posh'. The mix-up arises because some Standard English speakers also have a Received Pronunciation (RP) accent. This is the kind of accent you hear on old newsreels and, occasionally, from television and radio newsreaders. It is, in fact, perfectly possible to speak Standard English with any regional accent.

In some parts of England, the local dialect is very similar to Standard English but, for most people, Standard English is a dialect they learn at school. If you live in an area where many people speak a dialect, you will need to learn about the differences between your local way of speaking and Standard English so that you can adapt your speech when it seems necessary to do so.

If you speak with a very pronounced or strong regional accent, there may be some situations where you have to adapt that, too, in order to to make yourself understood. If you are talking to people who live a long way from where you live, for example, they may not be familiar with your way of speaking.

Your written English will be almost entirely Standard English. Of course, it is easier to write than to speak, because you have more time to think and to make changes when you are writing. Speech is immediate and you can't really alter it once you've opened your mouth, so you may need to practise Standard English until it becomes a habit and feels natural.

AT2 Reading

The National Curriculum states that pupils should be able to:

4 **(a)** read aloud expressively, fluently and with increased confidence from a range of familiar literature.

(b) demonstrate, in talking about a range of stories and poems which they have read, an ability to explore preferences.

(c) demonstrate, in talking about stories, poems, nonfiction and other texts, that they are developing their abilities to use inference, deduction and previous reading experience.

(d) find books and magazines in the class or school library by using the classification system, catalogue or database and use appropriate methods of finding information, when pursuing a line of inquiry.

5 (a) demonstrate, in talking and writing about a range of stories and poems which they have read, an ability to explain preferences.

(b) demonstrate, in talking or writing about fiction, poetry, nonfiction and other texts, that they are developing their own views and can support them by reference to some details in the text.

(c) show, in discussion, that they can recognise whether subject matter in non-literary and media texts is presented as fact or opinion.

(d) select reference books and other information materials and use organisation devices to find answers to their own questions and those of others.

(e) show, through discussion, an awareness of a writer's choice of particular words and phrases and the effect of the reader.

6 (a) read a range of fiction and poetry, explaining their preferences through talking and writing, with reference to details.

(b) demonstrate, in talking and writing about literature, nonfiction and other texts that they are developing their own insights and can sustain them by reference to the text.

(c) show, in discussion or in writing, that they can recognise whether subject matter in non-literary and media texts is presented as fact or opinion, identifying some of the ways in which the distinction can be made.

(d) select from a range of reference materials, using appropriate methods to identify key points.

(e) show, in discussion of their reading, an awareness that words can change in use and meaning over time and demonstrate some of the reasons why.

7 (a) read a range of fiction, poetry, literary nonfiction and drama, including pre-20th century literature, explaining their preferences through talking and writing, with reference to detail.

(b) talk and write about literature and other texts, giving evidence of personal response and showing an understanding of the author's approach.

(c) show, in discussion, that they can recognise features of presentation which are used to inform, to regulate, to reassure or to persuade, in non-literary and media texts.

(d) select, retrieve and combine information independently from a wide range of reference materials.

(e) show, in discussion or in writing, an awareness of writers' use of sound patterns and some other literary devices and the effect on the reader.

8 (a) read a range of fiction, poetry, literary nonfiction and drama, including pre-20th century literature.

(b) talk and write about literature and other texts, giving evidence of personal response and showing an understanding of the devices and structures used by the writers, with appropriate reference to details.

(c) show, in discussion and in writing, an ability to form a considered opinion about features of presentation which are used to inform, regulate, reassure or persuade, in non-literary and media texts.

(d) select, retrieve, evaluate and combine information independently and with discrimination, from a comprehensive range of reference materials.

(e) discuss and write about changes in the grammar of English over time, encountered in the course of their reading.

9 (a) read a range of fiction, poetry, literary nonfiction and drama, including pre-20th century literature.

(b) talk and write clearly about literature and other texts, giving sustained evidence of personal response and showing an understanding of the devices and structures used by the writers, making comparisons within texts and between different texts.

(c) show, in discussion and in writing, an ability to recognise techniques and conventions of presentation in non-literary and media texts, and judge the effectiveness of their use.

(d) select, retrieve, evaluate and combine information independently and with discrimination, from a comprehensive range of reference materials, making effective use of the information.

(e) demonstrate some understanding of the use of lexical and grammatical effects in the language of literature.

10 (a) read a range of fiction, poetry, literary nonfiction and drama, including pre-20th century literature.

(b) talk and write cogently and knowledgeably about literature and other texts, giving sustained evidence of personal response and showing an understanding of the devices and structures used by the writer, making comparisons within texts and between different texts.

(c) show, in discussion and in writing, an ability to evaluate techniques and conventions of presentation in non-literary and media texts, and judge the effectiveness of their use.

(d) select, retrieve, evaluate and combine information independently and with discrimination, from a comprehensive range of reference materials, making effective and sustained use of the information.

(e) demonstrate, in discussion and in writing, some understanding of attitudes in society towards language change and of ideas about appropriateness and correctness in language use.

In the same way as for Speaking and Listening, it is possible to pick out the main areas which you must study and the things which you must do for assessment in Reading:

- reading a range of texts;
- responding to literature;
- reading non-literary texts;
- using reading skills to study;
- reading about language.

The syllabuses also want you to look at as wide a range of literary and non-literary texts as possible. Literary texts are books, short stories, plays, poems which someone has written – the words to a song could be a literary text. Non-literary texts are magazine or newspaper articles, sets of instructions or advertisements. You may also have to keep a record of the books you have read and the other materials you have studied. There is more detail on exactly what you have to do for this part of your English course in Section Five.

AT3 Writing

The National Curriculum states that pupils should be able to:

4 (a) produce, independently, pieces of writing showing evidence of a developing ability to structure what is written in ways that make the meaning clear to the reader; demonstrate in their writing generally accurate use of sentence punctuation.

(b) write stories which have an opening, a setting, characters, a series of events and a resolution and which engage the interest of the reader; produce other kinds of chronologically organised writing.

(c) organise non-chronological writing for different purposes in orderly ways.

(d) begin to use the structures of written Standard English and begin to use some sentence structures different from those of speech.

(e) discuss the organisation of their own writing; revise and redraft the writing as appropriate, independently, in the light of that discussion.

5 (a) write in a variety of forms for a range of purposes and audiences, in ways which attempt to engage the interest of the reader.

(b) produce, independently, pieces of writing in which the meaning is made clear to the reader and in which organisational devices and sentence punctuation, including commas and the setting out of direct speech, are generally accurately used.

(c) demonstrate increased effectiveness in the use of Standard English (except in contexts where non-standard forms are needed for literary purposes) and show an increased differentiation between speech and writing.

(d) assemble ideas on paper or on a VDU, individually or in discussion with others, and show evidenced of an ability to produce a draft from them and then to revise and redraft as necessary.

(e) show in discussion the ability to recognise variations in vocabulary according to purpose, topic and audience and whether language is spoken or written, and use them appropriately in their writing.

6 (a) write in a variety of forms for a range of purposes, presenting subject matter differently to suit the needs of specified known audiences and demonstrating the ability to sustain the interest of the reader.

(b) produce, independently, pieces of writing in which the subject matter is organised and set out clearly and appropriately and in which sentences and any direct speech are helpfully punctuated.

(c) demonstrate the ability to use literary stylistic features and those which characterise an impersonal style, when appropriate, using Standard English (except in contexts where non-standard forms are needed for literary purposes).

(d) recognise when redrafting and revising are appropriate and act accordingly, either on paper or on a computer screen.

(e) demonstrate, through discussion and writing, grammatical differences between spoken and written English.

7 (a) write in a wider variety of forms, with commitment and a clear sense of purpose and awareness of audience, demonstrating an ability to anticipate the reader's response.

(b) produce well-structured pieces of writing, some of which handle more demanding subject matter; punctuate their writing so that meaning and structure are clear to the reader.

(c) make a more assured and selective use of a wider range of grammatical and lexical features, characteristic of different styles, that are appropriate for topic, purpose and audience; use Standard English (except in contexts where non-standard forms are needed for literary purposes).

(d) demonstrate an increased awareness that a first draft may be changed, amended and re-ordered in a variety of ways.

(e) show in discussion and in writing an awareness of what is appropriate and inappropriate language use in written texts.

8 (a) write in a wide variety of forms, with a clear sense of purpose and audience, demonstrating an ability to judge the appropriate length and form for a given task and to sustain the interest of the reader.

(b) produce, independently, well-structured pieces of writing, providing evidence that the function of paragraphing has been grasped; punctuate writing so that meaning and structure are clear to the reader.

(c) make an assured and selective use of a wide range of grammatical constructions, which are appropriate for topic, purpose and audience; use Standard English (except in contexts where non-standard forms are needed for literary purposes).

(d) demonstrate knowledge of organisational differences between spoken and written English.

9 (a) write in a wide variety of forms, with an assured sense of purpose, organising and presenting subject matter appropriately for specified audiences, both known and unknown, showing awareness of the need to sustain the interest of the reader; present subject matter from a point of view other than their own, showing evidence of commitment to the topic; produce a sustained piece of writing when the task demands it.

(b) organise and present complex subject matter in coherently linked sentences within paragraphs; punctuate writing so that meaning and structure are clear to the reader.

(c) make an assured and selective use of a wide range of grammatical constructions which are appropriate for topic, purpose and audience, demonstrating awareness of the means whereby a writer may choose to achieve a desired emphasis; show an ability to sustain the chosen style; use Standard English (except in contexts where non-standard forms are needed for literary purposes).

(d) demonstrate in discussion and in writing knowledge of ways in which language varies between different types of texts.

10(a) write, selecting an appropriate length, in a wide variety of chosen forms, demonstrating an assured sense of purpose and audience and a commitment to the topic.

(b) organise complex, demanding or extended subject matter clearly and effectively; produce well-structured pieces of writing in which the relationship between successive paragraphs is clear; punctuate their writing so that meaning and structure are clear to the reader.

(c) sustain a personal style, making an assured, selective and appropriate use of a wide range of grammatical constructions and an extensive vocabulary, choosing to use Standard English (except in contexts where non-standard forms are needed for literary purposes) and maintaining the interest and attention of the reader.

(d) demonstrate, in discussion and in writing, knowledge of criteria by which different types of written language can be judged.

AT4 Presentation

Pupils should be able to:

4   (a) spell correctly, in the course of their own writing, words which display other main patterns in English spelling.
    (b) produce more fluent joined-up writing in independent work.

5   (a) spell correctly, in the course of their own writing, words of increasing complexity.
    (b) check final drafts of writing for misspelling and other errors of presentation.
    (c) produce clear and legible handwriting in printed and cursive styles.

6   (a) recognise that words with related meanings may have related spellings, even though they sound different; recognise that the spelling of unstressed syllables can often be deduced from the spelling of a stressed syllable in a related word.
    (b) check final drafts of writing for misspelling and other forms of presentation.
    (c) write fluently and legibly.
    (d) show some ability to use any available presentational devices that are appropriate to the task, so that finished work is presented clearly and attractively.

7   (a) spell (and understand the meaning of) common roots that have been borrowed from other languages and that play an important role in word-building; recognise that where words have been borrowed in the last 400 years, there are some characteristic sound-symbol relationships that reflect the word's origin.
    (b) check final drafts of writing for misspelling and other errors of presentation.
    (c) write fluently and legibly.
    (d) show an increased ability to present finished work appropriately, clearly and attractively.

The Attainment Target for Writing is grouped with two other Attainment Targets at Key Stage 4: Spelling and Handwriting. Together, these two are called Presentation (AT4). It is easiest to think of them as always included with Writing because, even where they are separately assessed, the marks are added together to give a Grade for Writing and Presentation combined. The main areas where you have to show what you can achieve in writing are similar to those for the other Attainment Targets:
• writing for a range of audiences and purposes;
• structuring and organising writing;
• using Standard English;
• drafting and redrafting;
• writing about language;
• spelling correctly;
• using legible handwriting and presenting work neatly.
   Section Four gives more details of exactly what you have to do for the writing element of English.

What is English Literature?

English Literature has been a popular GCSE subject for many years. It gives you the chance to read a range of well-known books and to write about them. In many ways, the reading that you do in English is very similar to that you have to do in English Literature. Basically, the study of English Literature adds four new aspects to the reading you have done for English. To study English Literature, you have to:
• read more books;
• study set books (chosen from a list) and answer questions on them in the examination;
• link some of the books you read by connecting them to a theme;
• compare the books you read and write about them in more detail.

There are no separate Attainment Targets in English Literature and the result is one single grade for the subject as a whole.

Level 4
The candidate will show the ability to explore and explain personal preferences and be able to demonstrate, in talking about stories, poems, non-fiction and other texts, a developing ability to use inference, deduction and previous reading experience.

Example
Referring to the subject material or sequencing of story or play.

Level 5
In addition to achievement at Level 4, the candidate will show a growing ability to explain personal preferences by referring to some details in texts.

Making reference to character or action and distinguishing fact from opinion.

Level 6
In addition to achievement at Level 5, the candidate will show the developing ability to explain personal preferences with sustained references to the text. The candidate will be able to make personal judgements about characters, actions and narrative sequence.

Putting forward an opinion in relation to, or supported by, close textual reference.

Level 7
In addition to achievement at Level 6, the candidate will show the ability to respond to a growing range of fiction, poetry, and drama (including pre-twentieth century literature), giving evidence of a sustained and structured personal response and an understanding of the writer's approach. The candidate will be able to show an awareness of the writer's use of literary devices and their effect on the reader.

Making a sustained response to a text, or texts which acknowledge the role of the author and his or her use of language.

Level 8
In addition to achievement at Level 7, the candidate will be able to respond to a range of more difficult texts. The candidate will be able to write clearly about literature, giving clear evidence of personal response and showing an understanding of the devices used by writers.

Making a sustained and critical response to more demanding texts.

Level 9
In addition to achievement at Level 8, the candidate will be able to show evidence of a personal and critical response revealing an understanding of the devices and structures used by the writer and making comparisons within texts and between different texts. The candidate will be able to demonstrate some understanding of the use of language in literature.

Relating a number of texts by reference to features of style and language. Making confident use of literary terms in the close study of demanding texts.

Level 10
In addition to achievement at Level 9, the candidate will be able to write cogently and knowledgeably about literature giving sustained evidence of personal response, showing an understanding of the devices and structures used by the writer, and making detailed comparisons within texts and between different texts.

Sustaining an assured, critical style across a variety of texts in order to compare and analyse in depth. Presenting a clear, detailed overview of an area of study and contributions made to it by different authors and texts.

Chapter 3

English and English Literature Syllabuses

When you are entered for a GCSE examination in English or English Literature, you follow the syllabus set down by one of the examining groups. For English, this syllabus must include everything required by the National Curriculum Attainment Targets and Programmes of Study. For English Literature, the syllabus must add the study of more works of literature (books, plays and poems) in a more demanding way than they are studied for English. Two documents, the GCSE National Criteria for English and for English Literature, set down exactly for the examining groups how their syllabuses must relate to the National Curriculum.

That is why all the English and English Literature syllabuses are so similar. Often, they take their exact wording from the criteria documents so that they read in exactly the same way. There are some differences, however, in they way that the syllabuses organise the work which has to be done and in the way that teachers must record and assess it. There can be differences in the amount of coursework required or the type of record for speaking and listening which is included with it. The examination papers can vary in length, while a single paper may cover only one attainment target or two. Sometimes an attainment target likeAT4/5 is only assessed in coursework.

Reading the English syllabus

At school, you are unlikely to have any choice over the English syllabus you follow. Your teachers will already have made that decision and the similarities between syllabuses are so extensive that it would be a waste of your time to try and change or to follow a syllabus that is not taught by your school. However, if you are taking English GCSE as a mature or an external candidate, it might be worth your while to shop around the different syllabuses and to make a choice. In every syllabus you will find the same kinds of main headings.

1 A statement about weightings

For English, the attainment targets are weighted. This means that some attainment targets make a greater contribution to your final level or grade. These weightings are laid down by the National Criteria for English. They are the same for all GCSE English syllabuses.

AT1	Speaking and Listening	20%
AT2	Reading	40%
AT3	Writing	30%
AT4/5	Presentation	10%

The same National Criteria also state that AT1 must be assessed through coursework and that coursework as a whole can only add up to 40% of the assessment in total. The syllabus therefore shows the combination of terminal examination and coursework which is used.

	Terminal examination	Coursework
Speaking and Listening		20%
Reading	30%	10%
Writing and Presentation	30%	10%
Totals	60%	40%

② A statement about syllabus overlap

To make it easier for teachers, and to reduce the burden of coursework, all GCSE English syllabuses overlap with similar syllabuses in English Literature. Schools are encouraged to teach both subjects in the same lesson and to keep just one coursework folder. Then the same coursework may be used for both subjects and English coursework can be based on the set books studied for the English Literature terminal examination. The completed folder containing work for both subjects will then be checked by only one marker (the teacher) and one moderator (an examining group assessor).

③ Aims and objectives

The aims and objectives of the syllabus are closely related to the National Curriculum Statements of Attainment as given on pp. 13–18. They may be broad statements, outlining what the course should aim to achieve.

❶ Successful candidates should be able to express themselves effectively in a range of speaking and listening activities, matching style and response to audience and purpose;

❷ They should show the ability to read, understand and respond to all types of writing and develop information-retrieval strategies;

❸ They should show the ability to construct and convey meaning in written language using correct grammar and standard English, matching style to audience and purpose.

Often, the broad aims are turned into specific objectives.

Candidates must demonstrate that they can:

- recount personal experience, views and feelings;
- share and exchange views and ideas;
- use language to inform and explain;
- take a central part in group presentations;
- show an awareness of how spoken communication varies according to situation, purpose and audience;
- read a wide range of texts (including fiction, poetry, nonfiction and drama);
- respond to literature;
- select, retrieve, evaluate and combine information from reference materials;
- plan, organise and paragraph using appropriate punctuation and use correct grammar and Standard English;
- correct, edit and revise their own writing
- spell common words;
- write legibly;
- present finished work clearly and attractively.

Or, a list of possible activities is given.

Candidates must:

- undertake a wide range of activities, including giving instructions, problem solving activities, group presentations, debating and argument;
- read a wide range of literary, non-literary and media texts, including the works of Shakespeare and other pre-20th century texts;
- discuss, and comment in writing on, a range of informative and media texts including newspapers and magazines, advertising materials and reference books;
- in talking and writing about literature, use an appropriate critical vocabulary and support personal views and responses with textual references;
- produce writing which is varied in form, topic, purpose and audience;
- write diaries, letters, reports, accounts, reviews, newspaper articles and promotional materials and also a range of narratives, poems and scripts;
- plan, organise, draft, redraft and revise their writing with attention to its communicative success and its presentational impact – including layout, the accuracy of spelling and the neatness of handwriting.

④ A scheme of assessment

In English, the final assessment is made up from a number of components. Marks from the separate components are added together to give levels for Attainment Targets and a grade for the subject. These components could include:

An oral record giving evidence for AT1 about your performance in speaking and listening, and for AT2 where you have commented on your reading by talking about what you have read.

GCSE English
Speaking and Listening Record

Name _____ Teaching Group ___ AT1 ___ AT2 ___ Year 199 ___

Date	Activity	AT1	AT2	Teacher Comment

Candidate Summative Comment

Teacher Summative Comment

Coverage of strands

Describing & Narrating 1a
Explaining 1b
Collaborating & discussing 1c
Talking about language 1d

A reading log or diary showing the books you have studied and the range of your reading for AT2 assessment.

GCSE English

Reading Record

Name _____ Teaching Group _____ Year 199 ___

Date	Title	Comment
	Author	
	Author	
	Author	
	Author	

Written coursework showing how well you can write for AT3, the level of your spelling and handwriting for AT4/5 and your response to reading for AT2.

Examination papers 1 and 2 showing how well you can write for AT3 and respond to reading for AT2. In some syllabuses, one paper tests AT2 and the other tests AT3 while in others, both papers test both attainment targets. Examination papers usually test spelling and, sometimes, handwriting AT4/5.

You can see from this that, for AT2 and AT3, up to three components contribute to your final level. The advantage of this is that if you do badly in the examination, your coursework can then help to give you a higher grade. The disadvantage is that to do really well, you have to achieve high marks for each component.

One other complication is that the examination papers are **tiered**. In a tiered system, different examination papers are set for (or target) a limited range of levels. The idea behind this is that candidates who expect to do very well at English can be set a paper with difficult reading material or questions which might be too hard for the average candidate. Because the examination is designed to show how well you can do against a scale of levels of difficulty from 4–10, it is important that the questions target levels quite closely. To understand this better, imagine taking a test in a foreign language which you knew enough of to chat to people, to shop and to order food in restaurants. If a test asked you to do these things, then you would probably score quite highly. But suppose your test asked you to translate a highly technical article or a complicated novel and left you completely confused. Then you would do worse than you deserved to and your grade would not be a fair one.

In some National Curriculum tests there are **four** tiers: in many GCSE subjects there are **three** but for English and English Literature there are only **two**. There is usually a lower tier, sometimes called Standard or Basic, which covers **Levels 4–6** and a higher tier covering **Levels 6–10**. Apart from the overlap at Level 6, the lower tier allows you to be given any level in the range 4–7 while the higher tier allows for any level in the range 5–10. For different syllabuses, the levels covered may vary very slightly but they are broadly the same. Because the higher tier covers all but one of the GCSE levels, many teachers believe that almost all candidates can be entered for that examination.

To answer an obvious question, you are not allowed to enter for both tiers! The examinations take place at the same time and the regulations forbid it. Remember also that only the examination is tiered – the coursework and other records are always the same.

⑤ The examination papers

As indicated above, the examination papers vary in how they test attainment targets. They also vary in length and in the kinds of things they ask you to do. For one syllabus you could be asked to write a report, for another an imaginative story. Some papers set more questions than others. Some papers are set with a common theme for all of the questions. In assessment terms, the form of the examination paper will probably not make any difference to your overall result but, if you have a choice, this is one section of the syllabuses you should definitely look at.

For each paper in the syllabus you should find the following information:

Title	Tier code	Target levels	Allowed levels	Duration	Weighting
e.g. Understanding Response Paper 3	Higher	6–10	5–10	2 hours	30%

The syllabus will also contain a more detailed description of each examination paper.

e.g. **Higher Tier Paper   Understanding and response   2 hours 100 marks**

Section A (60 marks)
Candidates will be given a number of tasks based on an at least two unseen texts on

related themes. At the highest levels, they will be expected to use detailed reference to the texts in support of their insight and opinions, to make detailed comparisons within and between texts, to discuss language and form using an appropriate critical vocabulary, and to give sustained evidence of personal response. All the questions must be answered.

Section B (40 marks)
A choice of tasks will be given to elicit an imaginative and creative response to the material. Candidates will be expected to interpret and reflect the ways in which a writer has used subject material, style and language for effect.

⑥ Coursework

All English syllabuses give detailed guidance on the coursework which you must submit at the end of the course. These regulations are very important. Submitting an incomplete folder can severely reduce your marks. The folder is supposed to give evidence of your highest attainment in the subject and for each attainment target. That means it will be assessed as if it is your best work. Most syllabuses ask that some of the coursework has been supervised by a teacher. This is done so that the teacher can guarantee that the work is your own and that you are not getting an unacceptable level of help from other people.

The precise contents of the coursework vary from syllabus to syllabus, although between them the coursework and the examination papers must cover all aspects of the attainment targets. For AT1, Speaking and Listening, where coursework is the only evidence of performance, the record must show that most of the statements of attainment at a certain level have been covered. For AT2 Reading, AT3 Writing and AT4/5 Presentation, coursework must cover those Statements of Attainment for which it is most suited, especially those which cannot be assessed in the examination paper. Skills such as redrafting written work or attempting a range of types of writing would come into this group.

There are slight differences between the coursework requirements for different English syllabuses, but in general the completed folder must contain records and enough written work to provide evidence of:
• achievements in speaking and listening;
• the range of your reading, including literary and non-literary texts;
• the study of language;
• the study of whole works of literature;
• a response to the work of Shakespeare;
• the redrafting and revision of writing and its neat presentation.

While this may seem a lot of work, the pieces can overlap so that a single piece covers more than one of the requirements. For example, a detailed piece of writing on the use of language in a particular Shakespeare play would, if carefully redrafted, be evidence of at least the last four of these.

In practice there is a lot of discussion about how much work should be included. The sensible principle to work on is that you do not need to show the moderator that you can do something more than once, but you do need to include your best work. As a rough guide, expect to have to include:
- around five pieces of written work, some of which must be handwritten;
- a written record of speaking and listening activities;
- a written record of the texts you have studied, with dates and short comments.

The five pieces of written work could include a piece on a Shakespeare play, a piece on another work of literature – poetry or fiction – and a piece based on some non-literary material like a newspaper report, advertising materials or a television programme. Then the other pieces could be imaginative or creative writing, letters and reports, persuasive speeches or other forms of writing. However, it is important to check this against the fine print of your chosen syllabus, as there are significant variations between syllabuses.

The syllabus will also give advice on the presentation of the coursework folder. It should normally:
- be A4 in size with a flat cover – not a ring binder;
- be clearly labelled with your name and examination codes and numbers;
- include a form – supplied by the examining group – which lists its contents.

In addition, each piece of writing should:
- be clearly headed with your name and the date;
- include a title and, where relevant, the source or text upon which your work is based;
- have been marked by your teacher;
- not have been altered by you after marking.

There will often be a statement for you to sign which states that the work in the folder is your own and that you have completed it without an unreasonable amount of help. There is more advice on coursework in Section 5.

Reading the English Literature syllabus

English Literature syllabuses tend to be slightly different from each other. However, you will find the same basic sections in the syllabuses. The aims and objectives and schemes of assessment are simpler because English Literature does not have Attainment Targets which have to be weighted. Also, the balance between coursework (30%) and written examination papers (70%) does not vary.

The main differences between the syllabuses are in the books you have to read and the way the reading is assessed. As you study these syllabuses, look out for these features:

The Examination Paper

Usually, there is a single paper in English Literature of around two hours in length. The tiers for English Literature are the same as for English. Look at the balance between unseen material and any extracts which are given out to candidates beforehand as a pre-released anthology. Look at the number of set books you are asked to answer questions on in the examination. Remember that studying a number of books may add to your revision, but will give you more choice when you come to sit the examination paper.

Coursework

The coursework at its simplest will ask for three pieces of work on three separate texts – a play, a book and a poem. But there are some complications to watch out for. The first is to do with the combined choice of books for the coursework and the examination where you may have to study a Shakespeare play and one other pre-twentieth century text to achieve Grade C or higher. The second is that some examining groups link the examination papers for English and English Literature so that one paper counts towards the level for both English AT2 and for Literature. Finally, remember that the coursework can overlap, so that the study of one Shakespeare play can meet the requirements for both syllabuses.

Choosing the right syllabus

Some of the information in this section is quite complicated and there are differences between syllabuses. If you are uncertain about exactly what a syllabus is asking from you, ask a teacher to help to clarify exactly what it says.

Most advice suggests that it makes sense to follow the same examining group's syllabuses for English and English Literature, but you should also study the coursework requirements and the set books you will have to study before making up your mind.

Special syllabuses for older students

There are some syllabuses intended for mature candidates in full-time or part-time education and for external candidates, who do not attend a college. The content of these courses is different, since they are meant to appeal to older students who have probably already taken a GCSE syllabus and want to do something different at college. However, their structure is identical to other syllabuses and the work involved is exactly the same. They all have coursework. This may mean in the future that if you are not in full-time education and would like to take an examination in English you will have to become part of a class at a college of further education or take school evening classes.

Revision file: your syllabuses

Complete copies of this chart to make sure that you know all the details of each syllabus you are following. Ask your English teacher to lend you the syllabuses. He or she should be able to give you some help as well. It is possible to buy syllabuses direct from the examination groups. Their addresses are listed in the Appendix at the end of this guide.

Syllabus title: English

Examining group:

Syllabus code or number:

Component no.	Title	ATs	Weighting	How assessed?	No. of pieces/ length of examination
Speaking and Listening (i.e. oral coursework)					
Written coursework					
Examination Paper 1					
Examination Paper 2					

Chapter 1
Your own language

Building on what you know

You certainly are not starting from scratch as a speaker and listener. You have been doing these things since before you can even remember: at home, at school, with your friends, in shops, maybe even at work. So, what more is there to learn? If you want to gain a Grade C or higher in your GCSE, the answer is, quite a lot. This section aims to show you what you have to do and how to do it better.

It also goes into the detail of what your assessment of speaking and listening should consist of and the way in which your work in this area will be assessed. Of course, exactly how this is done will depend on where you are studying. A college of further education or an evening class may have to provide more structured opportunities for this kind of work than a school does.

This section shows you the skills and knowledge you need to reach the higher levels of speaking and listening assessment. It also gives you some ideas for activities you can undertake to practise the skills you will need to use in school.

In your area there is probably a local dialect and a local accent. If you have lived there a long time then you may not notice it – probably because you speak it to some extent! Listening to old people talking can often give you a chance to hear good examples of local accents and dialects. The reason why this is so gives you an insight into dialects and Standard English.

Only a hundred years ago, people rarely travelled far out of their own local area. Books were very expensive compared to their cost today, there were few national newspapers and no radio or television. In fact, most people spent their time talking and listening. Only a limited amount of reading and writing went on and many people were illiterate (unable to read or write). In these circumstances local dialects flourished and people spoke the way their ancestors had spoken for generations. A woman from Cornwall would only have to travel as far as London to find herself in a place where people spoke what was almost a different language.

Sometimes it is hard to take in just how much things have changed. You are used to owning books and having them around, to reading magazines and newspapers and to a choice of national television and radio. You watch video tapes and know about satellite broadcasting and cabled television and you, and everyone around you, is used to travelling not just in the British Isles but all over the world. Distances have shrunk. It might have taken that Cornishwoman three days to travel to

London. Now it takes less than two hours by air, less than four hours by train and less than six by road.

The result of this is that the language we use is becoming more national and the old regional accents and dialects are dying out. Writing, printing and broadcasting have speeded up this process as one dialect has come to be used by more and more people. This is the dialect called Standard English which was first used outside London in the south and east Midlands. From there it became the standard form for writing and printing and, later still, the standard form for speaking in formal situations.

Workbench assignment

Why is talk important?

Find four people, two male and two female; two between the ages of 30 and 50 and two over the age of 50. Ask them if they would answer these questions for you. If you can, tape their answers.

• What do you remember about talking in school?

• What do you remember about listening?
• What do you think children need to be taught about speaking and listening in school nowadays?
• How important is it to be good at talking? Do you need to be a good speaker and listener to do your job?
• Do you think it is as important to be a good speaker and listener as it is to be a good reader and writer?
• In what ways are speaking and listening important to you in your home life?
• What does talking properly mean to you? What is the right way to talk?
• Do you think that you speak with any accent or dialect? Have you noticed that accents and dialects are now heard less often than they used to be?

If you can, carry out this investigation with a friend. Discuss your findings. Ask yourself what you have learned about:
  the nature of spoken language;
  how spoken language changes;
  social attitudes towards spoken language.

Even if you don't follow up your initial investigations, you will have found out that the English language is something everyone knows about and has opinions about. You may even have heard opinions that you disagreed with. One thing you will almost certainly have discovered is that we take our ability to talk very much for granted. Only people who for some reason have found it difficult to learn to speak, such as people with hearing or speech impairments, appreciate how difficult it would make our everyday lives to be without it.

You may have discovered from your interviews that, for many older people, talking at school was often considered 'bad behaviour', even though it is important to be able to talk well when work and social situations demand it. But times change and the National Curriculum in English recognises changing attitudes to the importance of talk by putting it first on the list of things you must learn to use in English.

Chapter 2

Speaking and listening in the National Curriculum

As you know from Section 1, your skills as a speaker and listener will account for 20% of your final assessment. Unlike reading or writing, all of your talk will be assessed by your teacher, as there is no final examination, so this is one area where you will need to improve your skills and demonstrate them in school or college right the way through your English course. You will find the advice in this section useful in other subjects where talk plays a part in your work.

There are five distinct areas of skills that are assessed. In classroom activities, these will often overlap. They will sometimes be connected with your reading and writing activities. You will find plenty more opportunities to practise your talk in later sections as well.

What do I need to know how to do?

The speaking and listening achievements which the National Curriculum assesses are sometimes broken down into smaller areas known as **strands**. English has five of these, depending on how the Statements of Attainment are grouped together.

1. Describing and narrating
2. Working together and discussing
3. Explaining
4. Performing
5. Talking about language

Or, in more detail:

1. **Describing and narrating** – your ability to talk about your own experiences, your ideas, opinions and your feelings

   This could involve anything, from having a conversation with your friends about what you did at the weekend, to giving a talk to the class about a book you have read, or making a persuasive speech about a controversial topic.

2. **Collaboration and discussion** – your ability to work as a member of a group and to collaborate and discuss with others

   Any activity you do with a partner or in a group will demonstrate this. You will already be experienced in doing plenty of group work in English.

3. **Information and explanation** – your ability to understand and give instructions and explanations

At the simplest level, this could be a matter of seeing if you do what you are told. At the most complex level, it could involve you in demonstrating to a group of total strangers how to undertake a fairly complicated task, for example, explaining how you use tape and video recorders to help you with oral work on a school Open Evening.

4 **Performance and audience** – your ability to take part in group work that leads to a public performance

This could be making a public speech, performing an improvised drama, acting in a play or role-playing a meeting in class.

5 **Knowledge about language** – your ability to show that you have some knowledge about how spoken English works and how people feel about it

This will involve you in acquiring some specific knowledge about the grammar of spoken English, how people communicate non-verbally, how different styles of speaking are necessary in different situations, etc. The action research at the beginning of this section was an example of this, and the language project ideas at the end of it are intended to develop this knowledge further.

Different syllabuses set them out in slightly different ways, but these are the skills your English teacher will assess. For the rest of this section, each skill is looked at in turn.

1 Personal account

Telling stories

A Cream Cracker under the Settee

(Doris is in her seventies and the play is set in the living room and hallway of her semi-detached house. She is sitting awkwardly on a low chair and rubbing her leg. It is morning.)
It's such a silly thing to have done.
Pause.
I should never have tried to dust. Zulema says to me every time she comes, "Doris. Do not attempt to dust. That's what the council pay me for. You are now a lady of leisure." Which would be all right providing she did dust. But Zulema doesn't dust. She half-dusts.
When she's going she says, "Doris. I don't want to hear you've been touching the sweeper. You're on trial here." I said, "What for?" She said, "For being on you own. For not behaving like a woman of seventy-five who has a pacemaker and dizzy spells and doesn't have the sense she was born with." I said, "Yes, Zulema."
She says, "What you don't understand, Doris, is that I'm the only person that stands between you and Stafford House. I have to report on you. They bend over backwards to keep you in your own home. But, Doris, you've got to meet them half way. Pull your horns in. Let the dirt wait. I'm here every week."
I was glad she'd gone, dictating. I sat for a bit looking up at me and Wilfred on the wedding photo. And I though, "Well, Zulema, I bet you haven't dusted on top of that". So I got the stool and climbed up. And she hadn't. Thick with dust. Home help! Home hindrance. You're better off doing it yourself. And I was just wiping it over when, oh hell, the flaming stool went over.
Pause.

I think I'm all right. My leg's a bit numb. I'm just going to sit and come round a bit.
Pause.
Shan't let on I was dusting.
She looks down at the wedding photo on the floor.
Cracked the photo. We're cracked, Wilfred.
Pause.
The gate's open again. Dogs coming in, all sorts. You see Zulema should have closed that, only she didn't.
Pause.
The sneck's loose, that's the root cause of it. I kept saying to Wilfred, "When are you going to get round to that gate?" But oh no. It was always the same refrain. "Don't worry, Mother. I've got it on my list." I never saw no list. He'd no system at all, Wilfred. "When I get a minute, Doris." Well, he's got a minute now, bless him.
Pause.
Feels funny this leg. Not there.
Pause.
Some leaves coming down now. Zulema won't touch them. Says if I want leaves swept it's Parks Department. They're next door's leaves. We've only got one bush and it's an evergreen, so I'm certain they're not my leaves. Only other folks won't know that. I ought to put a not on the gate. 'Not my leaves!'; Not my leg either, the way it feels. Gone to sleep.
Pause.
I didn't even want the bush. I said, "Dad, is it a bush that'll make a mess?" He said, "Doris. Rest assured," and fetches out the catalogue. "'This labour-saving variety is much favoured by retired people.' Anyway," he says, "the garden is my department." I said, "Given a choice, Wilfred, I'd have concrete." He said, "Doris, concrete has no character." Well, he's got his little garden now. Only I bet it's covered in leaves. Graves, gardens, everything's to follow.
I'll make a move in a minute. Put the kettle on. Come on leg. Wake up.
Black out.
Come up on Doris sitting on the floor with her back to the wall.
Fancy, there's a cream cracker under the settee. She's not half done this place, Zulema. I'm going to save that cream cracker and show it her. I'll say, "Don't Stafford House me, lady. I've only got to send this cream cracker to the Social Services Department and you'll be on the carpet. Same as the cream cracker. I'll be in Stafford House, Zulema, but you'll be in the Unemployment Exchange".
I'm en route for the window only I'm not making much headway. I'll bang on it. Alert somebody. Don't know who. Don't know anybody round here now. Folks opposite, I don't know them. Used to be the Marsdens. There for years. Then he died, and she died and the daughter went away somewhere and folks started to come and go. You lose track. I don't think they're married half of them. You see all sorts.
Ought to have had a dog. Then it could have been barking for someone. Wilfred was always hankering after a dog. I wasn't keen. Hairs all up and down, then having to take it outside every five minutes. Wilfred said that would be his province. I said, "Yes, and whose province would all the little hairs be?" We never got one either. It was the growing mushrooms saga all over again. He never got round to it. Like the fretwork, making toys and forts and whatnot. No end of money he was going to make. Then there was this phantom allotment. "We can be self-sufficient in the vegetable department, Doris." Never materialised. I was glad. It'd've meant muck somehow.

She looks in the place where the pram was.
I wanted to call him John. The midwife said he wasn't fit to be called anything and had we any newspaper? Wilfred said, "Oh yes, she saves newspapers. Shoeboxes as well." I must have fallen asleep because when I woke up she'd gone. I wanted to see him. Wrapping him in newspaper as if he was dirty. He wasn't dirty, little thing. I don't think Wilfred minded. A kiddy. Same as the allotment and the fretwork. Just a craze. He said, "We're better off, Doris. Just the two of us." Then he started talking about a dog.

If it had lived I might have had grandchildren now. Wouldn't have been in this fix. Daughters are the best. They don't migrate.
Pause.

We were always on our own, me and Wilfred. We weren't gregarious. He thought he was, but he wasn't. Mix. I don't want to mix. Comes to the finish and they suddenly think you want to mix. I don't want to be stuck with a lot of old lasses. You go daft there. Wearing somebody else's frock. They even mix up your teeth. I am H.A.P.P.Y. I am not H.A.P.P.Y. I am un H.A.P.P.Y. Or I would be.
And Zulema says, "You don't understand, Doris. You're not up to date. They have lockers now. Flowerbeds. They go on trips to Wharfedale." I said, "Yes, smelling of pee." She said, "You're prejudiced, you." I said, "I am where hygiene is concerned."
When people were clean and the streets were clean and it was all clean and you could walk down the street and folks smiled and passed the time of day, I'd leave the door on the latch and go on to the end for some toffee, and when I came back Dad was home and the cloth was on and we'd have our tea. And I'd wash up while he read the paper and we'd eat the toffees and listen to the wireless all them years ago when we were first married and I was having the baby.
Doris and Wilfred. They don't get called Doris now. Or Wilfred. Museum, names like that. That's what they're all called in Stafford House. Alice, Mabel, Doris. Antiques. Keep them under lock and key. "What's your name? Doris? Right. Pack your case."
A home. Not me. No fear.

Long pause.
You've done it now, Doris. Done it now, Wilfred.
Pause.
I wish I was ready for bed. All washed and in a clean nightie and the bottle in, all sweet and crisp and clean like when I was little on Baking Night, sat in front of the fire with my long hair still.
Her eyes close and she sings a little to herself.
Pause.
Never mind. It's done now, anyway.
Light fades.

We all tell stories about our experiences. We tell them in conversations to entertain our friends; we tell them to explain our feelings and to illustrate points we are making. Some stories are mainly intended to teach the listener something. Consider how often your teachers in school use anecdotes to help you understand and remember something they are explaining to you.

Storytelling is something you have been doing all your life, both in and out of school, quite spontaneously. You will be well aware that some people are better at this than others: they hold their listeners spellbound while they talk about their experiences. How do they do it?

Workbench assignment

Listening to and telling stories

Spend a day listening to the way people use anecdotes: on the bus, at school, at home, on the television and radio. Make brief notes about as many of the stories as you can. Use these headings to help you:
- Who was telling it?
- Who to?
- For what reason?
- How? As a monologue or as part of a conversation? Was it rehearsed or spontaneous?
- What skills did the teller have (or not have) that made it a good (or bad) story?

At the end of the day, consider all the information you have collected and decide which were the best three stories you heard. Use the notes you have made to put together a list of rules for good storytelling.

Now have a go yourself. Think about something interesting that you did recently, or a vivid memory. Find two people to tell it to, such as a younger sister or brother, an older member of the family or a neighbour, or one of your friends.

• Tape yourself so you can listen to the two different versions afterwards.
• Think in advance about the interesting details you want to keep in and the boring bits you want to leave out.
• Think how you would begin and end your story.
• Think about where you might need to include descriptive details of people and places, and where you might want to comment on how you felt about the events that happened. Make some brief notes if you are not sure you can trust your memory.
• Think about the importance of eye-contact: how can you tell your listener is understanding you, or is interested in what you are saying? What do you do if they are not?
• Think about ways in which the speed, the intonation and gestures you use might help to make your storytelling better.

Afterwards, listen to your tape. As you listen, think about how the story was changed to suit the different audiences. For example, you would probably use simpler vocabulary when talking to a child, and tell the story more slowly, perhaps with more explanation of unfamiliar experiences, than you would if you were talking to a close friend. Talking to someone older, who is less familiar to you, you might find that you avoided slang and choose to highlight slightly different events in the story.

Remember that suiting the way you talk to a particular audience, and being able to explain the choices you make, is a skill you need to develop to become a 'high-level' talker.

Talking about feelings and reactions

Being able to talk about emotions and responses, both your own and those of others, is a little different from many of the other sorts of talk you will read about in this section. Most talking skills will be useful to you in many of your school subjects. Talking about feelings is something you are more likely to do in your English classroom than anywhere else. You will find yourself discussing your feelings about your own experiences, the books you read, and the feelings of the characters in the books you read.

Empathy (the ability to identify with the feelings of other people) is a skill you cannot be without to succeed in English. The starting point is being able to talk about how you feel about things yourself.

This is not easy for some people: British culture seems to encourage an attitude that feelings are private, and only for sharing with a circle of intimate friends. Talking about feelings in groups can be quite awkward for a lot of people. Don't worry if you find it difficult at first, and remember that talking about the difficulties faced by characters in books or on television and film may be much easier than talking about similar problems in your own life.

② Collaboration and discussion
Giving your views in a group

You will spend a great deal of time working and talking together with other members of your class. Your skills as a **collaborative** talker will be assessed by many of your teachers: nearly all GCSE subjects have statements of attainment relating to oral communication. What are the skills your teacher is watching for when you are being assessed?

Being a better listener

There is a lot more to good listening than simply sitting in silence. It is possible to do that and be thinking of something completely different from what you are hearing. Two reasons why people are poor listeners are either that they find it hard to sustain concentration listening to others, or that they are very confident talkers and prefer that to listening.

If you recognise these faults, practise these skills:

- Show that you are listening. Making eye contact with the person speaking is one way of doing this. So is appropriate body language: face the speaker; lean towards them; nod or shake your head; smile; look interested; look puzzled. Your facial expressions show whether you are listening and understanding what you are hearing.
- Verbal encouragement is useful too. Say 'mm' and 'yes' if you agree. Ask for more details or for clarification if they are trying to make a point that you cannot understand.
- Don't be in a tearing hurry to make your contribution. Ask others in the group if they agree or disagree, and listen to what they have to say.
- Rephrase or summarise what has been said so far, if it seems useful. You do not always have to make a new point.
- Give quieter members of the group time to talk. Encourage good listening skills in the others.
- Try not to interrupt or change the subject until you are sure the speaker has finished.
- Being able to explain what you think and your reasons for holding an opinion are skills you need to work hard at during your English course. Forming and explaining well-thought-out points of view will be influenced by:

   how well you listen to the opinions of others

   how carefully you read materials that help you form opinions

   how you use all these other sources of information to make sense of what you think yourself.

Making your point

Reading newspapers and taking an interest in current affairs programmes on radio and television is a good way of building up information, so that the views you express are based on evidence rather than prejudice. Reading a broadsheet quality paper, like the *Independent*, *Telegraph* or *Guardian* is a good idea. All newspapers have some sort of bias, but you will find more reasons and explanations backing up the points of view in the quality papers, whereas the tabloid papers like the *Sun* and the *Star* tend to present their readers with opinions which appeal to emotions rather than logical thought.

Editorial and opinion columns from any newspaper are a good starting point for discussing points of view. The less reasoned they are, the more you will find to say to put an opposing point of view.

Workbench assignment

Read this newspaper article. It is taken from a Sunday newspaper – *The News of the World*. You should be able to detect four separate opinions being presented here:

1. that football hooliganism is a disgrace;
2. that German football hooligans are as bad as English ones;
3. that English teams should only be banned from European football if German ones are;
4. that the cause of football hooliganism could be violence on television.

This article presents one person's opinion. There is very little justification given for any of the opinions presented, and anyone might disagree with some or all of them.

What are your views on the last argument – that television encourages football violence? You might think that the causes of football hooliganism are a lot more complicated than the programmes people watch on television. After all:

- millions of people watch television and do not become football hooligans;

THE VOICE OF REASON

Woodrow Wyatt

English football hooligans disgraced us in Sweden. German football hooligans disgraced Germany after they were beaten by Denmark.

They were just as violent as the English. It'd be monstrous if English teams were prevented from competing on the Continent unless German teams were too.

Perhaps TV provokes the terrifying behaviour. Flicking from channel to channel, scenes of brutality are an all day, every day matter.

That's whether it's the news or what passes for entertainment. As the young everywhere see people beat each other about the head they've begun to think this is normal life.

- some psychologists even say that watching violence makes people less likely to want to participate in it;
- there are many more theories to explain football hooliganism: poor home backgrounds, mob pressure, etc. Recently, a government politician suggested that if children were taught more English grammar in school, it would reduce hooliganism!

Now add two more reasons of your own to explain why you either agree or disagree with the theory that there is a link between violence on television and hooliganism. Ask friends or relatives to discuss the topic. If possible, audiotape your discussion so you can listen to it afterwards.

Tip box

- State your points of view clearly and back them up with well-thought-out reasons for what you say.
- Listen to the points of view of the person you are talking to.
- Be ready to ask them to explain in more detail if you do not see the logic in what they are saying.
- Be prepared to explain why you think some of the points they make are unsound. Use evidence to do this.
- Be willing to modify your opinion if they make a good point which you had not thought of.
- Be careful not to resort to prejudice, or to rely on comments like, 'It's obvious', or 'everyone knows that.'

Remember that you do not have to 'win' an argument to have a good discussion. You *may* persuade someone to agree with you, but even if you still hold different points of view, you should have better understanding of your reasons for holding them.

As you listen to your tape, check off which of these skills you used. Ask the other person or people you talked to for their assessment as well.

Working in larger groups

Sometimes you will be expected to work in larger groups. The bigger the group, the more skilful you need to be: once a group gets to be bigger than four people, you need all your skills to make it work: confident talkers tend to take over and quieter members get left out. Make sure you do not take on the same role every time you work in a group. It is easy for quieter members to find they are always secretary, while the more confident members of the group do the chairing and reporting. Make sure roles are swapped: you will not learn how to do a job if you never try it out. Also, the roles of Chair and Secretary are highly skilled jobs. If you show you can do these well, you will be on your way to achieving a high mark for your collaborative skills.

③ Information and explanation

Talking facts

By the time you start your new GCSE English course, you will have had plenty of practice at following instructions and acting on information, both at home and at school. In fact, at the highest assessment levels, it is more or less taken for granted that you are able to listen carefully and to carry out accurately the task you have been given. In real life, of course, we all know that some very simple instructions, like: 'Tidy that bedroom, NOW!' and 'Give your homework in tomorrow morning', are very difficult for the average GCSE student to follow.

Giving information and instructions clearly and accurately is something you will need to do outside school and in many other lessons apart from English, so it is worth practising. Most of us have had the experience of asking someone in a strange town how to find the railway station, for example, and been given information like this:
'Well, you take the first, no, the second left. No, it's not, it's right. Then you walk down the High Street until you get to Boots, or is it WH Smith's? Well, if you get there you've gone past it, but this is the easiest way...' and so on, and so on!

Workbench assignment

Giving instructions

Could you do better? Practise, with a friend, giving as wide a variety of instructions as you can. The less familiar the listener is with what they are being told, the better. As far as possible, use words only: use diagrams and demonstrations as a last resort.

Try out these ideas. Tell each other how to:
- get from one place to another;
- programme your video recorder;
- dub a tape on your stereo;

- play a card game;
- cast off a row of knitting;
- get to the next level or 'world' in a computer game.

It doesn't really matter *what* the task is, though if you intend to follow each other's instructions as they are given, avoid tasks which could result in danger or damage if things went wrong! Finally, each of you should compile a list of between five and ten instructions about how to give clear, precise information. Compare your lists.

④ Performance and audience

Making a speech

Once you feel confident about arguing your case in conversation, you will be ready to practise something more difficult: presenting a well-thought-out, extended statement of your opinion on a difficult subject is one of the skills that will help you to gain the highest possible level for your speaking and listening assessment. Many people, including very articulate adults, find this a nerve-racking experience. If the thought of making a speech to your own class at school, let alone to a larger group of complete strangers, fills you with trepidation, you can be sure you are not alone in feeling like that.

Case study

Jessica has been asked to give a talk to her class on a topic she feels strongly about. She is a vegetarian, so it seemed natural to talk about that. That topic seemed too broad for a short talk so her teacher suggested that she focus on one idea – the way that animals are raised with factory farming methods.

 The first thing Jessica did was to think hard about the opinions people hold on the subject.

I'm a Rastafarian, so I don't eat meat, though I do eat fish, because that's what my religion teaches.

My religion forbids the eating of meat. It teaches that all life is sacred. I'm a Jain, which is a type of Hindu.

I eat meat because I like the taste. It's a matter of freedom of choice. No one has any right to tell me what to eat.

I'm a vegetarian because I think it's healthier. I do make a point of buying free-range eggs as I don't think animals should suffer so we can eat.

I'm a vegan because I believe that animals should have the same rights as people, so I don't eat any animal products at all.

I don't eat beef for environmental reasons: cows eat cereal and that could be used to feed people, and sometimes they are grazed on land where rainforest has been destroyed. But I eat lamb, because keeping sheep doesn't damage the earth to that extent.

Then she did some reading in the library.

The *Indy* guide to life without meat

Vegetarians are growing in number and are no longer considered freaks. **Anne Churchward** and **Louise Hurst** explain how to take the meat out of your diet. They reveal the life in a factory farm and name some famous veggies along the way.

BECOMING A vegetarian doesn't just mean giving up the odd beef doorstep sandwich from your school lunch, and existing on a diet of soggy lettuce and nut roast.

Here are a few tips which might make life a little easier if you decide you want to be a veggie and don't warm to the prospect of boiled cabbage and Brussels sprouts for dinner every night.

1 You don't have to subject yourself to eating mounds of Brussels sprouts for dinner and sticks of celery for lunch! There are loads of good vegetarian cookbooks around, so pop down to your nearest bookshop to investigate.

2 Quorn is a form of soya protein which can take the place of meat as the protein content of your diet. When cooked, e.g. in a vegetable stew, it takes the flavour of what it is cooked in.

3 If you decide to become a vegetarian because you are opposed to the cruelty inflicted upon factory-farmed animals, then you may also choose to eat free-range eggs, laid by chickens who live happily out in a farmyard, instead of battery-farmed eggs.

4 The invisible ingredients warning: many everyday foods and sweets contain ingredients derived from animals. You may think that by not eating meat or fish you are excluding animal foods from your diet, and are a fully-fledged vegetarian. But if you are serious about becoming a vegetarian you should try to *avoid* the following.

a Gelatine – this is glue-like and derived from a protein called collagen which is found in animal tissues. Gelatine often crops up in chewy sweets and similar confectionery.

b Animal fat – this is used in a wide variety of foods, ranging from margarine, suet, cooking fats, biscuits and cakes to sweets; look carefully if you want to avoid it.

c Rennet – rennet is obtained from calf's stomachs and is used to curdle milk. This means it turns up in hard cheeses, such as cheddar. If you want to avoid rennet it is best to steer well clear of pizzas, cauliflower cheese, cheese sandwiches or any other foods which contain non-vegetarian cheese.

5 Many people who want to become vegetarians are put off by their mum or dad. If your parents moan and say, 'No you can't become vegetarian... I'm not cooking two separate dinners... don't be such a pain!', try sitting down and reasoning with them.

Explain why you want to become a vegetarian, and suggest that your mum or dad tries cooking some vegetarian meals for the whole family. You could even volunteer to help with the cooking, but make sure they are sitting down when you tell them, so they don't collapse from shock!

6 You are now ready to become a successful vegetarian. Remember, when you go into fast-food restaurant, beefburgers are out of the question. However, Wimpy do sell beanburgers as an alternative.

Why be a vegetarian?

Being a vegetarian does not make you an anaemic, pale-faced freak!
* The vegetarian diet is very similar to the recommendations issued by the government on medical aspects of food policy.
* The average fibre content of a vegetarian diet is almost twice that of a meat-eater.
* The total daily calorie intake of fat per person could be reduced by 10 per cent by cutting out meat.
* British milk is among Europe's worst, as most of our cows are pumped full of antibiotics.
* Diseases such as diabetes, gout and kidney stones are more common among meat-eaters.
* Millions of children in Third-World countries go blind because they do not get enough of vitamin A, which is abundant in a vegetarian diet.

Eating without meat is healthy and kind says **Joe Newman**, age 15 of Simonstock School, Maidstone

Why I am a vegetarian

I TURNED vegetarian three years ago, when I was twelve, and have not eaten meat since. At first it was difficult and there were many problems. One of these was eating at someone else's house. Gradually I and other people got used to it. Half of my family were already vegetarian.

The change of diet was difficult though. Now I check the ingredients of every type of food before I eat it. For example, Polos have gelatine in which is made from animals.

I turned vegetarian when I found out what was going on within the meat industry and, more importantly, on the factory farms. The most disturbing was the animal cruelty going on there.

I do not eat eggs either because battery hens are put into cages measuring four inches wide. In such a small space there is no room to walk, make dustbaths, spread their wings, lay their eggs in nests, scratch or peck.

Pigs are also kept in appalling conditions, where they are kept in crates on cold concrete floors. These crates are only two feet wide, where there is no room to even turn around.

The same kind of treatment is given to cows, chickens, turkeys and sheep. None of these animals take exercise, feel fresh air, experience freedom of movement or natural companionship with their own species. They face a sentence of life imprisonment.

Another reason I turned vegetarian was because it is more healthy than a meat eating diet. Meat has a high fat content. A vegetarian diet has a high fibre content. It also provides carbohydrates, some fat, vitamins and minerals, which all add up to a healthy, balanced diet.

Such a diet can reduce the risks of heart disease, cancer of the colon (in your stomach), obesity and hernias (internal ruptures). A reduction in fatty foods can reduce the risk of cardiovascular disease (in the heart's blood vessels) which is the UK's biggest killer, with 180,000 deaths each year.

The meat industry is also responsible for environment damage, such as water pollution and loss of wildlife. Tropical rainforests the size of Wales are cut down every month to make way for cattle ranching.

One hectare of land will feed enough animals to produce meat to make just 1,000 hamburgers, each costing half a tonne of rainforest.

Next time you are eating your dinner, think about it.

The shocking facts for you meat eaters

Many people are now choosing not to eat meat because they object to the cruel process of factory farming

* Almost half-a-billion animals every year are killed for food in Britain alone.
* Battery hens are kept in rows of wire cages about the size of a piece of typing paper (they cannot spread their wings for the whole of their lives).
* The cramped space makes them susceptible to illness and disease.
* The hens become aggressive in small spaces, so the farmers cut their beaks off to stop them pecking their neighbours to death. This causes severe pain, yet more than 1,000 hens per farm per day are still mutilated.
* Pigs are stunned with electric shocks before being killed. However, this does not always make them unconscious to pain.

* Many pigs are still fully awake when they are hung upside down to have their throats slit!
* Most hens are killed on a conveyor belt system, by an automatic throat slitter. If the birds are too large or too small then the knife will miss their throats and cut their heads or lower neck.
* In some abattoirs (slaughter-houses) sheep are stunned through the eyeball.
* In a lifetime one British person eats on average 8 cows, 346 pigs, 36 sheep, 750 poultry.
* There are 2 million vegetarians in Britain alone, and the number is constantly increasing.
* 1 in 9 students are vegetarians.
* 2 million battery hands die in their cages every year.
* 6 million livestock die each year before they reach the abattoir.
* Vegetarian have a 20 per cent lower blood cholesterol level on average than meat eaters.
* 100 acres of tropical rainforest is destroyed every minute. A lot of the land is used to rear

Types of vegetarians

14 per cent of under-16s in Britain are one of three types of vegetarian.
1) Ovovegetarians eat a diet of vegetables, milk, cheese and eggs.
2) Lactovegetarians eat a diet of all vegetables, milk, cheese but no eggs.
3) Pure vegetarians, vegans, eat a diet of all vegetables, and will not eat any product of animal origin, (i.e. milk or eggs).

She made some notes:

Many methods of raising animals for meat are inhumane.

There are laws which should prevent real cruelty.

Raising animals for meat is wasteful and damages the environment.

Some people have moral and religious reasons for not eating meat.

People should be allowed to choose for themselves.

A meatless diet is healthier than one containing meat.

Jessica now had the beginnings of her speech.

Jessica's notes

Burgers
Rainforest

What she said

> Remember tucking into your last Big Burger? The fresh warm bun; the tasty ozone-layer relish; the succulent burger? But did you think about where that burger came from? A lump of minced-up cow, grazed on land that ought to be rainforest. Did you ever think that you were doing your bit for the destruction of the ozone layer?

Technical Tips: Notice three things Jessica does to make what she says strike home. She asks a series of questions which set a trap for the listeners and makes them question their behaviour. She uses emotive words ('minced-up cow', 'destruction') which help sway the audience to adopt her point of view. She also lists things in groups of three. This is sometimes called the rule of three. It is a way of reinforcing your point by making it three times in slightly different ways.

Once Jessica had the attention of her audience, she could use any number of persuasive techniques. She could:
- shock them with facts about factory farming;
- scare them by emphasising health risks;
- appeal to their sympathy by describing the suffering of animals;
- appeal to their common sense.

The end of a speech is as important as the beginning. Jessica needed to leave her audience in no doubt about the main point she was trying to make.

Jessica's notes

No meat
Health
Suffering of animals
Damage to environment
Big Mac

What she said

> So, I think you'll agree that it's best not to eat meat. For the sake of your own health; to avoid causing unecessary suffering to animals; to protect our planet. Next time you pick up a juicy Big Burger, just think about all that!

Talking Standard English

In this kind of public performance you have to think about your use of Standard English. Look back at Section Two for an outline of what Standard English is. If you have already carried out the Workbench assignment on telling stories, you will have begun to consider the way you adapt how you speak to suit different listeners: a child, a friend your own age or an elderly relative, for example.

Skilful talkers also need to be aware of how we need to adapt our use of English to suit different occasions. Suppose you turned up at a party dressed very casually and then realised you were the only one there not wearing a formal suit or a long dress. You would feel quite out of place, because your clothes were not appropriate for the occasion.

There are some occasions which call for the language equivalent of 'best clothes'. This is one of the skills you will need to develop during your English course. To achieve Grade C or above, you will need to show that you recognise where it is appropriate to use Standard English and to demonstrate that you are capable of adapting your everyday speech to do this.

Formal situations, where you are attempting to make a good impression, are the most likely to require Standard English. These might include:
• job interviews;
• speeches to a large audience;
• showing an important visitor around your school;
• phoning to make an appointment or a complaint, etc.

Which dialect features might I need to alter?

Vocabulary is the simplest part of language to change. If you know you sometimes use words which are local dialect words, you need to 'translate' these into words which any English speaker might also understand. In formal situations, you will also need to avoid slang and colloquial expressions. Even though these might be understood by anyone, they will not be appropriate in formal speech.

Grammar is more difficult to adapt. You will need to know how your local grammar differs from Standard English.

This might include the way you form verb tenses.

In the North of England you might hear a local dialect speaker say, "I were stood at the bus stop for more than an hour," where a Standard English speaker would say "I was standing…".

It might include the way you use adverbs.

In Yorkshire you might hear someone say, "I waited while the rain stopped," where the Standard English speaker would say 'I waited until…'.

You might find there are different pronouns in your dialect.

In some Irish dialects there is a plural form of 'you': "Which one of youse did this?", where Standard English uses the same word for singular and plural.

You may notice different use of prepositions.

Some Scottish speakers say, "We went by my house," where a Standard English speaker would say, "We went to my house."

Being a local dialect speaker is not a disadvantage. You will learn a great deal about English grammar by taking an interest in dialect and by talking about it to other people, and you will also improve your skills in writing and speaking Standard English.

Workbench assignment

Making a formal speech

Now, prepare a short speech giving **your** views on the causes of football hooliganism. First, note down your opinions and then try to back up each one with evidence or examples. Keep the points you want to make as clear and simple as you can. Make a conscious attempt to use Standard English.

If you are able to, videotape your performance. If that is not possible, try giving your speech as you look in a mirror. You will find it very hard to give a speech to just one or two friends. Speeches are 'public' and sound odd in personal situations or small groups.

Tip box

• Making speeches really does get easier with practice: the more times you do it, the more confident you will become.

- Advance preparation is essential. Know your facts and prepare notes in advance. Trying it out either on a friend, or on tape or in front of a mirror, will make you feel much more confident when you finally face a larger audience.
- Take a few deep breaths before you start. Having a table in front of you on which to steady yourself will make you feel less like a quivering jelly.
- Work from notes – not a written speech. Make your notes on a bundle of cards (about postcard size), one point to each card. If your hands shake with nerves, it is a lot less obvious to those watching you if you are holding small cards, rather than a large, quivering sheet of paper! Grip your cards in one hand, and hang onto the table with the other.
- Use visual aids (posters, pictures, facts on an overhead projector) to emphasise your points, but make sure your audience can see them properly.
- Make each point clearly. Use 'tricks of the trade' to involve your audience. Vary tone, volume and pace of voice. Use pauses to give your audience time to think. Try to use eye contact and gestures.
- Start with something to make your audience to sit up and take notice. Shock them, surprise them. Make sure you have a strong beginning and end to your speech.

Endnote: using role-play

You will probably already have had experience of taking part in a variety of larger group performances during your English course. You might be taking on roles of people with different opinions to argue out differing points of view about various topical issues, improvising scenes, sometimes of your own invention, sometimes based on your reading, and acting out scripted plays, written by members of your class, or plays you were studying.

Many of you will have already have demonstrated the skills required to reach Level 6: you have helped to plan and taken part in a group performance. That is the highest possible level for this aspect of Speaking and Listening as far as English is concerned. At Key Stage 4 you will continue to practise these skills because they make a contribution to other aspects of your English work.

Working in a group on a drama or role-play allows you to develop your collaborative skills.

Role-playing allows you to demonstrate your ability to argue a case or to give information.

Group performances based on the books you are reading, either for English or for English Literature, allow your teacher to assess your understanding of what you have read as an alternative to written essays.

Role-playing may be used to help you gather information in preparation for writing essays about varying points of view on a topic. Improvisation can help you to refine ideas for writing a script or a story.

All of these are skills which you can develop to reach the highest levels in Reading and Writing, in addition to Speaking and Listening.

⑤ Knowledge about language

Talking about words

The National Curriculum expects you to think about the words you use and reflect on why you use them in particular ways. This is called Knowledge about Language. For example, did you know that girls are generally better listeners than boys and that, contrary to popular belief, boys tend to talk more than girls in group discussions? That is a piece of useful knowledge about language which you could use in different ways. You could test it out by observing different people talking in groups and, in your own groups, you could encourage the boys to listen and give the girls space to talk.

As another example, an American linguist called Deborah Tannen has suggested that there are two different ways of interrupting. One way is to talk over the top of what someone else is saying, changing the subject and showing that you were not listening to or did not care about what they were saying.

The other sort of interruption, she suggests, is when someone is so interested in what another person is saying that they join in and start relating it to their own experience and feelings. She suggests that men usually interrupt the first way (maybe because they are not such good listeners), whilst women usually interrupt in the second way. Try observing people working in groups at school and see if you think she is correct!

Workbench assignment

Roles in groups

Working in pairs is easy enough, so long as you are both prepared to listen and both take part in talking. Once groups get larger than two, they take more organising and more understanding about how language works in groups. It can help if different members of the group take on different jobs and all members know what their job is.

Groups usually function best if they have:

A chairperson, who
• should make sure the group is clear about the task;
• should make sure the task gets done;
• should make sure everyone in the group is involved in the task.

A secretary, who
• should make sure that any conclusions the group reaches are written down, especially if information is to be passed on or shared with other groups during or after the activity.

A reporter, who
• is the group's messenger or spokesperson and should be able to pass on information or conclusions from the group to other groups.

In a way, everything you have read in this section has involved knowledge about spoken language.

Revise what you have learned by looking at who does what in a good group meeting or discussion.

List four of the speaking and listening skills outlined above which you think a good chairperson would need.

1 _____

2 _____

3 _____

4 _____

Which four speaking and listening skills do you think a good secretary would need?

1 _____

2 _____

3 _____

4 _____

Which four speaking and listening skills do you think a good reporter would need?

1 _____

2 _____

3 _____

4 _____

Which four speaking and listening skills would be the most important to group members?

① _____

② _____

③ _____

④ _____

Case study

Gemma, Carl, Nasreen and James have been given the task of discussing a poem, *Song of the Battery Hen*. Here is the transcript of the start of their discussion. Look at how they choose their roles and then begin to make use of them.

James: OK then, this poem. Nasreen can read it and Gemma can make notes.
Nasreen: James, Gemma was secretary last time. Don't you think she should have a go at chairing?
Carl: Yeah, and James can report. I hate doing that.
Gemma: Nas, I'm no good, why did you...
James: Go on then Nas. Gemma chairs, Carl reports.
Carl and
Gemma: Oh no!
Nasreen: Go on Gem, you can.
Gemma: All right. Nas, read the poem. Then we've got to, er...
James: Discuss whether...
Nasreen: Go on, Gem.
Gemma: Yeah, we have to say whether factory farming is cruel. We have to say why it's, er... unhuman...
Carl: Inhumane.
Gemma: Oh, yeah, inhumane for the hens. And we have to decide whether... er... there are advantages for people that, like... er...
Nasreen: Justify it?
Gemma: Yeah. Justify it.
Carl: 'Course it's worth it, because free range eggs cost a fortune, don't they? And besides, they're only a load of hens...
Gemma: Carl, let's read the poem first. OK, Nasreen?
(Nasreen reads)

Song of the Battery Hen

We can't grumble about the accommodation:
we have a new concrete floor that's
always dry, four walls that are
painted white, and a sheet-iron roof
the rain drums on. A fan blows warm air
beneath our feet to disperse the smell
of chicken-shit and, on dull days,
fluorescent lighting sees us.

You can tell me: if you come by
the North door, I am in the twelfth pen
on the left-hand side of the third row
from the floor; and in that pen
I am usually the middle one of three.

But, even without directions, you'd
discover me. I have the same orange-
red comb, yellow beak and auburn
feathers, but as the door opens and you
hear above the electric fan a kind of
one-word wail, I am the one
who sounds loudest in my head.

Listen. Outside this house there's an
orchard with small moss-green apple
trees; beyond that, two fields of
cabbages; then, on the far side of
the road, a broiler house. Listen:
one cockerel grows out of there, as
tall and proud as the first hour of the sun.
Sometimes I stop calling with the others
to listen, and wonder if he hears me.

The next time you come here, look for me.
Notice the way I sound inside my head.
God made us all quite differently,
and blessed us with this expensive home.

Edwin Brock

James: Well, that's all about inhumanity isn't it? I mean, look at what it says about it never seeing daylight. That's really...

Gemma: Good point, James. Hey... no one's taking notes. James, would you? Write it down before you forget. Carl, do you still think it doesn't matter because they're only hens?

Carl: Well... er... this bit here is a bit tight...

Nasreen: Which? Read it to us.

Carl: Where it says...

James: I think...

Gemma: Can Carl explain why, first? Sorry, James. Are you writing it down, then?...

Recording your achievements

At the end of the course, your teacher has to send a detailed written summary of your speaking and listening skills to the examination board. Some boards leave it to schools to decide how this should be presented, others have a form for teachers to complete. The form opposite is an example.

Self-assessment

Sometimes your teacher may ask you to fill in ready-prepared forms to record and assess what you have done in lessons where most of the work is speaking and listening. Sometimes you may be asked to observe another pupil and to record what they have done. All of this is useful in helping you to develop your own speaking skills, as well as providing your teacher with much more information than it would be possible to record when watching twenty or thirty pupils at the same time.

All the way through this section, you have been building up your own knowledge about speaking and listening skills. If you put these into practice, you will be a better talker and listener. Reflecting on your own performance as a talker is useful, because:

- if you know what your strengths and weaknesses are, then you will be able to make efforts to improve specific skills;
- most of the talking you do in school goes on in a busy classroom, and a great-deal of it vanishes into thin air: it would not be possible to tape or video every single thing you said for the two years of your GCSE course. Written records of self-assessment will be a great help to your teacher when it comes to recording your overall achievement.

Teacher Summary of Oral Coursework

Centre Name..   Centre No....................................

Candidate Surname...................................   Candidate No.............................

Other Names ....

Brief Details of the Oral Activities on which Assessment is based

Activity	Text used if any
....	....
....	....
....	....
....	....
....	....
....	....
....	....
....	....
....	....
....	....
....	....

Please use the heading below to summarise the candidate's achievement

Achievement in Speaking and Listening (AT1)

Explain, explore and present events, feelings and points of view

....
....
....

Develop and refine ideas, plans and arguments through discussion

....
....
....

Reflect on and evaluate the ways in which s/he and others use spoken and written language in different contexts for different purposes

....
....
....

Achievements in Reading (AT2)

Personal response, ideas and opinions

....
....
....

Ability to consider and distinguish features of texts

....
....
....

Discussion of the way language is used in the texts studied

....
....
....

Signed...
Teacher

Keeping a talk log

The most thorough way of recording your speaking and listening is to keep a diary in which you can record all your significant achievements. This is most useful because it allows you to write about talk in other lessons, not just English, as well as any achievements out of school, like taking part in a play or a debating competition.

If you have not done this before, it might be difficult to decide what is worth writing about, so here are some ideas to start you off:

You can write about work you have done in pairs

What was the work you did? Who did you work with? Did you work well together? Did you help each other get the work done well? Did you solve any problems together? Could you make any improvements if you worked with that person again?

You can write about group work

Who was in your group? What was the work you did? Did you have a particular job (chair, secretary)? Did your group work well? What did you (or other people) do that helped to get the work done? What did you (or other people) do that made it difficult to work? Could you make any improvements if you worked with that group again?

You can write about drama work – role-play, improvisation, working with a script, etc.

Who did you work with? What was the work you did? What part did you play? Did you do well? What about the others in the group?
Were there any problems with the work? Were they anybody's fault?
Could you improve the work if you had to do it again?

You can write about performances you have been involved in – acting out your drama work for the class, doing a talk or a reading, etc.

Did you work on your own or with other people?
What went well? What went badly? What would you improve next time you do something like this?

You can write about any special conversations you have with your teacher

Did you start them, or did the teacher? What did you talk about?
Was the conversation helpful? Will it help you to do better with your work in future?

Chapter 3
Investigating talk

Some examination groups specify that part of your coursework should be a written unit which is language-based. In other words, it should show evidence of your knowledge about language. Trying out some of the Workbench activities in this section will have shown you that talk is a very interesting area to research. It is all around you and most people have quite a lot to say about it. Here are a few possible topics and practical tips for getting started on a Talk Project.

Talk project one: Baby talk

If there is a small child in your family, observing and writing about the way children learn words and begin to put them together into sentences is a fascinating study.

It is still a mystery to linguists who study language acquisition quite how children do learn to talk: in the first four years of life, a child learns a vocabulary of about 2000 words, and a complex set of grammatical rules, without any difficulty. You only have to think how difficult you found it to learn a foreign language to appreciate the achievement.

Background information

Between about four months and a year old, babies experiment with sounds by cooing (vowel sounds) and babbling (repeated consonant and vowel sounds like Ba–ba–ba.) Towards the end of this time, they only make sounds that they hear in the language spoken by those around them.

At about a year old, babies begin to communicate with single words: but they don't just name things. By using intonation like that of the adults around them, they make their single words into questions or commands, as well as statements. This is called the Holophrastic stage by linguists, because the one word is a 'whole' sentence in meaning.

When they are one to two years old, toddlers begin to put two words together. They are beginning to develop a kind of grammar. Usually, they have a set of phrases in which one word remains, but the second word may be varied, e.g. 'all-gone dinner', 'all-gone teddy', 'all-gone daddy'.

Between about two and four years old, children learn masses of new words and begin to work out all kinds of rules to do with meaning of words and the grammatical patterns that combine them into sentences. This is probably the most interesting age to study, because children make mistakes, though they are not so much mistakes as evidence that they are thinking hard about the rules of language.

One example of this is what linguists call 'over-extension': this occurs when a child has worked out a language rule, but uses it too widely. You will notice this where children over-extend the meaning of a word (e.g. calling all men 'Daddy' or all four-legged animals 'pussy').

You will also notice over-extended grammatical rules. For example, you will hear three-year-olds talking about 'mouses' and making up verb past tenses like 'I holded', though they would have been using the words 'mice' and 'held' at two years old. These changes are sure signs that the child is almost at the final stage of learning to talk.

By about five years old, the miracle has happened, and the child is speaking English, using the same rules as any adult speaker, though still with many more words to learn.

Workbench assignment

Try doing at least two of the following, and write up your findings.

1. Construct a questionnaire for parents or carers of young children, and collect examples of the kinds of early words and sentences their children said. Ask them about how they helped their child to learn to talk; whether they used special games and activities; how they altered their normal way of speaking to communicate with the child.

2. Tape record a child once a month for a period of six months, and see what progress in language development has taken place.

3. Transcribe a short extract of conversation between a child and its carer which demonstrates some of the signs of development shown above.

4. Listen carefully to the special way the adult talks to the child and consider how adult talk plays a part in helping the child to progress towards an adult use of English.

Talk project two: Girl talk/boy talk

Linguists have done a great deal of research into the differences between the way males and females talk, either when they are together in mixed gender groups, or when they are in groups of their own gender. Some of these findings are mentioned earlier on in this unit.

Background information

Some major findings include:

- In single gender groups, women are inclined to be cooperative and supportive of what each other says, whilst men are more likely to be competitive: they compete for talking time and compete to be the one who is right (or funniest).
- In mixed groups, men talk more (and more loudly!) than women, and women listen more than men.
- In mixed groups, men tend to be 'task-focused' (i.e. they want to get the job done quickly), while women tend to be 'relationship-focused' (i.e. they want to include people in the group and make them feel valued).
- In mixed groups, men interrupt women more than they interrupt other men. (Though remember the two different types of interruption mentioned on p.48.)
- In general, men talk more about facts, while women talk more about feelings.

Workbench assignment

Try doing at least two of the following and write up your findings.

1. Construct a questionnaire to find out whether a variety of people of different ages are aware of these differences, or whether they

believe they are true from their own experience.

2 Tape some conversations, of mixed gender and single-gender groups. Design a record sheet for collecting statistical evidence which either proves or disproves that these differences do exist.

3 Transcribe some short extracts which show definite evidence of the above differences, or definite evidence of the exact opposite.

Talk project three: Body language

"It's not what you said, it's the way you said it!" How often have you heard someone say that?

Talk is more than just words. Part of our meaning is expressed by our faces. The way we stand or sit and the way we arrange our arms and legs may also be part of the message. We are not always aware that we are doing this. The intonation we use can either emphasise or contradict the literal meaning of the words we say. The curriculum requirements for knowledge about language are specifically concerned with demonstrating an understanding of body language at the higher levels of attainment.

Why at higher levels only? There are many things about body language that even very small children understand: They know the difference between a smiling and an angry face. But they will not know that what gives them away when they are not telling the truth is that, without thinking about it, they cover up their mouth with their hands. Even adults may retain a shadow of this gesture, though when adults tell a lie, it may look more as if they are scratching their nose.

Background information

One basic distinction is between **open** and **closed** body language. When people who trust each other are talking together, they tend to sit or stand with their arms spread and their legs uncrossed. If they are agreeing with each other, they may even 'mirror' each other's position. This is **open** body language.

Closed body language is shown by tightly folded arms and crossed legs. This might demonstrate lack of trust, disagreement, dislike or nervousness.

Seating yourself so that you are physically higher than the person you are talking to is a way of indicating power (how often has a teacher told you off while you're sitting and they are standing?). Leaning on, or putting your feet on, objects is an unconscious way of saying, "I own this". Putting your hands on your hips, or your thumbs in your belt, is a way of looking wider and larger and is an aggressive gesture. Avoiding eye contact is a sign of mistrust. Making eye contact with someone's face is a normal expression of social interest. Looking them up and down usually signifies a more intimate interest!

Workbench assignment

Try doing the following, and write up your findings. Ideally, you need a video recorder to tape people in conversation and to study their body language, though you could try taping and drawing stick diagrams of interesting positions people adopt during a conversation.

1 Listen carefully to the intonation used on the tape. Do you spot any instances where intonation contradicts the words? Transcribe some extracts where this seems to be happening.

2 Find out how well other people can read body language: you could show them some of the pictures in this book and see how they would interpret those gestures or positions.

Talk project four: Varieties of English

You will already have found that people hold all kinds of opinions about accents and dialects. To attain the higher levels for knowledge about language, you need to be able to show that you are aware of how this may affect their attitudes towards others.

Workbench assignment

Try doing at least two of the following and write up your findings.

1 Construct a questionnaire that will help you find out about 'language biographies'. What factors influence the kind of accent or dialect people speak? (You may well be able to do this with your own family. If you have moved around the country, you may find that everyone in your family speaks with a slightly different accent. Accounting for these differences would be a good project.)

2 Conduct a survey on people's attitudes to their own accent, those of other areas and the RP accent. Find out how aware they are of modifying their accent or dialect in different situations.

3 If you live in an area where some people are bilingual or multilingual, this can be the basis for a fascinating project. Find out what languages people speak; when, where and to whom they speak them; and what purposes they use their different languages for. Find out which languages they can *write*, as well as speak: does it make a difference if a language is *only* spoken?

4 Tape the interviews you carry out. Transcribe extracts of conversation which highlight interesting discoveries.

Writing a transcript of spoken English

Taking a few sensible precautions when taping saves a lot of frustration: carry spare batteries if you are using a portable recorder, so it does not stop taping in the middle of your best interview. Make a copy of any tape you are going to transcribe, as winding tapes backwards and forwards can make them break. Do not try to transcribe more than a few minutes of talk – it is very time-consuming.

Use conventional transcription symbols like these:

=	one speaker follows another with no pause
[	two speakers talk at the same time
(.)	very brief pause
: :	a lengthened sound
<u>word</u>	a word with strong stress
°word°	a word said quietly
↑word↑	rising intonation
↓word↓	falling intonation

Revision file

There is no examination of Speaking and Listening but make sure that:
• you have covered at least three of the AT1 strands in the work you have done and that this is clearly shown on your record sheets;
• your teacher has seen you at your best – taking a variety of roles in a range of situations;
• if you have talked about reading or your use of language, that these discussions are also recorded as achievements against AT2 and AT3.

Chapter 1

What makes a good reader?

Danesh is a good reader. He loves Roald Dahl and can read his favourite books out loud with very few mistakes. He likes looking up information from the books in the school book corner and has just finished making his own book about different kinds of dinosaur. He even used a junior encyclopedia for some of the information, though he found that rather difficult to understand.

Kylie is a good reader. She belongs to the local library and has read every single book it has by Enid Blyton. Recently she has started reading Nina Bawden's novels and is surprised by how different they are from each other, 'not like *The Famous Five*'. She reads comics and newspapers at home. She worries about the environment and is doing a lot of research about pollution that is damaging the ozone layer. In school she has just produced a poster to persuade her classmates not to use aerosols. She found some information in her older sister's science text book that she included in this.

Iannis is a good reader. Private reading is his favourite English lesson and you will often see him chuckling away at Michael Rosen's poetry. Recently he read *Oliver Twist* and wrote a script about the part where Oliver learns to pick pockets. He directed a group of his friends acting this out in drama. All his teachers agree that his comprehension is excellent. He did a traffic survey for Geography that involved reading some complicated town planning documents. He is good at reading in exams, too: fast, accurate and able to write well-expressed and full answers that show a grasp of both the detail and the overall message of what he's read.

Waynetta is a good reader. She knows she is. She always has been. She likes reading. She reads a lot. She finds it easy. What she wants to know is how she can prove it and make sure she is awarded the high level she's sure she deserves for her GCSE.

Building on what you know

The very fact that you are reading this book shows that you are already an experienced and skilful reader. Not only do you know how to decode the words on the page, you also have enough experience of reading to know about the different purposes reading may serve.

You did not pick up this book simply to pass the time: it would hardly count as light entertainment. But you know that it contains some information which will be useful to you. You may have started off by **scanning** the contents page to get a general idea of what the book was about. No doubt there will be some sections that you already feel you know enough about, so you will **skim-read** those. Some parts will contain information you don't know, so those will need close reading. Some parts may be difficult to understand, so you'll find yourself **back-tracking** and **re-reading** to make sense of what is being said.

You will have been developing all of these skills right the way through school. You read without much effort and take it for granted, just like your ability to talk. You may find it hard to imagine what more there is to learn about reading during the two years of your GCSE course.

Reading in the National Curriculum

Your skills as a reader contribute 40% to your final assessment. Work that you do during your English course will be worth 10%. This work may be oral or written. The other 30% of your mark will depend on how well you perform in the written exam at the end of your course.

This section aims to show you the five areas of skill which will be assessed by your English teacher. It also includes some Workbench assignments to back up the work you do in English and to help you prepare for the final exam. These will demonstrate what it is you need to be able to do to reach the higher levels of attainment.

Some of the skills you develop will merge into the skills you need to succeed if you also take English Literature. Some of these skills will also help you become a more efficient reader for the purposes of other subjects you are studying in school.

Tip box

Obviously, it's perfectly possible to be a very good reader and never say or write a word about what you have read, but that would hardly allow your teacher to assess your ability. If you wish to demonstrate that you are a good reader, you will have to use your Speaking and Writing skills to show it, so you will need to read this section in conjunction with Sections 2 and 4 to do your best.

This book, on its own, will not turn you into a good reader. Good readers READ. They read books and newspapers and magazines. They think about what they read. They watch films, plays and television in the same thoughtful manner.

If an extract printed here interests you, follow it up: take the book out of the library. Change the newspaper you read. Take a look at that magazine where the interesting article was published and see what else it has to offer.

What do I need to know how to do?

These are the skills your English teacher will assess:
1. Reading a range of texts
2. Responding to literature
3. Reading non-literary texts
4. Using reading skills to study
5. Reading about language

In more detail, these mean:

1 Your experience of, and enthusiasm for, reading of literary writing

You will need to show that you have read a good selection of books: novels, poetry, plays, diaries, travel books, and that you have enough reading background to say what you like and dislike about them. Some work on Shakespeare's plays is compulsory for all GCSE students. To reach the higher levels you need to read books written before this century. You also need to demonstrate that you know about the books in some detail.

2 Your ability to express your personal response to the books you have read, either in talk or writing

This could involve talking to your class about a book you have read, or producing a piece of writing about it. To reach the higher levels, your response work must show you know the book in detail and also that you understand the author's approach to writing, so you need to be able to comment on style and technique as well as the 'story' of the book.

3 Your ability to read non-literary and media texts

This means that you need to develop critical reading skills which will enable you to explain, for example, how an advertisement or a political pamphlet uses language to persuade the reader to a particular point of view. Media texts include films and television programmes, as well as written pieces.

4 Your ability to use reference materials to do research

This will involve you going off to the library to do some independent work to back up what you're studying in class. You need to show that you know how to use all kinds of sources, from an encyclopedia to a computer database, and that you can bring the information you discover together in a piece of work of your own: a talk for your class, or a written project.

5 Your ability to show that you have some knowledge about the language of written texts

This could involve you in studying pieces of writing which are hundreds of years old, and talking about the way language has changed between then and the present day. You will also add to your knowledge about the various techniques used by writers. People's attitudes towards written English is another topic you may investigate.

Whichever syllabus you are following, your English course will aim to help you develop all of these skills and your coursework will provide evidence of the level you have reached in each. It would be difficult to assess the breadth of your reading or your research skills in an exam, so your coursework will need to show what you can do in those areas. The final exam will test your response to literary texts (the second skill area.) Apart from that, it varies a great deal from exam board to exam board. For example, most of the exam boards specify that you must include coursework showing that you have studied Shakespeare, but NEA tests that in the final exam. NEA does not test your ability to read media texts in the exam, so your coursework must provide evidence of that. LEAG and SEG expect your knowledge about language to be shown in a piece of coursework, rather than testing it in the exam.

More details about the requirements of the different syllabuses are shown in Section 1. Your teacher will give you guidance about the contents of your coursework folder and the skills you will need to practise to prepare for the particular exams you will sit.

Chapter 2
Extending your range

You are a unique individual. No one else has had a life exactly like yours. No one else has shared every one of your experiences and feelings. No one else will have shared your experience of reading either. You will have your own personal tastes and preferences. You will have read a great deal that you have forgotten about. You will have read (and re-read) certain things which are not just memorable, but actually part of you: part of the way you

think and understand the world around you.

Reading is a very personal and private activity: often it's just you, alone with a book. All kinds of thoughts go through your mind as you are reading and these are yours and yours alone. Even when you read with your class in school, every single one of you will be thinking your own unique thoughts about the book, because each of you will be making sense of it according to your different experiences in life and different histories as readers.

Your development as a reader is a lifelong journey. During your GCSE course, your teacher has the responsibility of finding out how far you have already got, encouraging you and guiding you further along your own personal route, then assessing the point you have reached at the end of the course.

The journey is your own. If you're already a keen reader, this part of your English work will often be very enjoyable, even though some of it might be challenging. If you are starting out from a point where you know that reading is not something that you would choose to do for fun, or, at least, not the kind of reading your English teacher wants you to do, then you have some hard work ahead of you. What you need to remember is that your own personal route may be different, but you'll find it if you put the effort into searching for it.

Where am I now?

Complete this questionnaire to find out exactly what type of reader you are.

What kind of reader are you?

1 When did you last read a book?
(a) ages ago
(b) within the last month
(c) within the last week

2 Who was it by?
(a) I don't know
(b) I can't remember
(c) I can tell you

3 What was it about?
(a) I don't know
(b) I sort of know
(c) I can tell you in detail

4 Why did you read it?
(a) told to read it at school
(b) given it as a present
(c) I wanted to

5 Did you finish it?.
(a) no
(b) I pretended I had
(c) yes

6 Did you enjoy it?
(a) Not at all
(b) it was okay
(c) yes

7 Do you have a favourite author or authors?
(a) no
(b) I used to have
(c) yes

8 How many books do you own?
(a) one or two
(b) at least five
(c) ten or more

9 If someone gave you a £5.00 book token today would you...?
(a) try to sell it for £2.50
(b) have a vague idea of what you might buy
(c) buy something you know that you want to get

10 How do you read newspapers and magazines?
(a) look at the pictures
(b) flip through and read what catches my eye
(c) start at the front and read all the way through

11 What reading do you do in other subjects?
(a) as little as possible
(b) what I'm told to
(c) I use reading to find extra information

12 Do you have a hobby or interest which encourages you to read?
(a) no
(b) I have had in the past
(c) yes

13 Do the rest of your family read much?
(a) no
(b) occasionally
(c) regularly

14 When did you last visit your local library?
(a) can't remember
(b) in the last year
(c) in the past month

How did you score?

If most of your answers were (c)s: you're probably too good to be true! Seriously though, it shows that you have the reading habit and enjoy reading – two vital things. You need to make sure that you don't get 'stuck' in one reading groove and always be on the lookout for new reading matter.

If most of your answers were (a)s: you don't enjoy reading and you don't see any point in doing it. Overcoming that feeling has got to be your starting point in becoming a reader. You may find reading difficult as well. Finding the right books to get started with is going to be your next problem: your teacher should be able to advise you.

If most of your answers were (b)s: you're a lazy reader but you know what's involved in being a responsive reader. You need to find a few really good stories to read and then start to enjoy reading for its own sake.

The skill this section focuses on is about your development as an independent reader of literary texts. Let's start with a snapshot of your reading over the past year. What kinds of reading have you done? What kind of use have you made of all the different places you might go to find books to read?

This year I have read:

	Town Library	Home	School Library	School (English)	School (other)	Bookshop	Friend, etc
Folk tales							
Myths and legends							
Animal fiction							
School fiction							
Family fiction							
Adventure fiction							
Historical fiction							
Fantasy fiction							
Science fiction							
Romance fiction							
Poetry							
Plays							
Short stories							
Auto/biography							
Nonfiction							
Picture books							
Comics/Comic books							
Magazines							
Newspapers							
Stories, etc. by other pupils							

Tick the boxes which show **what** you read and **where** you got the book from.
Now take a look at the gaps.
● You may have read masses of books, but realise when you are filling in the chart that they all fall into one category. If you are hooked on a certain type of bestseller, like horror or romantic fiction, extending your reading range will mean branching out into a much wider variety of reading.

- There may well be types of books you haven't read this year. Is this because you've tried them and don't like that kind of literature? Or is it a type of reading you have never tried at all? Extending your reading range will involve having another attempt, or a first attempt at types of reading you don't normally do.
- You may find that almost all your reading has been done in your English lessons. Extending your range will mean taking more responsibility for your own reading and taking advantage of some of the other sources of reading material.

A quick activity like this has its uses, but it doesn't provide the kind of information your teacher would need to assess your reading skills. That requires more detailed information about which books you have been reading and what you thought of them.

Workbench assignment

If you are at the beginning of your GCSE course, now is a good time to take stock of where you are up to and how you got there.
Get together with a friend, or better still two or three friends, and discuss the questions below.

If you can, include both boys and girls in the discussion: the similarities between your development as readers will be interesting in reminding you of books you may not remember on your own; the differences will show you just how individual every reader is and may help you spot areas of reading experience that, so far, you have missed out.

1. Before you started reading, did you like looking at picture books? Did you have stories read to you or told to you at home, or at play group? What do you remember about the ones you liked and the ones you disliked?

   Do you think watching television had any effect on your early experiences of stories?

2. When you learnt to read, how did you learn – at home or at school? What do you remember about the first books you read for yourself? What sort of reading (comics, etc.) did you do at home at this age?

3. As your reading developed, which books do you remember particularly enjoying between the ages of 7 and 11? What else did you read? (Newspapers, encyclopaedias, cereal packets?) Which books do you remember from school?

4. Reading now. You have matured a great deal over the past three years – is this reflected in the things you read?

5. Which books have you read at home which were important to you? What else do you read at home?

6. What about the influence of television and video? Does it stop you reading (many adults say it does!) or encourage you to read?

7. What about the books you read in school? Try to cover plays and poems as well as novels and stories.

8. What do you want to read next? What do you hope to get out of your English or English Literature course?

Tip box

This assignment would make a useful introduction to a Key Stage Four Reading Journal. If you haven't kept a reading journal previously, further advice about keeping a record of your reading on pp. 102–3 will help you to do this.

Where do I go from here?

Your GCSE course will seek to build on the reading you have already done. Unless you are a prolific reader, you are bound to come into contact with some types of book you had never read at all before the course started.

The wider your own range of reading, the better you will cope with the books you have to study in your English lessons. Areas of reading you will need to cover, particularly if there are currently gaps in your experience of reading, include the following:

- Modern novels and short stories written for adults
- Classic works written by great authors from the past
- Playscripts
- Nonfictional literary writing like autobiography, travel writing, and letters and journals
- Poetry
- Literature from other cultures

The pages which follow are intended to give you a taste of the kinds of books you might read.

Modern novels and short stories written for adults

The past twenty years has seen an explosion of fictional writing aimed at the teenage reader and it is quite likely that a great deal of your reading so far, both in and out of school, has been of this sort. Names you probably know will include Judy Blume, Jan Needle, Nigel Hinton and Jan Mark.

Now you are embarking on GCSE, you will be expected to extend your reading to include a much wider range of prose fiction, including books that were not written with younger readers in mind. You may already have read quite a number of adult books and it can come as a surprise when your English teacher tells you that, although James Herbert and Jackie Collins, for example, write extremely popular and readable stories, these are not counted as 'literature'. Part of what you need to learn as a reader is what is considered to be worth reading for the purposes of study. Your GCSE course will give you guidance on this, too.

One of the main differences beteen popular best sellers and literature is that the main purpose of best sellers is to entertain the reader: to amuse, excite or to shock. They don't usually set out to challenge the way the reader thinks about the world. Good literature sets out to make you think. The author will be attempting to put across a serious point. Of course, good literature can also be humorous, entertaining and shocking. It may even use the same genres as the best seller: romances, science fiction and detective stories can all be found in books which are generally agreed to be 'great' literature.

Another thing that might surprise you is that 'modern' can mean anything written this century, not just in the last ten years or so. You would certainly find that some books written during the early 1900s seem almost as difficult to read and as far away from the world you live in as the 'classic' novels of earlier centuries. Even so, authors such as D H Lawrence, James Joyce and Virginia Woolf still count as modern writers. Writers like these will certainly be worth reading, but are probably not the best starting point if your experience of reading so far has been confined to teenage and popular fiction.

The extracts that follow are taken from three modern novels and one complete short story. They all make a point about how children are educated in the values of a particular society: how children learn to 'fit in'. Each one is, in some way, concerned with 'learning the rules', 'discipline' or 'punishment'. Apart from that, each of the books is very different.

Workbench assignment

As you read each extract, consider the following questions:

• Who speaks the text? Is it a first-person or third-person narrative? Is the author adopting the omniscient (all-knowing) perspective, or is there one character whose thoughts and feelings you are invited to share?

• What genre of fiction is this? Is it realistic, or does it have elements of fantasy? Is the author adapting autobiographical experience in his or her writing, or is this a world of the imagination?

• Which of the characters do you sympathise with? How does this affect your opinion of the experience the extract describes?

• Is the message of the extract clear, or would you need to read more of the book to check your first impressions? What thoughts about education has it made you have? Does it remind you of anything you have experienced yourself?

• Think about the style of writing. Was the extract difficult or easy to read? Was the vocabulary used simple or complex? Did the author use much description or dialogue to help narrate the events?

• Which did you enjoy reading most, and why? Would you want to read the rest of the book, or look for other books by any of these writers?

Brave New World by Aldous Huxley

Aldous Huxley wrote this novel in 1932. It tells of a future world, where science is used to create order. Huxley's other great novels include *Eyeless in Gaza* and *Point Counterpoint*. He also wrote short stories and travel books.

In this extract, the Director of Hatcheries and Conditioning (the D.H.C.) is explaining to a group of students how Delta-type babies are educated for their future. There are five ranks of people in this society, named after letters of the Greek alphabet. Alphas are superior and Epsilons are inferior. Deltas are the group above Epsilons.

 M. Foster was left in the Decanting Room. The D.H.C. and his students stepped into the nearest lift and were carried up to the fifth floor.

INFANT NURSERIES. NEO-PAVLOVIAN CONDITIONING ROOMS, announced the notice board.

The Director opened a door. They were in a large bare room, very bright and sunny; for the whole of the southern wall was a single window. Half a dozen nurses, trousered and jacketed in the regulation white viscose-linen uniform, their hair aseptically hidden under white caps, were engaged in setting out bowls of roses in a long row across the floor. Big bowls, packed tight with blossom. Thousands of petals, ripe-blown and silkily smooth, like the cheeks of innumerable little cherubs, but of cherubs, in that bright light, not exclusively pink and Aryan, but also luminously Chinese, also Mexican, also apoplectic with too much blowing of celestial trumpets, also pale as death, pale with the posthumous whiteness of marble.

The nurses stiffened to attention as the D.H.C. came in.

'Set out the books,' he said curtly.

In silence the nurses obeyed his command. Between the rose bowls the books were duly set out – a row of nursery quartos opened invitingly each at some gaily coloured image of beast or fish or bird.

'Now bring in the children.'

They hurried out of the room and returned in a minute or two, each pushing a kind of tall dumb-waiter laden, on all its four wire-netted shelves, with eight-month-old babies, all exactly alike (a Bokanovsky Group, it was evident) and all (since their caste was Delta) dressed in khaki.

'Put them down on the floor.'

The infants were unloaded.

'Now turn them so that they can see the flowers and books.'

Turned, the babies at once fell silent, then began to crawl towards those clusters of sleek colours, those shapes so gay and brilliant on the white pages. As they approached, the sun came out of a momentary eclipse behind a cloud. The roses flamed up as though with a sudden passion from within; a new and profound significance seemed to suffuse the shining pages of the books. From the ranks of the crawling babies came little squeals of excitement, gurgles and twitterings of pleasure.

The Director rubbed his hands. 'Excellent!' he said. 'It might almost have been done on purpose.'

The swiftest crawlers were already at their goal. Small hands reached out uncertainly, touched, grasped, unpetalling the transfigured roses, crumpling the illuminated pages of the books. The Director waited until all were happily busy. Then, 'Watch carefully,' he said. And, lifting his hand, he gave the signal.

The Head Nurse, who was standing by a switchboard at the other end of the room, pressed down a little lever.

There was a violent explosion. Shriller and even shriller, a siren shrieked. Alarm bells maddeningly sounded.

The children started, screamed; their faces were distorted with terror.

'And now,' the Director shouted (for the noise was deafening), 'now we proceed to rub in the lesson with a mild electric shock.'

He waved his hand again, and the Head Nurse pressed a second lever. The screaming of the babies suddenly changed its tone. There was something desperate, almost insane, about the sharp spasmodic yelps to which they now gave utterance. Their little bodies twitched and stiffened; their limbs moved jerkily as if to the tug of unseen wires.

'We can electrify that whole strip of floor,' bawled the Director in explanation. 'But that's enough,' he signalled to the nurse.

The explosions ceased, the bells stopped ringing, the shriek of the siren died down from tone to tone into silence. The stiffly twitching bodies relaxed, and what had become the sob and yelp of infant maniacs broadened out once more into a normal howl of ordinary terror.

'Offer them the flowers and the books again.'

The nurses obeyed; but at the approach of the roses, at the mere sight of those gaily-coloured images of pussy and cock-a-doodle-doo and baa-baa black sheep, the infants shrank away in horror; the volume of their howling suddenly increased.

'Observe,' said the Director triumphantly, 'observe.'

Books and loud noises, flowers and electric shocks — already in the infant mind these couples were compromisingly linked; and after two hundred repetitions of the same or a similar lesson would be wedded indissolubly. What man has joined, nature is powerless to put asunder.

'They'll grow up with what the psychologists used to call an "instinctive" hatred of books and flowers. Reflexes unalterably conditioned. They'll be safe from books and botany all their lives.' The Director turned to his nurses. 'Take them away again.'

Still yelling, the khaki babies were loaded on to their dumb-waiters and wheeled out, leaving behind them the smell of sour milk and a most welcome silence.

One of the students held up his hand; and though he could see quite well why you couldn't have lower-caste people wasting the Community's time over books, and that there was always the risk of their reading something which might undesirably de-condition one of their reflexes, yet… well, he couldn't understand about the flowers. Why go to the trouble of making it psychologically impossible for Deltas to like flowers?

Patiently the D.H.C. explained. If the children were made to scream at the sight of a rose, that was on grounds of high economic policy. Not so very long ago (a century or thereabouts), Gammas, Deltas, even Epsilons had been conditioned to like flowers — flowers in particular and wild nature in general. The idea was to make them want to be going out into the country at every available opportunity, and so compel them to consume transport.

'And didn't they consume transport?' asked the student.

'Quite a lot,' the D.H.C. replied. 'But nothing else.'

Primroses and landscapes, he pointed out, have one grave defect: they are gratuitous. A love of nature keeps no factories busy. It was decided to abolish the love of nature, at any rate among the lower classes; to abolish the love of nature, but *not* the tendency to consume transport. For of course it was essential that they should keep on going to the country, even though they hated it. The problem was to find an economically sounder reason for consuming transport than a mere affection for primroses and landscapes. It was duly found.

'We condition the masses to hate the country,' concluded the Director. 'But simultaneously we condition them to love all country sports. At the same time, we see to it that all country sports shall entail the use of elaborate apparatus. So that they consume manufactured articles as well as transport. Hence those electric shocks.'

'I see,' said the student, and was silent, lost in admiration.

Second from Last in the Sack Race by David Nobbs

David Nobbs wrote this novel in 1983. It tells the story of the childhood of Henry Pratt in Yorkshire during the 1930s and 1940s. Nobbs is best known for having created the television character Reginald Perrin. His novels are never likely to be judged amongst the greatest works of literature, but they do fall into a category where popular fiction begins to merge into literature.

In this extract, young Henry has just passed his eleven-plus and, along with a few of his friends, has started at the local Grammar School.

Another September. Another beginning. Henry got off the Thurmarsh tram at the stop before the terminus. The grammar school was in Link Lane, next to the fire station.

Boys were converging on the school from all sides, in black blazers and black-and-yellow-striped ties. The new boys stood out among the scruffy stream like barristers in a public bar.

The school building was long, brick, many-windowed, uninspired but also unforbidding. He was looking for Martin Hammond, but found only Norbert Cuffley. Although he didn't want to be seen as an ally of such an outrageous goody, they clung together in that vast strangeness.

He caught sight of Martin Hammond in the school hall. The boys sat in rows, with the younger boys at the front. The masters filed in, and sat facing the boys. The hubbub subsided, and the headmaster, Mr E. F. Crowther, entered.

They stood and sang a hymn. They sat and the headmaster intoned a prayer. Henry also noticed Milner and Trellis from Brunswick Road. He was surprised to find that he was feeling quite excited.

Mr E. F. Crowther addressed the school. Mr Quell stifled a yawn.

'Welcome back, old boys. Welcome to Thurmarsh Grammar, new boys,' began Mr E. F. Crowther. 'You see before you our staff, as fine as body of men as can be found… in this building.'

Mr Crosby had heard this joke twenty times before, but he still laughed exaggeratedly at it.

'Thurmarsh. It is not perhaps a name that resounds throughout the educational world. It is not an Eton or a Harrow. But is it any the worse for that?' Mr E. F. Crowther paused, as if defying some miserable urchin to say 'yes'. Nobody did. Nobody ever had. 'I am proud to be headmaster of Thurmarsh Grammar,' he continued at last. 'Perhaps I am biased, because I am Thurmarsh born and Thurmarsh bred.'

'And Thurmarsh bread is very nice when it's fresh,' whispered Henry to Norbert Cuffley. He hadn't expected to say it. It just came to him. He was a budding humorist, an emerging character, and he felt exhilarated. Besides, it terrified Norbert Cuffley.

The headmaster paused, and looked in his direction. Careful, Henry.

'In the great war that strained the civilised world almost to breaking point,' resumed Mr E. F. Crowther, 'Old Thurmarshians have been up there beside Old Etonians and Old Harrovians. I am sure that in the battle to rebuild our nation and take up once again our rightful place in the forefront of history, there will once again be Thurmarshians in the van.'

'The bread van,' whispered Henry.

The headmaster turned towards him.

'Did somebody speak?' he asked.

Oh, miserable and aptly-named Pratt.

'Who spoke?' thundered the headmaster.

The room resounded to the loud silence of six hundred boys. You could have heard an earwig breathe.

'The whole school will stay in for one hour, unless somebody owns up,' said Mr E. F. Crowther.

'It were me, sir,' said Henry in a small voice.

'Stand up,' commanded Mr E. F. Crowther.

Henry stood up.

'Who are you?' said Mr E. F. Crowther.

'Pratt, sir.'

There was laughter.

'Silence,' said Mr E. F. Crowther. 'There is nothing funny about a boy's name. People who find names funny are puerile. You're new, aren't you, Pratt?'

'Yes, sir.'

'You have passed your eleven plus, and are therefore considered fit to come here rather than fester away in a secondary modern school,' said Mr E. F. Crowther. 'Allow us to share the epigrammatical delight of your secret discourse, Pratt, and help us to judge whether we find you fit.'

'Sir?'

'What did you say?'

His mind was a blank. He could think of nothing except the truth.

'The bread van, sir.'

'The bread van, Pratt?'

'Yes, sir. Tha said tha hoped there'd be Thurmarshians in the van. I said "the bread van".'

'Are you related to Oscar Wilde, by any chance, Pratt?'

'No, sir.'

'I thought not. You're an imbecile, Pratt. What are you?'

'An imbecile, sir.'

'You will come and see me in my study after school.'

'Yes, sir.'

After the day's chaotic activities were over, and a relatively ordered basis for the future had been established, Henry made his way uneasily towards the headmaster's study.

'Good luck, bread van,' said a senior boy, whom he met in he corridor.

He knocked.

'Come in,' said Mr E. F. Crowther.

He entered.

Mr E. F. Crowther sat behind a large desk on which there were several piles of papers arranged on spikes. His study was airy. The walls were liberally festooned with rosters and graphs. The room stated, 'Things get done here. We are plain, practical men, concerned with achievement, not pretension.'

'Good afternoon, Pratt,' said Mr E. F. Crowther.

'Good afternoon, sir,' said Henry.

'Thought up any more little gems, Pratt?'

'No, sir.'

'A pity. I've had a hard day. I was looking forward to being entertained.'

Mr E. F. Crowther picked up his cane, then let it fall onto the top of his desk.

'Can you furnish me with any arguments that might persuade me not to cane you, Pratt?' he enquired.

'Yes, sir.'

The headmaster raised his eyebrows in eloquent surprise.

'Then do so.'

'I were excited, sir.'

'It's "I was excited," Pratt. You'll have to learn to speak grammatically here. After all, it is the grammar school.'

'I *was* excited sir.'

'Why?'

'Coming to Thurmarsh Grammar, sir.'

Mr E. F. Crowther gave Henry a searching glance. He prided himself on his searching glances. Sometimes, he was so keen on making sure that his glance was searching that he forgot to look for the thing for which he was searching.

'I must warn you that I have the sole franchise for all sarcasm uttered between these four walls,' he said.

'Please, sir?'

'Are you seriously telling me that you said "the bread van" because you were excited about coming to Thurmarsh Grammar?'

'Yes, sir.'

Mr E. F. Crowther leant back in his chair. Behind him, a hazy autumn sun shone. There was a beam of dust in the air.

'Explain,' he said.

'Well, sir, I didn't like it that much at Brunswick Road because it were... it *was* mainly Reading, Writing and Arithmetic, with just a bit of Geography and that. I were... I *was* looking forward to learning all the different subjects, like, like History and French and that, and with seeing all the older boys and everything, I thought about everything I was going to learn and how after I left school I might get on in t'world and be summat, and I felt like my life was just starting at last, and I gor over-excited, sir. I'm only eleven.'

The headmaster stared at Henry with his mouth slightly open.

'Try to stay excited,' he said, 'but try not to get so carried away with your enthusiasm that you say "the bread van" while I'm talking. Run along now.'

'Yes, sir. Thank you, sir.'

The Fifth Child by Doris Lessing

Doris Lessing wrote this novel in 1988. The story concerns the problems of a family bringing up a strange, violent child called Ben. Doris Lessing is one of the great writers of the twentieth century. Since she started writing in the 1950s, her range of published work has been vast, from philosophy to science fiction. *Martha Quest* (a novel based on her experiences of growing up in Africa) and her short stories are also a good introduction to her writing.

In this extract, Ben has just started school. Earlier in the story his parents, fearing his effect on their four older children, put him into a psychiatric hospital but later removed him because he was desperately unhappy there. Ben's only friends are an adolescent motorbike gang who take him to school and pick him up every day.

After Ben had been at school for a month, and there had been no unpleasant news, she [his mother] asked his teacher how he was getting on. She heard, to her surprise, 'He's a good little chap. He tries so hard.'

Towards the end of the first term she was summoned on the telephone by the headmistress, Mrs Graves. 'Mrs Lovatt, I wonder if you...'

An efficient woman, she knew what went on in her school and that Harriet was the responsible parent of Luke, Helen, Jane, and Paul.

'We all find ourselves at a loss,' said she. 'Ben is really trying very hard. He doesn't seem to fit in with the others. It's hard to put one's finger on it.'

Harriet sat waiting – as she had done, it seemed to her, far too often in Ben's short life – for some kind of acknowledgement that here might be more than a difficulty of adjustment.

She remarked, 'He has always been an oddball.'

'The odd man out in the family? Well there's usually one, I've often noticed it,' said affable Mrs Graves. While this surface conversation went on, the sensitised Harriet was listening for the other, parallel conversation that Ben's existence compelled.

'These young men who come and collect Ben, it's an unusual arrangement,' smiled Mrs Graves.

'He's an unusual child,' said Harriet, looking hard at the headmistress, who nodded, not looking at Harriet. She was frowning, as if some annoying thought were poking at her, wanting attention, but she did not feel inclined to give it any.

'Have you ever known a child like Ben before?' Harriet asked.

This risked the headmistress saying, 'What do you mean, Mrs Lovatt?' And in fact Mrs Graves did say 'What do you mean, Mrs Lovatt?' but quickly, and then, to stop

Harriet telling her, she funked it with, 'He is hyperactive, perhaps? Of course that is a word that I often feel evades the issue. To say a child is hyperactive does not say very much! But he does have this extraordinary energy. He can't keep still long – well, a lot of children can't. His teacher has found him a rewarding little boy because he does try, but she says she has to put more effort into him than all the rest put together.... Well, Mrs Lovatt I'm glad you came in, it has been a help.' And as Harriet left she saw how the headmistress watched her, with that long, troubled inspection that held unacknowledged unease, even horror, which was part of 'the other conversation' – the real one.

Towards the end of the second term, she was telephoned: Would she come in at once, please? Ben had hurt someone.

Here it was: this is what she had dreaded. Ben had suddenly gone berserk and attacked a bigger girl in the playground. He had pulled her down, so that she fell heavily on the asphalt, bruising and grazing her legs. Then he had bitten her, and bent back her arm until it broke.

'I have spoken to Ben,' said Mrs Graves, 'He doesn't seem to be remorseful in any way. You might even think he doesn't know he did it. But at that age – he is six, after all – he should know what he is doing.'

Harriet took Ben home, leaving Paul to be picked up later. It was Paul she wanted to take with her: the child had heard of the attack, and was hysterical, screaming that Ben would kill him, too. But she had to be alone with Ben.

Ben sat on the kitchen table, swinging his legs, eating bread and jam. He had asked if John would come here to pick him up. It was John he needed.

Harriet said, 'You hurt poor Mary Jones today. Why did you do that, Ben?'

He seemed not to hear, but tore lumps of bread off with his teeth, and then gulped them down.

Harriet sat down close to him, so that he could not ignore her, and said, 'Ben, do you remember that place you went to in the van?'

He went rigid. He slowly turned his head and looked at her. The bread in his hand was trembling: he was trembling. He remembered, all right! She had never done this before – had hoped she would never have to.

'Well, *do* you remember, Ben?'

His eyes had a wild look; he could have jumped down from the table and run off. He wanted to, but was glaring around into the corners of the room, at the windows, up the staircase, as if he might be attacked from these places.

'Now listen to me, Ben. If you ever, ever, ever hurt anyone again, you'll have to go back there.'

She kept her eyes on his and hoped that he could not know she was saying inwardly, But I'd never send him back, never.

He sat shivering like a wet, cold dog, in spasms, and he went through a series of movements, unconsciously, the vestiges of reactions from that time. A hand went up to shield his face, and he looked through the spread fingers as if this hand could protect him; then the hand fell, and he turned his head away sharply, pressing the back of the other hand to his mouth, glaring in terror over it; he briefly bared his teeth to snarl – but then checked himself; he lifted his chin, and his mouth opened, and Harriet saw that he could have emitted a long animal howl. It was as if she actually heard this howl, its lonely terror...

'Did you hear me, Ben?' Harriet said softly.

He slid down off the table, and thumped his way up the stairs. He left behind him a thin trail of urine. She heard his door shut, then the bellow of rage and fear he had been holding back.

Girl by Jamaica Kincaid

This is a short story taken from a collection of short stories called *At the Bottom of the River*. The writer is from the Caribbean and the stories were first published in 1985. In this story, the learning which takes place is the kind which goes on at home rather than in school.

Because this kind of story is literature from another culture, you may find some of the ideas, and the vocabulary used to describe the ideas, unfamiliar, unless you are lucky enough to have family or friends who are familiar with the life, language and writing of the Caribbean. A discussion with a friend about the difficulties you encountered in understanding this story, and using a dictionary to check the meaning of unfamiliar words will involve you in some high-level Knowledge about Language work.

> Wash the white clothes on Monday and put them on the stone heap; wash the color clothes on Tuesday and put them on the clothesline to dry; don't walk barehead in the hot sun; cook pumpkin fritters in very hot sweet oil; soak your little cloths right after you take them off; when buying cotton to make yourself a nice blouse, be sure that it doesn't have gum on it, because that way it won't hold up well after a wash; soak salt fish overnight before you cook it; is it true that you sing benna in Sunday school?; always eat your food in such a way that it won't turn someone else's stomach; on Sundays try to walk like a lady and not like the slut you are so bent on becoming; don't sing benna in Sunday school; you mustn't speak to wharf-rat boys, not even to give directions; don't eat fruits on the street – flies will follow you; *but I don't sing benna on Sundays at all and never in Sunday school*; this is how to sew on a button; this is how to make a button-hole for the button you have just sewed on; this is how to hem a dress when you see the hem coming down and so to prevent yourself from looking like the slut I know you are so bent on becoming; this is how you iron your father's khaki shirt so that it doesn't have a crease; this is how you iron your father's khaki pants so that they don't have a crease; this is how you grow okra – far from the house, because okra tree harbors red ants; when you are growing dasheen, make sure it gets plenty of water or else it makes your throat itch when you are eating it; this is how you sweep a corner; this is how you sweep a whole house; this is how you sweep a yard; this is how you smile to someone you don't like too much; this is how you smile to someone you don't like at all; this is how you smile to someone you like completely; this is how you set a table for tea; this is how you set a table for dinner; this is how you set a table for dinner with an important guest; this is how you set a table for lunch; this is how you set a table for breakfast; this is how to behave in the presence of men who don't know you very well, and this way they won't recognize immediately the slut I have warned you against becoming; be sure to wash every day, even if it is with your own spit; don't squat down to play marbles – you are not a boy, you know; don't pick people's flowers – you might catch something; don't throw stones at blackbirds, because it might not be a blackbird at all; this is how to make a bread pudding; this is how to make doukona; this is how to make pepper pot; this is how to make a good medicine for a cold; this is how to make a good medicine to throw away a child before it even becomes a child; this is how to catch a fish; this is how to throw back a fish you don't like, and that way something bad won't fall on you; this is how to bully a man; this is how a man bullies you; this is how to love a man, and if this doesn't work there are other ways, and if they don't work don't feel too bad about giving up; this is how to spit up in the air if you feel like it, and this is how to move quick so that it doesn't fall on you; this is how to make ends meet; always squeeze bread to make sure it's fresh; *but what if the baker won't let me feel the bread?*; you mean to say that after all you are really going to be the kind of woman who the baker won't let near the bread?

Classic works written by great authors from the past

If you are aiming for a Level 7 or above in either English or English Literature, you will be expected to read some books written before the twentieth century. Sometimes these will seem quite difficult, since the language which writers used in the past is not always as easy to understand as the sort of writing you are used to in modern literature. It can be helpful to begin by looking at the differences between pieces of writing with a similar story line, or theme, and comparing the way the writers deal with the story.

The three extracts which follow have in common that they are all taken from novels which tell the story of a romance. In each one, the significant event taking place is the hero's proposal of marriage to the heroine.

Workbench assignment

As you read the extracts, consider the following:
- What similarities do you notice in the story lines? Are there any obvious differences?
- Compare the major characters: what do they have in common and how do they differ? Look at the descriptions of strongly felt emotion and the way this is reflected in the dialogue spoken between the central couple in each extract.
- Compare the description of the setting of each of the extracts and consider how the writer uses it to create a particular atmosphere.
- Think about the different styles of writing and how these are similar because they are typical of romantic novels, but differ because the books were written at different times and for different readers.
- Which of the extracts did you feel was the most successful piece of writing? Which would be most likely to prompt you to go away and read the rest of the book? Why? (Be honest with yourself here: being able to recognise and talk about some of the difficulties of reading English written a long time ago is an important area of your Knowledge about Language skills.)

Jane Eyre by Charlotte Brontë

This is one of the most famous love stories of all time. It was first published in 1846 and has always been the best known of Charlotte Brontë's novels. Even if you have not yet read the book, the story will probably be familiar to you through television and film adaptations. It has always been a popular set text for GCSE English Literature and could well be one which your teacher will choose for you to study in class.

The events which lead up to this extract are that Jane Eyre has been working at Thornfield Hall as a governess to Adèle, who is the ward of her wealthy employer, Mr Rochester. Jane has fallen in love with Mr Rochester, but believes that her dreams are hopeless as he seems to be planning to marry a lady of his own status, Blanche Ingram.

A splendid Midsummer shone over England: skies so pure, suns so radiant as were then seen in long succession, seldom favour, even singly, our wave-girt land. It was as if a band of Italian days had come from the South, like a flock of glorious passenger birds, and lighted to rest them on the cliffs of Albion. The hay was all got in; the fields round Thornfield were green and shorn; the roads white and baked; the trees were in their dark prime; hedge and wood, full-leaved and deeply tinted, contrasted well with the sunny hue of the cleared meadows between.

On Midsummer-eve, Adèle, weary with gathering wild strawberries in Hay Lane half the day, had gone to bed with the sun. I watched her drop asleep, and when I left her, I sought the garden.

It was now the sweetest hour of the twenty-four: 'day its fervid fires had wasted', and dew fell cool on panting plain and scorched summit. Where the sun had gone down in simple state – pure of the pomp of clouds – spread a solemn purple, burning with the light of red jewel and furnace flame at one point, on one hill-peak, and extending high and wide, soft and still softer, over half heaven. The east had its own charm of fine, deep blue, and its own modest gem, a rising and solitary star: soon it would boast the moon; but she was yet beneath the horizon.

I walked a while on the pavement; but a subtle, well-known scent – that of a cigar – stole from some window; I saw the library casement open a hand-breadth, I knew I might be watched thence; so I went apart into the orchard. No nook in the grounds more sheltered and more Eden-like: a very high wall shut it out from the court on one side; on the other a beech avenue screened it from the lawn. At the bottom was a sunk fence, its sole separation from lonely fields: a winding walk, bordered with laurels and terminating in a giant horse-chestnut, circled at the base by a seat, led down to the fence. Here one could wander unseen. While such honeydew fell, such silence reigned, such gloaming gathered, I felt as if I could haunt such shade for ever; but in treading the flower and fruit parterres at the upper part of the enclosure, enticed here by the light the now rising moon cast on this more open quarter, my step is stayed – not by sound, not by sight, but once more by a warning fragrance.

Sweet-brier and southernwood, jasmine, pink, and rose have long been yielding their evening sacrifice of incense: this new scent is neither of shrub nor flower; it is – I know it well – it is Mr Rochester's cigar. I look round and listen. I see trees laden with ripening fruit. I hear a nightingale warbling in a wood half a mile off: no moving form is visible; no coming step audible; but that perfume increases: I must flee. I make for the wicket leading to the shrubbery, and I see Mr Rochester entering. I step aside into the ivy recess; he will not stay long: he will soon return whence he came, and if I sit still he will never see me.

But no – eventide is as pleasant to him as to me, and this antique garden as attractive; and he strolls on, now lifting the gooseberry-tree branches to look at the fruit, large as plums, with which they are laden; now taking a ripe cherry from the wall; now stooping towards a knot of flowers, either to inhale their fragrance or to admire the dew-beads on their petals. A great moth goes humming by me; it alights on a plant at Mr Rochester's foot: he sees it, and bends to examine it.

'Now he has his back towards me,' thought I, 'and he is occupied too; perhaps, if I walk softly, I can slip away unnoticed.'

I trod on an edging of turf, that the crackle of the pebbly gravel might not betray me: he was standing among the beds at a yard or two distant from where I had to pass; the moth apparently engaged him. 'I shall get by very well,' I meditated. As I crossed his shadow, thrown long over the garden by the moon, not yet risen high, he said quietly, without turning –

'Jane, come and look at this fellow.'

I had made no noise: he had not eyes behind – could his shadow feel? I started at first, and then I approached him.

'Look at his wings,' said he; 'he reminds me rather of a West Indian insect; one does not often see so large and gay a night-rover in England; there! he is flown.'

The moth roamed away. I was sheepishly retreating also; but Mr Rochester followed me, and when we reached the wicket he said –

'Turn back: on so lovely a night it is a shame to sit in the house; and surely no one can wish to go to bed while sunset is thus at meeting with moonrise.'

It is one of my faults, that though my tongue is sometimes prompt enough at answer, there are times when it sadly fails me in framing an excuse; and always the lapse occurs at some crisis, when a facile word or plausible pretext is specially wanted to get me out of painful embarrassment. I did not like to walk at this hour alone with Mr Rochester in the shadowy orchard; but I could not find a reason to allege for leaving him. I followed with lagging step, and thoughts busily bent on discovering a means of extrication; but he himself looked so composed and so grave also, I became ashamed of feeling any confusion: the evil – if evil existent or prospective there was – seemed to lie with me only; his mind was unconscious and quiet.

'Jane,' he recommenced, as we entered the laurel walk and slowly strayed down in the direction of the sunk fence and the horse-chestnut, 'Thornfield is a pleasant place in summer, is it not?'

'Yes, sir.'

'You must have become in some degree attached to the house – you who have an eye for natural beauties, and a good deal of the organ of Adhesiveness?'

'I am attached to it, indeed.'

'And though I don't comprehend how it is, I perceive you have acquired a degree of regard for that foolish little child Adèle, too; and even for simple Dame Fairfax?'

'Yes, sir; in different ways, I have an affection for both.'

'And would be sorry to part with them?'

'Yes.'

'Pity!' he said, and sighed and paused.

'It is always the way of events in this life,' he continued presently: 'no sooner have you got settled in a pleasant resting-place, than a voice calls out to you to rise and move on, for the hour of repose is expired.'

'Must I move on, sir?' I asked. 'Must I leave Thornfield?' 'I believe you must, Jane. I am sorry, Janet, but I believe indeed you must.'

This was a blow: but I did not let it prostrate me.

'Well, sir, I shall be ready when the order to march comes.'

'It is come now – I must give it to-night.'

'Then you *are* going to be married, sir?'

'Ex–act–ly – prec–ise–ly: with your usual acuteness, you have hit the nail straight on the head.'

'Soon, sir?'

'Very soon, my — that is, Miss Eyre: and you'll remember, Jane, the first time I, or Rumour, plainly intimated to you that it was my intention to put my old bachelor's neck into the sacred noose, to enter into the holy state of matrimony – to take Miss Ingram to my bosom, in short (she's an extensive armful: but that's not to the point – one can't have too much of such a very excellent thing as my beautiful Blanche): well, as I was saying – listen to me, Jane! You're not turning your head to look after more moths, are you? That was only a lady-clock, child, "flying away home". I wish to remind you that it was you who first said to me, with that discretion I respect in you – with that foresight, prudence, and humility which befit your responsible and dependent position – that in case I married Miss Ingram, both you and little Adèle had better trot forthwith. I pass over the sort of slur conveyed in this suggestion on the character of my beloved; indeed, when you are far away, Janet, I'll try to forget it: I shall notice only its wisdom; which is such that I have made it my law of action. Adèle must go to school; and you, Miss Eyre, must get a new situation.'

'Yes, sir, I will advertise immediately: and meantime, I suppose —' I was going to say, 'I suppose I may stay here, till I find another shelter to betake myself to': but I stopped, feeling it would not do to risk a long sentence, for my voice was not quite under command.

'In about a month I hope to be a bridegroom,' continued Mr Rochester; 'and in the interim, I shall myself look out for employment and an asylum for you.'

'Thank you, sir; I am sorry to give —'

'Oh, no need to apologize! I consider that when a dependent does her duty as well as you have done yours, she has a sort of claim upon her employer for any little assistance he can conveniently render her; indeed, I have already, through my future mother-in-law, heard of a place that I think will suit: it is to undertake the education of the five daughters of Mrs Dionysius O'Gall of Bitternutt Lodge, Connaught, Ireland. You'll like Ireland, I think: they're such warm-hearted people, there, they say.'

'It is a long way off, sir.'

'No matter – a girl of your sense will not object to the voyage or the distance.'

'Not the voyage but the distance: and then the sea is a barrier —'

'From what, Jane?'

'From England and from Thornfield: and —'

'Well?'

'From *you*, sir.'

I said this almost involuntarily, and with as little sanction of free will, my tears gushed out. I did not cry so as to be heard, however; I avoided sobbing. The thought of Mrs O'Gall and Bitternutt Lodge struck cold to my heart; and colder the thought of all the brine and foam destined, as it seemed, to rush between me and the master at whose side I now walked; and coldest the remembrance of the wider ocean – wealth, caste, custom – intervened between me and what I naturally and inevitably loved.

'It is a long way,' I again said.

'It is, to be sure; and when you get to Bitternutt Lodge, Connaught, Ireland, I shall never see you again, Jane: that's morally certain. I never go over to Ireland, not having myself much of a fancy for the country. We have been good friends, Jane; have we not?'

'Yes, sir.'

'And when friends are on the eve of separation, they like to spend the little time that remains to them close to each other. Come! we'll talk over the voyage and the parting quietly, half an hour or so, while the stars enter into their shining life up in heaven yonder: here is the chestnut-tree: here is the bench at its old roots. Come, we will sit there in peace to-night, though we should never more be destined to sit there together.'

He seated me and himself.

'It is a long way to Ireland, Janet, and I am sorry to send my little friend on such weary travels: but if I can't do better, how is it to be helped? Are you anything akin to me, do you think, Jane?'

I could risk no sort of answer by this time: my heart was still.

'Because,' he said, 'I sometimes have a queer feeling with regard to you – I especially when you are near to me, as now: it is as if I had a string somewhere under my left ribs, tightly and inextricably knotted to a similar string situated in the corresponding quarter of your little frame. And if that boisterous Channel, and two hundred miles or so of land, come broad between us, I am afraid that cord of communion will be snapped; and then I've a nervous notion I should take to bleeding inwardly. As for you – you'd forget me.'

'That I *never* should, sir: you know —' Impossible to proceed.

'Jane, do you hear that nightingale singing in the wood? Listen!'

In listening, I sobbed convulsively; for I could repress what I endured no longer; I was obliged to yield, and I was shaken from head to foot with acute distress. When I did speak, it was only to express an impetuous wish that I had never been born, or never come to Thornfield.

'Because you are sorry to leave it?'

The vehemence of emotion, stirred by grief and love within me, was claiming mastery, and struggling for full sway, and asserting a right to predominate, to overcome, to live, rise, and reign at last: yes – and to speak.

'I grieve to leave Thornfield: I love Thornfield: I love it, because I have lived in it a full and delightful life – momentarily at least. I have not been trampled on. I have not been petrified. I have not been buried with inferior minds, and excluded from every glimpse of communion with what is bright and energetic and high. I have talked, face to face, with what I reverence, with what I delight in – with an original, a vigorous, an expanded mind. I have known you, Mr Rochester; and it strikes me with terror and anguish to see I absolutely must be torn from you for ever. I see the necessity of departure; and it is like looking on the necessity of death.'

'Where do you see the necessity?' he asked suddenly.

'Where? You, sir, have placed it before me.'

'In what shape?'

'In the shape of Miss Ingram; a noble and beautiful woman – your bride.'

'My bride! What bride? I have no bride!'

'But you will have.'

'Yes – I will! – I will!' he set his teeth.

'Then I must go – you have said it yourself.'

'No: you must stay! I swear it – and the oath shall be kept.'

'I tell you I must go!' I retorted, roused to something like passion. 'Do you think I can stay to become nothing to you? Do you think I am an automaton? – a machine without feelings? and can bear to have my morsel of bread snatched from my lips, and my drop of living water dashed from my cup? Do you think, because I am poor, obscure, plain, and little, I am soulless and heartless? You think wrong! – I have as much soul as you – and full as much heart! And if God had gifted me with some beauty and much wealth, I should have made it as hard for you to leave me, as it is now for me to leave you. I am not talking to you now through the medium of custom, conventionalities, nor even of mortal flesh: it is my spirit that addresses your spirit; just as if both had passed through the grave, and we stood at God's feet, equal – as we are!'

'As we are!' repeated Mr Rochester – 'so,' he added, enclosing me in his arms, gathering me to his breast, pressing his lips to my lips: 'so, Jane!'

'Yes, so, sir,' I rejoined: 'and yet not so: for you are a married man – or as good as a married man, and wed to one inferior to you – to one with whom you have no sympathy – whom I do not believe you truly love; for I have seen and heard you sneer at her. I would scorn such a union: therefore I am better than you – let me go!'

'Where, Jane? To Ireland?'

'Yes – to Ireland. I have spoken my mind, and can go anywhere now.'

'Jane, be still; don't struggle so, like a wild frantic bird that is rending its own plumage in its desperation.'

'I am no bird; and no net ensnares me; I am a free human being with an independent will, which I now exert to leave you.'

Another effort set me at liberty, and I stood erect before him.

'And your will shall decide your destiny,' he said. 'I offer you my heart, my hand, and a share of all my possessions.'

'You play a farce, which I merely laugh at.'

'I ask you to pass through life at my side – to be my second self, and best earthly companion.'

'For that fate you have already made your choice, and must abide it.'

'Jane, be still a few moments: you are over-excited: I will be still too.'

A waft of wind came sweeping down tile laurel-walk, and trembled through the boughs of the chestnut: it wandered away – away – to an indefinite distance – it died. The nightingale's song was then the only voice of the hour: in listening to it I again wept. Mr Rochester sat quiet, looking at me gently and seriously. Sometime passed before he spoke; he at last said –

'Come to my side, Jane, and let us explain and understand one another.'

'I will never again come to your side: I am torn away now, and cannot return.'

'But, Jane, I summon you as my wife: it is you only I intend to marry.'

I was silent: I thought he mocked me.

'Come, Jane – come hither.'

'Your bride stands between us.'

He rose, and with a stride reached me.

'My bride is here,' he said, again drawing me to him, 'because my equal is here, and my likeness. Jane, will you marry me?'

Still I did not answer, and still I writhed myself from his grasp: for I was still incredulous.

'Do you doubt me, Jane?'

'Entirely.'

'You have no faith in me?'

'Not a whit.'

'Am I a liar in your eyes?' he asked passionately. 'Little sceptic, you *shall* be convinced. What love have I for Miss Ingram? None: and that you know. What love has she for me? None: as I have taken pains to prove: I caused a rumour to reach her that my fortune was not a third of what was supposed, and after that I presented myself to see the result; it was coldness both from her and her mother. I would not – I could not – marry Miss Ingram. You – you strange, you almost unearthly thing! – I love you as my own flesh. You – poor and obscure, and small and plain as you are – I entreat to accept me as a husband.'

'What, me!' I ejaculated, beginning in his earnestness – and especially in his incivility – to credit his sincerity: 'me who have not a friend in the world but you – if you are my friend: not a shilling but what you have given me?'

'You, Jane, I must have you for my own – entirely my own. Will you be mine? Say yes, quickly.'

'Mr Rochester, let me look at your face: turn to the moonlight.'

'Why?'

'Because I want to read your countenance – turn!'

'There! you will find it scarcely more legible than a crumpled, scratched page. Read on: only make haste, for I suffer.'

His face was very much agitated and very much flushed, and there were strong workings in the features, and strange gleams in the eyes.

'Oh, Jane, you torture me!' he exclaimed. 'With that searching and yet faithful and generous look, you torture me!'

'How can I do that? If you are true, and your offer real, my only feelings to you must be gratitude and devotion – they cannot torture.'

'Gratitude!' he ejaculated; and added wildly – 'Jane, accept me quickly. Say, Edward – give me my name – Edward – I will marry you.'

'Are you in earnest? Do you truly love me? Do you sincerely wish me to be your wife?'

'I do; and if an oath is necessary to satisfy, I swear it.'
'Then, sir, I will marry you.'

Pride and Prejudice **by Jane Austen**

This is another famous love story, which is also a great favourite for study as a GCSE English Literature text. Elizabeth Bennett and Mr Darcy took an immediate dislike to each other at their first meeting, but are gradually drawn together by the twists and turns of events in the novel. By the time this extract is found, very near the end of the book, Elizabeth has already rejected Darcy once, and feels there is very little hope of a second offer of marriage, even though she finally admits to herself that she is in love with him, after she has played a part in helping to conceal the scandal caused by Elizabeth's youngest sister, Lydia, eloping with a soldier. Like Mr Rochester, Mr Darcy is a wealthy gentleman and his chosen bride is far from his equal in wealth or social status.

They walked towards the Lucases, because Kitty wished to call upon Maria; and as Elizabeth saw no occasion for making it a general concern, when Kitty left them, she went boldly on with him alone. Now was the moment for her resolution to be executed, and while her courage was high, she immediately said, 'Mr Darcy, I am a very selfish creature; and, for the sake of giving relief to my own feelings, care not how much I may be wounding your's. I can no longer help thanking you for your unexampled kindness to my poor sister. Ever since I have known it, I have been most anxious to acknowledge to you how gratefully I feel it. Were it known to the rest of my family, I should not have merely my own gratitude to express.'

'I am sorry, exceedingly sorry,' replied Darcy, in a tone of surprise and emotion, 'that you have ever been informed of what may, in a mistaken light, have given you uneasiness. I did not think Mrs Gardiner was so little to be trusted.'

'You must not blame my aunt. Lydia's thoughtlessness first betrayed to me that you had been concerned in the matter; and, of course, I could not rest till I knew the particulars. Let me thank you again and again, in the name of all my family, for that generous compassion which induced you to take so much trouble; and bear so many mortifications, for the sake of discovering them.'

'If you *will* thank me,' he replied, 'let it be for yourself alone. That the wish of giving happiness to you, might add force to the other inducement which led me on, I shall not attempt to deny. But your *family* owe me nothing. Much as I respect them, I believe, I thought only of *you*.'

Elizabeth was too much embarrassed to say a word. After a short pause, her companion added, 'You are too generous to trifle with me. If your feelings are still what they were last April, tell me so at once. *My* affections and wishes are unchanged, but one word from you will silence me on the subject for ever.'

Elizabeth, feeling all the more than common awkwardness and anxiety of his situation, now forced herself to speak; and immediately, though not very fluently, give him to understand, that her sentiments had undergone so material a change, since the period to which he alluded, as to make her receive with gratitude and pleasure, his present assurances. The happiness which this reply produced, was such as he had probably never felt before; and he expressed himself on the occasion as sensibly and as warmly as a man violently in love can be supposed to do. Had Elizabeth been able to encounter his eye, she might have seen how well the expression of heart-felt delight, diffused over his face, became him, made his affection every moment more valuable.

Runaway Nurse

This is an extract from a Mills and Boon romance: not a book you would be likely to study as an English Literature text! However, it does make an interesting contrast with the two earlier extracts.

The story that leads up to this extract, which is from very near the end of the novel, tells of a nurse, Toni Hammond, who has gone to work in Australia to escape from an unhappy love affair. There, whilst working for Mrs Partridge, she has met and fallen in love with Doctor Grant Hammond. Unfortunately, he seems to be more interested in Sara and Celia than he is in her.

Standing beside him in the dark enclosed porch as he fumbled with his key in the door she felt more aware of him, although she could scarcely see more than his outline, than almost any time before. She shivered but it was not because the night was now chillier and she had come out without a cardigan.

Grant led her down a cheerfully red-carpeted hallway, off which there were two consulting rooms which he showed her briefly. They were white painted, like the hall, and reproductions of Australian paintings hung on the walls. In the waiting-room were flower prints, piles of magazines, comfortable cane furniture and a big box of toys for children. Through a door at one end of the passage were the living quarters that Grant and Tom Wilson had shared.

Grant ushered her into the living-room, which was furnished in a comfortable old-fashioned and slightly shabby way. 'Things are still in a mess,' he apologised. 'Tom has left a few gaps. l shall have to spread myself out more.'

'You'll miss him,' Toni said, glancing round, taking it all in, feeling the stamp of Grant's character in the room even more than Tom's. 'When does the locum arrive?'

'Tomorrow, I hope.'

There was an awkward pause, at least it seemed so to Toni. She said, to fill it, 'Dolly and Tom will be sunning themselves on the beach by now.'

'In the middle of the night!' he teased, and she smiled, having spoken to fill the gap without thinking properly. 'I doubt it! They'll be tucked up in bed in their hotel.'

He stood there looking at her as though he had forgotten what it was he had come for.

'Well, if you don't fetch that petrol,' she said, '*you* won't be till all hours.'

She raised her eyes to his involuntarily, and met a look she did not recognise but which sent her whole being into a frantic turmoil. In a sudden convulsive movement he gathered her unresisting body into his arms and brought his mouth down hard on hers, persuading her lips apart with his, touching his tongue to hers, until she yielded completely and let her arms fold around his neck, her fingers sliding up into his hair until she was pulling his head down to hers, and pressing her body against his as hard as his was to hers. There was no stemming the rush of emotion as her pent-up feelings found relief in the violence of his kiss and in the close contact with the man she loved. She surrendered herself to the sweeping desire his nearness aroused and they swayed unsteadily on the carpet, almost overbalancing, until suddenly Grant groaned and released her.

'Toni…' His eyes were smouldering and the veins in his temples showed blue against his tanned forehead, showing her the extent of his emotion.

Then suddenly she remembered Celia and a wave of anger drowned her love. 'You didn't really run out of gas, did you?' she whispered in horrified realisation.

He smiled wickedly. 'For a minute back there in Jacaranda Street I thought you weren't going to fall for it!'

She backed away from him, outraged. 'How could you? How could you go on being the town playboy and flirt when…' Words failed her for a moment, but with a renewed burst of anger, she said tightly, 'I suppose it would have spoiled your record to let me go without first conquering me. Oh, Grant, I thought better of you than that, now…' Her disappointment in him welled up in tears. 'It isn't very fair to Celia, is it?'

He looked stunned at her vehemence. 'Toni, what on earth are you talking about?'

'You love Celia,' she stabbed at him accusingly. 'I know you were holding back because you were uncertain, but today after you saw that photograph of Annabel you felt completely free at last, didn't you?'

He wiped a hand across his brow and looked hard at her tearful and angry face. 'Yes, I do feel absolutely free now. But whatever gave you the idea I was in love with Celia?'

'You asked me,' she reminded him coldly, 'at that dinner party with Dolly and Tom and Sara what I would do if I loved someone and I wasn't sure if they loved me, or even that they were suitable. I thought you meant Sara… but you didn't, so the only other person it could possibly be was Celia.'

Grant was rocking back and forth with contained laughter which disconcerted her. What was the joke? So far as she was concerned it was no joke to kiss a woman the way he had just kissed her, when he was supposed to be in love with someone else. She was ashamed of herself for allowing him to get away with it. She just couldn't understand him.

'Your lapse just now was quite unforgivable,' she said primly.

He eyed her with grim amusement. 'Wasn't yours?' he countered and there was a light in his eyes that was not really mockery.

'Yes, it was,' she murmured, eyes downcast.

She felt his fingers under her chin, lifting it and forcing her to look at him again. He was smiling now, as he pushed her firmly on to the couch and then sat beside her.

'What I did just now,' he said, his face very solemn, very close to hers, 'told me something that I've been wanting to know for a long time but was afraid to ask.'

She held her lips tightly together and looked at him defiantly, determined to give nothing away, whatever he might think.

'Toni, don't try to deny it!'

She wriggled away from him, but he moved closer and laid a hand firmly across her knees so that she could not get up and run from him. The arm of the couch helped effectively to imprison her.

'I'm not denying anything,' she said coolly, staring at a threadbare patch in the carpet where someone had regularly rubbed the heels of their shoes restlessly. Had this been Grant's favourite place that she was now sitting in?

'Toni,' he said softly, 'you jumped to conclusions rather precipitately that night when I asked you what you'd do if you loved someone...'

'Well, you were always round at Mrs Partridge's,' she defended hotly, 'so naturally I thought – we all thought – that you came to see Sara. It seemed obvious that you didn't want to make a big thing of it because this time you were really serious.'

Laughter shook him again. 'Oh, what amateur detectives you were! And Sara, I'm afraid, indulging in a game of wishful thinking quite out of character for her.'

'Well, yes, she did realise that herself in the end. She wasn't hurt.'

'I'm glad,' he said, 'although I have to say it would have been her own fault if she had been. I never gave her the slightest encouragement, any more than I encouraged Celia to think I might be serious. Would you have me never take a woman out unless I were serious? Don't tell me you never go out with a man unless you are? What about Nolan?'

She was trapped. 'Yes, but... that night you said...'

'My dearest Toni – Celia was not the alternative I had in mind.' Her eyes opened wide. 'Then who...?'

He cupped her face in his hands and lightly brushed her lips with his.

'Who but you, my darling? Who else but you, love? It was you I was talking about, and for one unbelievable moment I almost thought... and then you went and said "Sara", and spoiled it.'

His words slid through her brain but did not stick. She couldn't believe she had heard him say 'love'. Not Grant, who despised her, mocked her, treated her curtly, brusquely, sometimes so contemptuously.

'But you never liked me from the start,' she protested, 'so how could you...?' Her words drifted away under the sweet tender pressure of his lips.

'How could I not? That was the whole trouble, my darling. The very first night I saw you, standing on Mrs Partridge's verandah, looking so pert in your nurse's uniform, yet so lost and alone, you did something to me that night that no woman had ever done before. You stirred some depth in me that had never been stirred before. But it was all wrong. You were too much like Annabel, even to your prestigious relatives. I didn't want to fall in love with you only to find that you'd turn out just like Annabel, using your vocation to catch a rich husband, leaving me with bitterness and regret – again. I was not going to be caught a second time.'

Slowly Toni's brain was taking it in, and a warm glow grew and spread through her, like taking a draught of mulled wine on a cheerless and chilly day.

'So you were horrid and sarcastic and very abrupt with me,' she murmured.

'I'm afraid I often was. I hated myself for it, but I had to cast you in the mould even if it didn't fit you, because I was afraid to be let down again.'

'And when you saw that photograph in the magazine today?'

He smiled ruefully. 'It was the final stone out of my shoe. Deep down I knew I was wrong about you, that you were not at all like Annabel – the night of the accident proved that – but there was a trace of bitterness lingering, the dregs of a feeling long since dead but not put to rest. Seeing her face put it finally to rest. I felt nothing, not even bitterness any more.'

'I know. I felt you were different. I thought it meant you now felt free to ask Celia to marry you. I was surprised you didn't rush straight off to see her after dinner, but then I remembered what you'd said that night and I thought you must be afraid she would say no.'

He touched his forehead to hers. 'Wrong again! I was dying to ask *you* to marry me but afraid you might say no. You didn't even like me, and with good reason, and also you'd said you were going back to Martin General for personal reasons which you said were a man – this Paul...'

'Very definitely past tense,' she said.

He looked puzzled. 'Then why wouldn't you stay and help out at the hospital? You made all my doubts about you come back by refusing to do that. It couldn't have been just because you disliked me.'

She smiled as he drew back and looked hard at her. 'Quite the opposite. Just as I ran away from Martin General because I couldn't bear working near Paul, I had to run away from here because I knew I couldn't bear being near you.'

He stroked her neck with his fingertips, a light gentle touch that sent shivers through her. 'Was it so awful then... at the first aid lectures...'

'Oh, Grant, you don't know how awful!'

'I do,' he said. 'It was agony for me, too, wanting you there, cursing you for the way you affected me, hating Nolan because I thought you were falling in love with him, wanting to kiss you every time we were alone together for more than ten seconds...'

'You did once,' she recalled wryly.

'And you nearly slapped my face!'

She suddenly coloured. 'Grant, I always wanted to apologise for walking off the dance floor that night at the church hall. It was terribly rude of me.'

He was laughing. 'It served me right for goading you. I think I began to realise that night that you were genuine, but I didn't dare believe it.'

'Did you suffer terribly? I felt I'd made a laughing stock of you.'

'There were a few giggles. The nurses up at the hospital were jubilant because the arrogant Doctor Thompson had been snubbed by a little English nurse – something they wouldn't have dared to do, you see.'

'You knew I was at the dance, didn't you? Did you go along specially so that you could upbraid me for leaving Mrs Partridge?'

'No. I called in to Mrs Partridge's and learned where you were. I was jealous as hell of Nolan. I just couldn't stop myself going along to see you, and then to stamp on my feelings I had to be horrid to you.'

Toni leaned against him and his arm slipped comfortingly around her shoulders. 'And I never thought,' she murmured, 'I never once dared to hope...'

'How will you like being the wife of a country G.P.?' he asked, taking the tip of her ear-lobe between his lips.

'I don't see why I shouldn't.'

'But Martin General called you back. You told Dolly you missed life in the big hospital. Things are pretty quiet around here as a rule.'

'Grant! You make me sound callous,' she reprimanded. 'As though I need illness and accidents to brighten up my life!'

He caught her in his arms and hugged her tightly to him. He toppled back full length on the couch, pulling her down on top of him, brushing his lips against hers, tantalisingly.

'I know very well that you don't,' he murmured huskily, 'but you might find it dull here after London. We can offer you some part-time nursing at the hospital, of course, and there's always the future first-aid courses.'

'You don't think I would be wasting my talents?' she asked in wry amusement.

'Knowing you,' he said tenderly, 'you will probably find plenty of ways to utilise them in the full.'

'Oh, Grant,' she murmured, snuggling closer to him, 'if I can just be where I'm needed, that's all I ask.'

He smiled into her eyes. 'Bless you, lovely one. I need you more than anyone ever needed anything or anyone. I love you very much, Toni.'

'And I love you, so much,' she whispered.

He kissed her long and thoroughly, but with the passion overlaid with tenderness and the quiet reassurance that love was not just one soul-searing kiss but a continuing and burgeoning experience.

At last she drew her mouth away from his reluctantly. 'Grant, poor Mrs Partridge will think we've had an accident.'

Playscripts

You are more likely to read a novel in your own time than to read a playscript. There are many good reasons for this, one being that playscripts are written to be performed, either on the stage or on the radio or television. You will get much more out of the plays you study for English and English Literature if you take this into account. Take an interest in serious drama presented on the television and the radio. Visit the theatre, particularly if you get the opportunity to see a performance of a set text. When your teacher uses videotaped versions of plays in school, take an interest in how the voices and actions of experienced actors help you to interpret the text. Make use of the skills you have developed in the 'performance' element of speaking and listening skills. At the very least, when you read a script you need to imagine a performance taking place in your head.

You will gain more from the following assignment if you get together with a group of friends and read the scripts out loud, or try to act them out. In fact, a dramatised reading, or full-scale acted out version of one of these scripts could be used both for assessment of your speaking and listening and as evidence of your range of reading, if your teacher can be persuaded to find time to let your class watch you perform.

Workbench assignment

The following extracts continue the theme of romance, though they describe the initial stages of falling in love, rather than a proposal of marriage. As you read, or act them out, you could consider and discuss the following:

- Compare the way the couples talk to each other: there are very obvious differences in style, though there are some similarities in the content of their words.
- Think particularly about all the words connected with light in the first extract and try to explain what they have in common with the song at the end of the second extract.
- In both extracts, there are indications of many obstacles to either of these couples finding long-lasting happiness together. What are these obstacles, and are there any which are common to both of the extracts?
- The first play was written to be performed on stage, whilst the second is a radio script. Would you have guessed from reading them? What difference does it make in the kind of stage directions given? Would changes need to be made to perform the stage script on the radio or the radio script on stage?

Romeo and Juliet by **William Shakespeare**

You may already have studied Shakespeare's story of young love as part of your Key

Stage 3 English course but, even if you have not, you will probably know about the balcony scene, in which seventeen-year-old Romeo and thirteen-year-old Juliet first reveal their passion for each other. The play has always been a popular GCSE English Literature text and is likely to remain so, even though quite a number of students in school will now be studying it in less depth, and at an earlier point in their English studies.

Remember that study of Shakespeare is compulsory for GCSE English students, and that you will need to show a good understanding of his writing to gain a Level 7, either in English or English Literature. As far as extending the range of your reading goes, Shakespeare's plays fall into two categories: they are great classic works from the past *and* playscripts.

Rom.   But, soft! what light through yonder window breaks?
It is the east, and Juliet is the sun.
Arise, fair sun, and kill the envious moon,
Who is already sick and pale with grief,
That thou her maid art far more fair than she:
Be not her maid, since she is envious;
Her vestal livery is but sick and green
And none but fools do wear it; cast it off.
It is my lady, O, it is my love!   10
O, that she knew she were!
She speaks, yet she says nothing: what of that?
Her eye discourses; I will answer it.
I am too bold, 'tis not to me she speaks:
Two of the fairest stars in all the heaven,
Having business, do entreat her eyes
To twinkle in their spheres till they return.
What if her eyes were there, they in her head?
The brightness of her cheek would shame those stars,
As daylight doth a lamp; her eyes in heaven   20
Would bring through the airy region stream so bright
That birds would sing and think it were not night.
See, how she leans her cheek upon her hand!
O, that I were a glove upon that hand,
That I might touch that cheek!
Jul.   Ay me!
Rom.   She speaks:
O, speak again, bright angel! for thou art
As glorious to this night, being o'er my head,
As is a winged messenger of heaven
Unto this white-upturned wondering eyes
Of mortals that fall back to gaze on him   30
When he bestrides the lazy-pacing clouds
And sailed upon the bosom of the air.
Jul.   O Romeo, Romeo! wherefore art thou Romeo?
Deny thy father and refuse thy name;
Or, if thou wilt not, be but sworn my love,
And I'll no longer be a Capulet.
Rom. [*Aside*]   Shall I hear more, or shall I speak at this?
Jul.   'Tis but thy name that is my enemy;
Thou art thyself, though not a Montague.
What's Montague? it is nor hand, nor foot,
Nor arm, nor face, nor any other part
Belonging to a man. O, be some other name!
What's in a name? that which we call a rose
By any other name would smell as sweet;
So Romeo would, were he not Romeo call'd,
Retain thy dear perfection which he owes
Without that title. Romeo, doff thy name,
And for that name which is no part of thee
Take all myself.

Rom.   I take thee at they word: 50
Call me but love, and I'll be new baptized;
Henceforth I never will be Romeo.
Jul.   What man art though that thus bescreen'd in night
So stumblest on my counsel?
Rom.   By a name
I know not how to tell thee who I am:
My name, dear saint, is hateful to myself,
Because it is an enemy to thee;
Had I it written, I would tear the word.
Jul.   My ears have not yet drunk a hundred words
Of that tongue's utterance, yet I know the sound:
Art thou not Romeo and a Montague?   60
Rom.   Neither, fair saint, if either thee dislike.
Jul.   How camest thou hither, tell me, and wherefore?
The orchard walls are high and hard to climb,
And the place death, considering who thou art,
If any of my kinsmen find thee here.
Rom.   With love's light wings did I o'er-perch these walls;
For stony limits cannot hold love out,
And what love can do that dares love attempt;
Therefore thy kinsmen are no let to me.
Jul.   If they do see thee, they will murder thee.   70
Rom.   Alack, there lies more peril in thine eye
Than twenty of their swords: look thou but sweet,
An I am proof against their enmity.
Jul.   I would not for the world they saw thee here.
Rom.   I have night's cloak to hide me from their sight;
And thou but love me, let them find me here:
My life were better ended by their hate,
Than death prorogued, wanting of thy love.
Jul.   By whose direction found'st thou out this place?
Rom.   By love, who first did prompt me to inquire;   80
He lent me counsel and I lent him eyes.
I am no pilot; yet, wert thou as far
As that vast shore wash'd with the farthest sea,
I would adventure for such merchandise.
Jul.   Thou know'st the mask of night is on my face,
Else would a maiden blush bepaint my cheek
For that which thou hast heard me speak tonight.
Fain would I dwell on form, fain, fain deny
What I have spoke: but farewell compliment!
Dost thou love me? I know thou wilt say 'Ay,'   90
And I will take thy word: yet, if thou swear'st,
Thou mayst prove false; at lovers' perjuries,
They say, Jove laughs. O gentle Romeo,
If thou dost love, pronounce it faithfully:
Of if thou think'st I am too quickly won,
I'll frown and be perverse and say thee nay,
So thou wilt woo; but else, not for the world.
In truth, fair Montague, I am too fond,
And therefore thou mayst think my 'haviour light:
But trust me, gentleman, I'll prove more true
Than those that have more cunning to be strange.   100
I should have been more strange, I must confess,
But that thou overheard'st, ere I was ware,
My true love's passion: therefore pardon me,
And not impute this yielding to light love,
Which the dark night hath so discovered.
Rom.   Lady, by yonder blessed moon I swear
That tips with silver all these fruit-tree tops –

Jul. O, swear not by the moon, the inconstant moon,
That monthly changes in her circled orb,   110
Lest that they love prove likewise variable.
Rom. What shall I swear by?
Jul. Do not swear at all;
Or, if thou wilt, swear by thy gracious self,
Which is the god of my idolatry,
And I'll believe thee.
Rom. If my heart's dear love –
Jul. Well, do not swear: although I joy in thee,
I have no joy of this contract to-night:
It is too rash, too unadvised, too sudden;
Too like the lightning, which doth cease to be
Ere one can say 'It lightens.' Sweet, good night!   120
This bud of love, by summer's ripening breath,
May prove a beauteous flower when next we meet.
Good night, good night! as sweet repose and rest
Come to thy heart as that within my breast!
Rom. O, wilt thou leave me so unsatisfied?
Jul. What satisfaction canst thou have to-night?
Rom. The exchange of thy love's faithful vow for mine.
Jul. I gave thee mine before thou didst request it:
And yet I would it were to give again.
Rom. Wouldst thou withdraw it? for what purpose, love?   130
Jul. But to be frank, and give it thee again.
And yet I wish but for the thing I have:
My bounty is as boundless as the sea,
My love as deep; the more I give thee,
The more I have, for both are infinite.

Lily and Colin by Elisabeth Bond

This is an extract from a radio script, written nearly four hundred years after *Romeo and Juliet*. Lily, like Juliet, is thirteen years old. Unlike Juliet, she is a deprived, abused child. She runs away from home with Colin, a small-time thief in his late thirties.

The extract describes their first night together in a station waiting room, which a guard has given them permission to sleep in.

A heavy-goods train rumbles through again.
Lily: (*sleepily*) A fella came round our way selling insurance. He said that were protection. He told me dad we're allowed five fires a year. We've already had two but they didn't pay much. And me dad's behind wi' t'payments, so I don't suppose we'll get any more.
Pause.
You asleep, Colin?
Colin: Not really.
Lily: It's nice here. It's dry and it's cold. I'm glad he let us stay.
Pause.
Lily: My love… come up close and I'll wrap me legs round you.
Colin. I'll be heavy on top of you.
Lily: Try. (*Pause.*) Shift your shoulder round a bit. That's it.
Colin: I can feel your heart beating very loudly beneath my ear. Bang, bang, bang – your life blood, banging into me.
Lily: I love the way you talk.
Colin: I've always tried to express myself using long words wherever possible. At least I can sound properly educated.
Lily: It's beautiful talk.
Pause.
Comfortable now?
Colin: I am. Yes.
You've taught me a lot, you have, Lily, and yet you're only young. I could easily

have gone under today if it hadn't been for you. I might have drowned in the emotions occasioned by each different event. It feels like drowning when I get upset. You've taught me to hold my head up, take things as they come. To be honest, you've taught me to rely on God less and myself more – something I'd never have thought possible.

Lily: It's because I love you, Colin, you know that.

Pause.

Where shall we go tomorrow?

Colin: (*sleepily*) I'm all for the Scottish Highlands.

Lily: By train or thumbing it, this time?

Colin: Perhaps we'd better thumb it, travelling by lorry, kings of the road.

Lily: Knight of the highway.

Pause.

Colin: I must be getting heavy for you.

Lily: I like your weight. I like to feel you on me.

Pause.

When I were a kiddie, five or six, we had a teacher at school, Miss Grayson. I thought she were beautiful. She smelt nice. I remember her smell, I'd never smelt anyone like that before. The other teachers smelt of parsnips, and in our house, it were all fags and beer and fish and chip papers.

If you got upset or if someone pushed you and you cried, Miss Grayson'd take you on her knee. I used to wish I could cry so I could go on her knee and smell her smell close to. I used to pinch mesel' but it never worked. And once, I pushed a girl who were nasty to me, so she would push me back and make me cry. But they told and she went on Miss Grayson's knee, not me. And I thought to mesel', I'll never go on her knee now, and I never did.

Pause.

Daft, eh, the things you remember.

Colin: One of the worst aspects of prison is the smell.

Lily: Tomorrow, we will go into Boots and spray on some of them testers. They don't like it but they can't get you for it.

Pause.

I can see you quite clearly in t'moonlight.

She sings.

I see the moon, the moon sees me,

Shining on the leaves of the old oak tree,

Please let the light that shines on me,

Shine on the one I love.

(*Sleepily*) Me nana used to sing that to me – it's a right oldie. Nana smelt of old ladies, but it didn't bother me.

Colin: Little Lily… my love…

They sleep. Fade out.

Literary nonfiction

Not all literary writing is fictional. To achieve the higher levels in English, you will be expected to have extended the range of your reading to have covered a variety of books where writers are writing about their own experience in a literary way.

The extracts which follow are intended to show you what kind of writing is included in this category and, possibly, to introduce you to some types of writing you have not read before. Most of these books would fit the description of having been written for adults, and some could also count as classics, especially those written before this century.

Literary non-fiction includes autobiographies, biographies, travel writing and also more intimate kinds of writing, such as personal letters and private diaries. The range of styles and different levels of formality in these kinds of writing varies enormously, as you will see in the examples which follow.

Autobiography

The story of a writer's own life is more like a novel than most of the other types of literary nonfiction. In fact, some of the novels you were introduced to earlier in this section have similarities with autobiographies: *Jane Eyre*, for example, is written as if it were an autobiography and owes something to Charlotte Brontë's own childhood, especially the part of the book which tells of Jane's experiences at school.

Second From Last in the Sack Race has its origins in David Nobbs's own childhood in Yorkshire, though many of the events in the book are obviously fiction and there is a great deal of exaggeration for humorous effect which would be out of place in a genuine autobiography.

The extracts which follow are taken from three twentieth-century autobiographies. Each is an account of the writer's childhood experiences, growing up in relatively deprived circumstances. For all three authors, their account of how they received the education which equipped them to become writers in later life is an important aspect of their life story. School, home and friends played different parts for each of the three.

Workbench assignment

As you read the extracts, consider the following questions:
- Who were the people who had the most influence on the education of these writers and what was the effect of the influence?
- How important does their reading seem to have been in influencing the development of their English skills?
- What differences do you notice in the style of writing of the three extracts? Can you detect in each one where the writers make use of dialect words and phrases remembered from the place they grew up in? How and where do they do this? Is it effective to mix Standard English and dialect in this way?

Lark Rise to Candleford by Flora Thompson

Flora Thompson (who calls herself Laura in her autobiographical writing) tells of her childhood and young adulthood in an Oxfordshire village during the closing years of the nineteenth century. The book was written in 1945. In this extract, she tells of the memories she has of her final years at her village school and of her teacher, Miss Shepherd.

But the most memorable day for Laura was that on which the Bishop came to consecrate an extension of the churchyard and walked round it in his big lawn sleeves, with a cross carried before him and a book in his hands, and the clergy of the district following. The schoolchildren, wearing their best clothes, were drawn up to watch. 'It makes a nice change from school,' somebody said, but to Laura the ceremony was but a prelude.

For some reason she had lingered after the other children had gone home, and the schoolmistress, who, after all, had not been invited to the Rectory to tea as she had hoped, took her round the church and told her all she knew of its history and architecture, then took her home to tea.

A small, two-roomed cottage adjoining the school was provided for the schoolmistress, and this the school managers had furnished in the manner they thought suitable for one of her degree. 'Very comfortable', they had stated in their advertisement; but to a new tenant it must have looked bare. The downstairs room had a deal table for meals, four cane-bottomed chairs of the type until recently seen in bedrooms, a white marble-topped sideboard stood for luxury and a wicker armchair by the hearth for comfort. The tiled floor was partly covered with brown matting.

But Miss Shepherd was 'artistic' and by the time Laura saw the room a transformation had taken place. A green art serge cloth with bobble fringe hid the nakedness of the deal centre table; the backs of the cane chairs were draped with white crocheted lace, tied with blue bows, and the wicker chair was cushioned and antimacassared. The walls were so crowded with pictures, photographs, Japanese fans, wool-work letter-racks, hanging pincushions, and other trophies of the present tenant's skill that, as the children used to say: 'You couldn't so much as stick a pin in.'

'Don't you think I've made it nice and cosy, dear?' said Miss Shepherd, after Laura had been shown and duly admired each specimen of her handiwork, and Laura agreed heartily, for it seemed to her the very height of elegance.

It was her first invitation to grown-up tea, with biscuits and jam – not spread on her bread for her, as at home, but spooned on to her plate by herself and spread exactly as she had seen her father spread his. After tea, Miss Shepherd played the harmonium and showed Laura her photographs and books, finally presenting her with one called *Ministering Children* and walking part of the way home with her. How thrilled Laura was when, at their parting, she said: 'Well, I think we have had quite a nice little time, after all, Laura.'

But, at the time of that tea-drinking, Laura must have been eleven or twelve, one of Miss Shepherd's 'big girls' and no longer an object of persecution. By that time the play was becoming less rough and bullying rarer, for the older children of her early schooldays had left school and none who came after were quite so belligerent. Civilization was beginning to tame them.

But, even in her earlier days, her life was easier after Edmund began school, for he was better-liked than she was; moreover, he could fight, and, unlike most of the other boys, he was not ashamed to be seen with his sister.

Often, on their way to school, Laura and he would take a field path which led part of the way by a brook backed by a pinewood where wood-pigeons cooed. By leaping the little stream, they could visit 'the graves'. These were two, side by side, in the deepest shade of the pines, and the headstones said: 'In Memory of Rufus' and 'In Memory of Bess'. They both knew very well that Rufus and Bess had been favourite hunters of a former owner of the estate; but they preferred to think of them as human beings – lovers, perhaps, who in life had been used to meet in that deep, mysterious gloom.

On other days they would scramble down the bank of the brook to pick watercress or forget-me-nots, or to build a dam, or to fish for minnows with their fingers. But, very often, they would pass along the bank without seeing anything, they would be so busy discussing some book they had read. They were voracious readers, although their books were few and not selected, but came to them by chance. There were the books from the school library, which, though better than nothing to read, made little impression upon them, for they were all of the goody-goody, Sunday-school prize type. But their father had a few books and others were lent to them, and amongst these were a few of the Waverley Novels. *The Bride of Lammermoor* was one of the first books Laura read with absorbed interest. She adored the Master of Ravenswood, his dark, haughty beauty, his flowing cloak and his sword, his ruined castle, set high on its crag by the sea, and his faithful servant Caleb and the amusing shifts he made to conceal his master's poverty. She read and re-read *The Bride* and dipped into it between whiles, until the heathery hills and moors of Scotland became as real to her as her flat native fields, and the lords and ladies and soldiers and witches and old retainers as familiar as the sober labouring people who were her actual neighbours.

At seven years old *The Bride* made such an impression upon her that she communicated her excitement to Edmund, himself as yet unable to read, and one night in their mother's bedroom they enacted the scene in the bridal chamber, Edmund insisting that he should be Lucy and Laura the bridegroom, although she had told him that a bridegroom was usually one of his own sex.

'Take up your bonny bridegroom!' he cried, so realistically that their mother came running upstairs thinking he was in pain. She found Laura crouching on the floor in her nightdress while Edmund stood over her with a dagger which looked very much like his father's two-foot rule. No wonder she said, 'Whatever will you two be up to next!' and took *The Bride of Lammermoor* away and hid it.

Then a neighbour who had bought a bundle of old books for a few pence at a sale lent them *Old Saint Paul's*, and the out-house door was soon chalked with a cross and the wheelbarrow trundled round the garden to the cry of 'Bring out your dead!'

Between the ages of seven and ten, Laura became such a confirmed reader that, when other books failed, she would read her father's dictionary, until this disappeared because her mother thought the small print was bad for her eyes. There was still the Bible, which could not be forbidden, and she spent many an hour over that, delighting in the Old Testament stories of the Pillar of Fire, and of Ruth and Esther and Samuel and David, and of Jonah and the whale, or learning by heart the parables in the New Testament to repeat at Sunday School. At one time she had a passion for the Psalms, not so much from religious fervour as from sheer delight in the language. She felt these ought to be read aloud, and, as she dare not read them aloud herself, lest she should be overheard, she would persuade Edmund or some other child to read them with her, verse and verse about.

Once, when Edmund was upstairs in bed with measles and her mother was out, she and another girl were having a fine time imitating the parson and clerk reading the Psalms in church, when Edmund, who could hear all that was going on downstairs, called out to ask whose Bible Alice was using. She was using his and when Edmund had his suspicions confirmed he was so enraged that he dashed downstairs in his nightshirt and chased Alice all down the garden to the gate. If his mother could have seen him out of doors with his spots, in his night shirt, brandishing his Bible and threatening the retreating Alice, she would have been horrified, for measles patients were then told that they must not put so much as a hand out of bed or the spots would 'go inward' and the simple measles would turn to black measles, when they would probably die. But no one saw him and he returned to his bed, apparently not a ha-penny the worse for his airing.

A little later, Scott's poems came into their lives and Edmund would swing along the field path to school reciting 'The way was long, the night was cold', or stop to strike an attitude and declaim,

Come one, come all this rock shall fly

From its stern bases soon as I,

or wave Laura on with 'Charge, Chester, charge! On, Stanley, on!' At that time their conversation when alone together was tinged with the language of their favourite romances. Sometimes Edmund would amuse his sister and himself by translating, when a battered old zinc bucket became 'ye antique pail', or a tree slightly damaged by the wind 'yon lightning-blasted pine', while some good neighbour of theirs whom they could see working in the fields would have given Edmund what he would have called 'a darned good bommicking' if he had heard himself referred to as 'yon caitiff hind'.

Sometimes they tried their hand at writing a little verse themselves. Laura was guilty of a terrible moral story in rhyme about a good child who gave his birthday sixpence to a beggar, and Edmund wrote a poem about sliding on the ice with the refrain 'Slide, glide, glide, slide, over the slippery pond'. Laura liked that one and used to sing it. She also sang one of her own, beginning, 'The snowdrop comes in winter cold', which ran, with a stanza for every flower, through the seasons, and to which she added yet another stanza every time she saw or remembered a flower hitherto neglected. One day her mother asked her what that 'unked thing' she was trying to sing was about, and, in an unguarded moment, she brought out the scraps of paper on which it was written. She did not scold or even laugh at her folly; but Laura could feel that she was not pleased, and, later that evening, she lectured her soundly on her needlework. 'You can't *afford* to waste your time,' she said, 'Here you are, eleven years old, and just look at this seam!'

A Ragged Schooling by Robert Roberts

The writer tells us of his growing up in the slums of Salford during the early 1900s. The book was written in 1974. In this extract he describes an incident remembered from his final years at school, at a time when most children left education at fourteen years old.

During my last two years at school I acted as 'number one' monitor, which meant release on most days from lessons, a freedom rather irksome, since learning drew me still. I lackeyed for the headmaster, running his errands, seeking truants, checking lists and, of course, going off every Monday afternoon with the leather bag. Through a riveted reading each week of the *Magnet* magazine some of us boys were aware of the profound respect that the scholars of Greyfriars College registered for their headmaster, that revered sadist, Dr Locke; but I felt none for mine, or the school either. Without scruple I read all correspondence and confidential notes, picking up a deal of curious information, which was distributed for the interest and amusement of classmates. This way they got early warning of the visits of His Majesty's Inspectors. We noticed then how our teachers developed the jitters, how they suddenly became more anxious, patient, friendly, pumping us with answers to questions which, it was hoped, the dreaded HMI's would ask on 'Judgement Day'. And the great ones duly arrived, putting the fear of God into everyone on the staff. But *we* loved·them! Like Dutch uncles they went round the classes, treating us with a sort of old-world courtesy, always enquiring, and making us feel that, in school at least, girls and boys were the people who mattered. Among these men were some of the pioneers who dragged the elementary education system 'kicking and screaming' into the twentieth century. They came, and their questions ranged far and wide. 'Where, my boy,' asked one inspector, addressing Sydney Carey in Standard V, 'is the city of Rome?'

'On the Ganges!' Syd told him. (In geography Sydney put most places on that holy river, a weakness due to our possession of Empire.) The great man looked sad, and our teacher, Miss Bethel, bit her lips.

'Sir!' I shouted, shooting up an arm. 'Capital of Italy, sir! Called the Eternal City!' The old gentleman gobbled with pleasure and spoke to his colleague. I then proceeded to paint the lily! 'Also known as the '*Internal* City', sir, because it's chockful of underground passages and caves and cellars where all them early Christians lived!'

Now this was news to them. They smiled together, murmured a moment, then the elder turned. 'Well, hardly, my boy, hardly. But a very good answer indeed!' I fell back on my laurels and Miss Bethel shot me a lovely smile.

They moved among us like visiting royalty. All canes disappeared, and after several days of gentle but effective buzzing about our hive they summed it all up. Later the Head and some of his minions got their roasting, a cooled-off version of which appeared in the school log afterwards. Certain members of the staff were 'incompetent', 'unintelligent', 'unqualified', 'unimaginative methods used; teaching conditions – appalling'.

Once a chief inspector came with an assistant who had visited us on an earlier occasion. In the aftermath old Rowley, the Head, looked, I thought, more shaken than usual. He stood by his desk after school closed and seemed to be in deep trouble. Putting books away, I busied about with both ears cocked. How pleasant it was to see the mighty humbled! The inspectors, I gathered, were deeply disturbed at his scholars' inability to express themselves. We appeared to lack something, mentioned several times, called 'oral facility'. I rolled the words over in my mind and, later, asked my mother about it all. 'They can't talk!' she said. The inspectors added that we had responded to their questions either not at all or in broken, ungrammatical sentences. 'Most disturbing!' Moreover we had been drilled, it seemed, into a sort of slavish passivity: the teacher addressed us pupils and we did nothing but sit and listen, and altogether there was no health in us. The chief inspector put his fist somewhere in the region of the master's chest, then brought it towards his own, spreading his fingers. 'Draw it *out*!' be said. 'Understand?' Rowley nodded dumbly. Expanded vocabulary, fluency, self-assurance, that's what they were after! Our Head defended himself weakly, pointing out the kind of children he had to deal with – 'the homes they come from…' But his critics now showed impatience; they had visited similar schools to ours and found the pupils far more articulate. Something had to be done, and that quickly. In among the ruck of words that followed I heard Rowley say emphatically that he too had boys who… and he caulled me over. This lad, for instance, from Standard VII…

The chief inspector gazed down on me kindly. 'I didn't see you, my boy, in the top class!'

'No, sir,' I said. 'I was washin' out Standard VI's inkwells all afternoon.' He then asked me about the family – how my father earned his living. Did my parents take a newspaper and read books?

'My mother reads all sorts,' I told him. 'History books, story books – everything. I'm in the liberry.'

'And do you talk at home?' the other inspector asked, 'in the family – conversation?'

'We've a shop, sir. It's talkin' all day!'

'Ah, well, now!' he said. 'That's understandable! Now can you tell me the meaning of the word "articulate" – ar-tic-u-late?'

'Able to speak well, I think, sir – express yerself, like?'

'Excellent! Thank you, my boy!'

Old Rowley was beaming. 'You can go now!'

The new regime to increase verbal flow and stimulate self-assurance began the very next week under the direction of a phthisic young Scotsman. In the hall Mr Mackie always made great show and taught us well, but behind a classroom door away from the Head's surveillance he fell at once into a coma of indifference, and precious little instruction any of us got. But now the heat was on. According to the log book, His Majesty's Inspector required clear evidence, next time round, of an improvement in 'oral facility'. In any case, our school was to be the subject of a special report to the Board of Education. Fortunately, Mr Mackie had a brainwave: we would establish, he said, a 'moot', of which the old Anglo-Saxons had been very fond. We knew about the Anglo-Saxons. In our moot, problems of the day would be thrashed out. 'Everyone will be allowed,' he said, 'to stand up in front of the class and say just what they like. But no reading! Talk! Self-expression! That's what I want! The Anglo-Saxons didn't read!'

Mr Rowley, much enthused, came and set the first moot point, chalking it up on the board – 'Children should go to school until they are fifteen'. 'But write a composition on it beforehand,' he told us, 'then you'll have plenty of thoughts to go at when it comes to the public speaking. You can be *for* this, or against it, just as you wish.'

I turned out an essay of several pages wildly in favour of the proposal, and Mackie chose me at once as a protagonist. Unfortunately, in spite of threat or cajolery, he couldn't find a single other pupil willing to stand before the class and put the opposing, or indeed any, point of view, and this not for want of ideas but through fear alone. Free speech didn't come easily to children kept down at home and in the classroom. Just before the time for debate arrived, however, at which Mr Rowley himself would preside, the teacher dragooned a terrified girl off the back row. 'After Robert has finished his address,' Mackie told her, '*you* say a few words. Just a sentence or two, if that's all you can manage, but say *something*!' Having chatted the theme over with my mother the night before, I got on the box provided and did my three-minute stint without trouble. Rich people, I remember saying, sent their children to schools and colleges until they were twenty-one, so there must be something good in it. We would become doctors and teachers and chemists and explorers – things like that, if we went to school until we were fifteen. I was all for it.

Although Mackie had informed us that the audience was quite free to heckle or clap, they heard me out in dead silence. But both adult listeners seemed very pleased; the Head even patted my shoulder. 'Well, well!' said Mr Mackie. 'Very well spoken indeed! You almost convinced me! I've a story book at home for you – a little present. Now, Weeton!' (They dispensed with Christian names at school, even for girls.) My opponent, Lily Weeton, a pallid girl with plaits, came out and stepped on the box. Her words were few but explosive. 'I think,' she said, 'we should gerrout to work at fourteen and fetch some money in for us parents.' Then she stepped off the box to a thunderclap of applause, cheering and clog-stamping that rocked the school. Bubbling excitement, our 'electorate' now went to the poll, and the headmaster, acting as returning officer, announced the result in professional style:

Roberts, Robert 2
Weeton, Lily 48

Storming cheers again for the victor. Eddie Franklin and a girl friend had given me a sympathy vote, but nevertheless admitted to being intellectually with the opposition. 'Even Mackie was against me!' I complained to my mother that evening.

'Humph!' she said. 'Shows how much sense *he's* got!'

I Know Why The Caged Bird Sings by Maya Angelou

The writer tells of her childhood during the 1930s in the small American town of Stamps, Arkansas. She had been abused as a child and had stopped talking. Mrs Flowers, described earlier in the book as the 'aristocrat' of the Black community in Stamps, befriends Marguerite (Maya's full name) and this extract tells of her attempts to encourage the little girl to talk again.

There was a little path beside the rocky road, and Mrs Flowers walked in front swinging her arms and picking her way over the stones.

She said, without turning her head, to me, 'I hear you're doing very good school work, Marguerite, but that it's all written. The teachers report that they have trouble getting you to talk in class.' We passed the triangular farm on our left and the path widened to allow us to walk together. I hung back in the separate unasked and unanswerable questions.

'Come and walk along with me, Marguerite.' I couldn't have refused even if I wanted to. She pronounced my name so nicely. Or more correctly, she spoke each word with such clarity that I was certain a foreigner who didn't understand English could have understood her.

'Now no one is going to make you talk—possibly no one can. But bear in mind, language is man's way of communicating with his fellow man and it is language alone which separates him from the lower animals.' That was a totally new idea to me, and I would need time to think about it.

'Your grandmother says you read a lot. Every chance you get. That's good, but not good enough. Words mean more than what is set down on paper. It takes the human voice to infuse them with the shades of deeper meaning.'

I memorized the part about the human voice infusing words. It seemed so valid and poetic.

She said she was going to give me some books and that I not only must read them, I must read them aloud. She suggested that I try to make a sentence sound in as many different ways as possible.

'I'll accept no excuse if you return a book to me that has been badly handled.' My imagination boggled at the punishment I would deserve if in fact I did abuse a book of Mrs Flowers'. Death would be too kind and brief.

The odors in the house surprised me. Somehow I had never connected Mrs Flowers with food or eating or any other common experience of common people. There must have been an outhouse, too, but my mind never recorded it.

The sweet scent of vanilla had met us as she opened the door.

'I made tea cookies this morning. You see, I had planned to invite you for cookies and lemonade so we could have this little chat. The lemonade is in the icebox.'

It followed that Mrs Flowers would have ice on an ordinary day, when most families in our town bought ice late on Saturdays only a few times during the summer to be used in the wooden ice-cream freezers.

She took the bags from me and disappeared through the kitchen door. I looked around the room that I had never in my wildest fantasies imagined I would see. Browned photographs leered or threatened from the walls and the white, freshly done curtains pushed against themselves and against the wind. I wanted to gobble up the room entire and take it to Bailey, who would help me analyze and enjoy it.

'Have a seat, Marguerite. Over there by the table.' She carried a platter covered with a tea towel. Although she warned that she hadn't tried her hand at baking sweets for some time, I was certain that like everything else about her the cookies would be perfect.

They were flat round wafers, slightly browned on the edges and butter yellow in the center. With the cold lemonade they were sufficient for childhood's lifelong diet. Remembering my manners, I took nice little lady-like bites off the edges. She said she had made them expressly for me and that she had a few in the kitchen that I could take home to my brother. So I jammed one whole cake in my mouth and the rough crumbs scratched the insides of my jaws, and if I hadn't had to swallow, it would have been a dream come true.

As I ate she began the first of what we later called 'my lessons in living.' She said that I must always be intolerant of ignorance but understanding of illiteracy. That some people, unable to go to school, were more educated and even more intelligent than college professors. She encouraged me to listen carefully to what country people called mother wit. That in those homely sayings was couched the collective wisdom of generations.

When I finished the cookies she brushed off the table and brought a thick, small book from the bookcase. I had read *A Tale of Two Cities* and found it up to my standards as a romantic novel. She opened the first page and I heard poetry for the first time in my life.

'It was the best of times and the worst of times...' Her voice slid in and curved down through and over the words. She was nearly singing. I wanted to look at the pages. Were they the same that I had read? Or were there notes, music, lined on the pages, as in a hymn book? Her sounds began cascading gently. I knew from listening to a thousand preachers that she was nearing the end of her reading, and I hadn't really heard, heard to understand, a single word.

'How do you like that?'

It occurred to me that she expected a response. The sweet vanilla flavor was still on my tongue and her reading was a wonder in my ears. I had to speak.

I said, 'Yes, ma'am.' It was the least I could do, but it was the most also.

'There's one more thing. Take this book of poems and memorize one for me. Next time you pay me a visit, I want you to recite.'

I have tried often to search behind the sophistication of years for the enchantment I so easily found in those gifts. The essence escapes but its aura remains. To be allowed, no, invited, into the private lives of strangers, and to share their joys and fears, was a chance to exchange the Southern bitter wormwood for a cup of mead with Beowulf or a hot cup of tea and milk with Oliver Twist. When I said aloud, 'It is a far, far better thing that I do, than I have ever done...' tears of love filled my eyes at my selflessness.

On that first day, I ran down the hill and into the road (few cars ever came along it) and had the good sense to stop running before I reached the Store.

I was liked, and what a difference it made. I was respected not as Mrs Henderson's grandchild or Bailey's sister but for just being Marguerite Johnson.

Childhood's logic never asks to be proved (all conclusions are absolute). I didn't question why Mrs Flowers had singled me out for attention, nor did it occur to me that Momma might have asked her to give me a little talking to. All I cared about was that she had made tea cookies for *me* and read to *me* from her favorite book. It was enough to prove that she liked me.

Travel writing

In a way, travel writing is a very particular type of autobiography, dealing with the experiences of the writers on journeys to places far away fom home: the people they meet, the ways of life they observe, and their thoughts about the differences between their usual way of life and the lives of others.

Workbench assignment

The following extracts come from two books which tell of the travels of English writers in the Middle East. Both writers seem fascinated by the changes to the traditional Arab way of life which have come about because of money from oil and the fact that this has brought the people of these countries into contact with western society. Not all the changes are necessarily seen as good.

• As you read the extracts, look particularly at what the writers learn by listening to the people they meet. Both writers highlight the separation of men and women which is required by those who follow Islam. They show how this affects the daily lives of the people they meet and they consider the positive and negative aspects, both now and in the future.

• Try to come to some conclusions of your own about what each writer has to say.

A Traveller On Horseback by Christina Dodwell

This is an account of the writer's travels through Turkey and Iran. It was written in 1987 and is particularly interesting because there are not very many women travel writers. In this extract, she writes of her stay in Tehran and is thinking about how Khomeni led a backlash against western values and tried to reintroduce a traditional Muslim way of life. Because she is a woman, she actually manages to talk to some Iranian women about their views and attempts to make it clear to her readers that opinions about separation and modest dress are by no means clear cut.

I had grown to love awakening at dawn out on the *talar*, and hearing all the horses slowly waking up and whinnying soft greetings as we washed and made coffee. And I adored my morning rides on the big white mare, those spacious horizons, and the scent of crushed sage under hoof.

But after a week I noticed that the river level was dropping. It would soon be totally dry. The wheat had ripened and I could hear its seed-heads clicking and rattling in the breeze, and the crack as the ears popped open. It was time to move pasture. We loaded all our gear, the saddlery, and some last sacks of vegetables for market into the jeep and left. Narcy teased me about their house in Tehran with its washing machine and cook. It was difficult to imagine him and Louise in a house, they had been such happy nomads.

There were many military road blocks because some trouble had flared up with insurgents in the mountains. Above the forest we re-crossed the Elburz Mountains, whose peaks you can still see from the main street in Tehran. The Firouz house is in the centre of the city with its own private shady garden, an old building with some of the comforts of life, but no bedsteads. Here, as before, we laid our sheets out on floor-pads.

During the Revolution when Louise and Narcy came back to Tehran they were arrested and put in prison. 'But that's nothing special,' Louise had said. 'Most people went to prison for a while.' Many people had also been killed. Louise was in solitary confinement for two weeks, which ended when she went on hunger strike. Narcy was jailed for two months. Louise came back to the house which had been sealed and was in chaos, with slogans like 'Death to America' scrawled in lipstick and excrement. One of the slogans, written in lipstick, has been left in place, as part of the decor.

One morning we wandered around the local antique shops. I especially liked the miniatures, in some the figures were stepping out of the picture on to their paper surround. Whenever I went out of the house I had to put on my scarf and *mantau*. It felt absurd to be dressing up as if for an English winter, the blazing heat surprised me every time. We also went to the bazaar which has an astonishing number of gold shops. I wondered who keeps them in business, there were few shoppers. Gaggles of merchants seemed to be selling to each other.

Traffic in Tehran is maniacal. Men drive cars just like they drive donkeys, leaving the thinking to the donkey. And since donkeys are driven at maximum speed, so are their vehicles, while traffic lights flash, all three lights at once, seeming more for decoration than for traffic control.

One day in a carpet shop I got into conversation with a man who spoke out frankly saying that the Iranian people made a mistake over installing Khomeni, though he admitted that he was among those who had wanted the Revolution. 'We all wanted it to come; if only the Shah hadn't hidden the facts of life from us.' Illogically, he added, 'It was wonderful when the Shah was here.' This line about how great things were under the Shah was one I heard many times as people were forgetting their earlier hardships in the light of the present ones. But they say there won't be another revolution, because Khomeni sends all the troublemakers to be killed in the fight against Iraq.

As for women, the Shah's twin sister and his wife had championed women's rights, and in the sixties they won emancipation into a male-dominated society, with equal pay laws following in the early seventies, but it's all rather irrelevant since a working wife is still an insult to her husband.

During the previous Shah's time, the wearing of the *chadoor* had been made illegal. The effect was as shattering for some women as to insist that all western women walk down the high street in a bikini.

Now of course the *chadoor* or *mantau* is compulsory. Actually I don't think the women mind as much as their liberated sisters would want them to. They quite enjoy wearing one as a means of flirtation, sometimes wearing little underneath, and it gives the plain girl the same start as the beauty. Their natures are lovely; and kinder, more generous people would be hard to find.

Being female meant I could associate freely with Iranian women, and over the full course of my journey I talked with an enormous number, whose background varied from local bus passengers to the wealthy upper class. Segregation of men and women applies in all spheres, even the beaches are segregated, and on the female beach the women still have to wear a *chadoor* or *mantau*. It would be terrifying to swim in such a garment. A wife cannot play tennis with her husband, unless the court is private and not overlooked by public buildings. Iranian women who resisted covering up risked having acid sprayed in their faces.

It was time for me to move on; my visa was half expired so I bought a ticket on the public bus to Kerman which is 1,000 kilometres south-east of Tehran.

Arabia by Jonathan Raban

This is also an account of the writer's travels to several Middle Eastern countries. In this extract, he travels out from the capital city of Abu Dhabi, which is very rich and very westernised, to a small village. Here he talks to a man who is trying to preserve the old way of life and protect his family from what he sees as dangerous changes.

 Just six years ago, the old man said, counting the years off on his fingers, their life had been very different from this. They had spent the summers in a mud fort a few miles down the road – quarters they shared with many other families. Then, for the winter, they had driven their sheep and camels south to Muscat, where they lived in tents. It had not been like this at all: they had been very poor; there had been no television, no motor cars. Now – he praised Allah and Sheikh Zayed – they had this fine house; they had 'a.c.'; life was very good; they wanted for nothing. He remembered when Al Ain had been only an oasis in the desert: now it was a fine city, with a Hilton hotel. (It also had a hotel called the 'Rolex'; the names of famous wristwatches are potent symbols in this part of the world.)

In the shadow beyond where we were sitting, I saw a woman's face pressed against the mosquito mesh of a door frame. When she saw me looking at her her face dissolved back into shadow.

Did he not, I asked, think that with the coming of the city there would come other, bad thing? Could a close family like his own survive in a world of tall buildings and superhighways?

His family would always stay together, he said. His eldest son, who was not here today, was an engineer; he had trained in Beirut and London. When he was away, he had written home every week. When he returned, he was still obedient to his father. The power of the bedu family was very strong; I must understand that. The city was good, the motor car was good; how one used these things depended on the character of the people.

'But,' I said, 'you have a television —'

'Two!' he interrupted me. He had two televisions: one for the women and one for the men.

'On television you see what goes on in cities in the West, like London and New York. You see the violence in the streets, the break-up of families; aren't you frightened that something like that can take place here?'

Television, said the old man, was a great teacher. One learned much about distant countries from it. There was much to praise in England and America.

While the father talked, I looked at the young men to see if their faces showed any flicker of scepticism or dissent. I thought that I caught the occasional hint of a smile – but perhaps that was only because I expected to find one there. When I addressed questions to them, it was the old man who nearly always answered on their behalf, finishing sentences which they had begun. His youngest son wanted to be a doctor. I said that to be a doctor he might have to train far away: the boy said that he would come home to his family every Friday. *Every* Friday, said the old man; theirs was a close family, and it was unthinkable for anyone not to be home on Friday.

Sitting among the leaves, sipping coffee and smelling incense and eucalyptus, I tried to threaten them with another world of thuggery, isolation and family breakdown. The more I talked, the more unreal the words sounded in my own head. The men and the boys listened politely while I spoke of marooned wives in tower blocks and juvenile delinquency. Nothing like that, they assured me, would ever happen here. It was obvious that they thought I was telling improbable travellers' tales. Yet they had come much further than I had. Six years away from being desert nomads, they were talking confidently about careers in engineering and medicine; one member of the family had already worked in Europe and the Lebanon; they gave every sign of having adapted gracefully to a life in which Modern Tissues, the Range Rover, the twin-tub washing machine, two televisions, floral Thermos flasks, air travel and the local Hilton were taken perfectly for granted. The veiled women fluttered behind dark screens: I wondered how many more years it would take for them to emerge, and what the consequences would be then. At present their exclusion from this male domain of freedom, ambition and machines was vital: the blithe way in which the bedu men were able to talk about the future depended on keeping the women in the past.

The old man said that he would like to show me his farm. He led me around the edge of the women's quarters – still inside the walled box – to a well. Beside the well, on a patch of earth just a few feet square, he was growing oranges, mangoes, dates, grapes and olives. They were clustered so thickly together that it was like standing in a shadowy greengrocer's shop, with fruits entwining with each other on their stalks.

I said that it seemed to me to be a miracle of intensive agriculture. He must be a very talented gardener to make so many things grow so richly in so small a space. He smiled self-deprecatingly, showing his two teeth, and said I must not compliment him: I should instead praise Allah and Sheikh Zayed.

As we drove away I looked back at the village through the car window. Its streets were just as empty, its dice-like houses just as small and squat, as they had seemed when we arrived. It gave away nothing to the world about what was going on inside. Its farms and leafy courtyards were well-kept secrets. The family I had met had gone through an extraordinary revolution. They had been suddenly exposed to the full blast of twentieth-century manners and things. Other people in other places had simply been smashed by the impact: half of Africa has been devastated by the gale damage. Here, though, it was different. The bedu had met the century head-on, but they had been able to deal with it in the family, protected by thick walls of breezeblock and cement. It seemed much the safest and most graceful way.

Letters and journals

Some writing which ends up published in books was never originally written with that intention. Many people write letters to their friends, or keep journals for their own private thoughts. These are particularly interesting when they are kept by writers who also produced more polished writing for public consumption.

Workbench assignment

• Compare the two journal entries. Does the fact that Hopkins was writing notes for his own personal use, whilst Dorothy Wordsworth

was writing an account she intended to share with her brother, make a difference to the way the diarists express their ideas?
- What similarities and differences can you see between the descriptions Hopkins includes in his journal and those in the poem? (His choice of adjectives and use of imagery deserve attention.)
- Consider how William Wordsworth takes ideas for his poem from Dorothy's journal and note what he adds to make it something more than an account of a memory from childhood.

Gerard Manley Hopkins

Hopkins is most famous for his poetry which was written during the second half of the nineteenth century, but he also kept a journal where he recorded details of things he observed whilst out walking in the countryside. These detailed descriptions and comparisons are very similar to those found in his poetry.

Oct. 19– I was there again with Purbrick, at the scaffolding which is left as a mark of the survey at the highest point. We climbed on this and looked round: it was a fresh and delightful sight. The day was rainy and a rolling wind; parts of the landscape, as the Orms' Heads, were blotted out by rain. The clouds westwards were a pied piece – sail-coloured brown and milky blue; a dun yellow tent of rays opened upon the skyline far off. Cobalt blue was poured on the hills bounding the valley of the Clwyd and far in the south spread a bluish damp, but all the nearer valley was showered with tapered diamond flakes of fields in purple and brown and green.

Nov. 8 – Walking with Wm. Splaine we saw a vast multitude of starlings making an unspeakable jangle. They would settle in a row of trees; then, one tree after another, rising at a signal they looked like a cloud of specks of black snuff or powder struck up from a brush or broom or shaken from a wig; then they would sweep round in whirlwinds – you could see the nearer and farther bow of the rings by the size and blackness; many would be in one phase at once, all narrow black flakes hurling round, then in another; then they would fall upon a field and so on. Splaine wanted a gun; then 'there it would rain meat' he said. I thought they must be full of enthusiasm and delight hearing their cries and stirring and cheering one another.

Nov. 11 – Bitter north wind, hail and sleet. On the hills snow lying and the mountains covered from head to foot. But they could scarcely be seen till next day, a Blandyke, which was fine and clear. I went with Mr Hughes up Moel y Parch, from the top of which we had a noble view, but the wind was very sharp. Snowdon and all the range reminded me of the Alps: they looked like a stack of rugged white flint, specked and streaked with black, in many places chiselled and channelled. Home by Caerwys wood, where we saw two beautiful swans, as white as they should be, restlessly steering and 'canting' in the water and following us along the shore: one of them several times, as if for vexation, caught and gnawed at the stone quay of the sluice close under me.

Pied Beauty

Glory be to God for dappled things –
For skies of couple-colour as a brinded cow;
For rose-moles all in stipple upon trout that swim;
Fresh-firecoal, chestnut-falls; finches' wings;
Landscape plotted and pieced – fold, fallow, and plough;
And all trades, their gear and tackle and trim.

All things counter, original, spare, strange;
Whatever is fickle, freckled (who knows how?)
With swift, slow; sweet, sour; adazzle, dim;
He fathers-forth whose beauty is past change:
Praise him.

Dorothy Wordsworth

In the early 1800s, Dorothy and William Wordsworth went to live in the Lake District. Dorothy kept a journal for her brother which was almost like a letter to him. She too recorded details of things she saw on country walks (one of the most famous entries in the journal is where she describes seeing the daffodils which are the subject of one of the best known of all English poems), though she also records details of her life and conversations with her brother, inspiring some poetry which you might not otherwise guess had its origins in autobiographical experience.

 [*March 14th,*] *Sunday Morning*. William had slept badly – he got up at nine o'clock, but before he rose he had finished *The Beggar Boys*, and while we were at breakfast that is (for I had breakfasted) he, with his basin of broth before him untouched, and a little plate of bread and butter he wrote the Poem to a Butterfly! He ate not a morsel, nor put on his stockings, but sate with his shirt neck unbuttoned, and his waist coat open while he did it. The thought first came upon him as we were talking about the pleasure we both always feel at the sight of a butterfly. I told him that I used to chase them a little, but that I was afraid of brushing the dust off their wings, and did not catch them. He told me how they used to kill the white ones when he went to school because they were Frenchmen. Mr Simpson came in just as he was finishing the Poem. After he was gone I wrote it down and the other poems, and I read them over to him. We then called at Mr Olliff's – Mr O. walked with us to within sight of Rydale – the sun shone very pleasantly, yet it was extremely cold. We dined and then Wm. went to bed. I lay upon the fur gown before the fire, but I could not sleep – I lay there a long time. It is now halfpast 5 – I am going to write letters – I began to write to Mrs Rawson. William rose without having slept – we sate comfortably by the fire till he began to try to alter *The Butterfly*, and tired himself – he went to bed tired.

To A Butterfly

Stay near me – do not take thy flight!
A little longer stay in sight!
Much converse do I find in thee,
Historian of my infancy!
Float near me; do not yet depart!
Dead times revive in thee:
Thou bring'st, gay creature as thou art!
A solemn image to my heart,
My father's family!
Oh! pleasant, pleasant were the days,
The time, when, in our childish plays,
My sister Emmeline and I
Together chased the butterfly!
A very hunter did I rush
Upon the prey: – with leaps and springs
I followed on from brake to bush;
But she, God love her, feared to brush
The dust from off its wings.

Literature from other cultures

One requirement of the Programmes of Study for National Curriculum English is that you should include literature about other cultures and by writers from other cultures in your range of reading. If you have worked your way through these extracts, you have encountered writers like Jamaica Kincaid, Doris Lessing and Maya Angelou, in addition to accounts by two travel writers of their contact with the Muslim culture of the Middle East.

The books you are required to study in school, and the pre-released materials upon which your final examinations are based, will also include some texts from other cultures. Some English Literature syllabuses have thematic sections which focus on writing from other cultures: for example, one of the NEAB's areas of study is Childhood and Family in Black Writing.

If literature from other cultures interests you, this is something you could follow up in your independent reading, since all the other categories of texts outlined above could well include literature set outside England, or written by writers who have grown up in other parts of the world where English is an important, if not the first, language.

Chapter 3
Writing about independent reading

So far this section will have given you some idea of the huge variety of reading you might undertake during your GCSE course, in addition to the books you study in class. Even if you wanted to, it would hardly be possible for you to do a detailed assignment on every one of the books. In order for your teacher to assess you, you will need some written proof that you have read a range of books. One of the exam boards (MEG) asks for this to be included in your coursework folder.

Recording reading

Your school may have prepared forms for you to use to record your reading. These may simply record factual details of the books you have read:

Title: _____	Title: _____
Authors/Editors: _____	Authors/Editors: _____
Publishers: _____	Publishers: _____
First Published: _____	First Published: _____
I.S.B.N. No.: _____	I.S.B.N. No.: _____
Date Begun: _____	Date Begun: _____
Date completed: _____	Date completed: _____
Where from? _____	Where from? _____
Book No.: _____	Book No.: _____

or may have space for you to make a short comment on your book:

Title: _____	Title: _____
Author: _____	Author: _____
Date Finished: _____	Date Finished: _____
Comments: _____	Comments: _____
Star Rating: ☆ ☆ ☆ ☆ ☆	Star Rating: ☆ ☆ ☆ ☆ ☆

Keeping a reading log

In Section 1 you will have read about the advantages of keeping a written log of your speaking and listening activities. Keeping a detailed log of your reading is useful for similar reasons. It will be more than just a record of titles and dates. Your comments may also help your teacher to assess your 'response' skills and possibly your knowledge about written language.

If you are reading a difficult and lengthy book, you will find it useful to 'think on paper' as you go along. Spontaneous thoughts and feelings of that kind will help you sort out your ideas in preparation for more formal assignment writing.

If you haven't kept a reading log before, it is often difficult to decide how best to do it. Here are some ideas for the kind of comment you may wish to write.

- When you choose a book you can write about your first thoughts.
  Look at the picture on the cover and the blurb on the back. Who is the author? What is the title? What attracted you to the book? What do you think it will be about?
- You can give a very brief summary of the story – just a paragraph about the important events (the plot) in each chapter.
- You can say what you think might happen next.
- You can compare one part of the book with another – or compare it with other similar stories – or a television or film version. You can ask questions about the book. What is going through your mind as you read? What do you what to find out about the story?
- You can write about the people in the book. What are they like? How do you feel about them? Do you sometimes want to give them advice, or criticise the way they behave, or feel sorry for them? You can predict how you think they might have changed by the end of the story.
- You can write about what kind of book it is and how well you think the author is dealing with that type of story. What does the author do well, or badly?
- When you finish the book you can recommend it to other readers, or say why you wouldn't recommend it.
- You can talk about problems (and good bits) you found as you were reading it.

If you use these suggestions alongside the advice this section gives about response and knowledge about language, you will be able to check whether the comments you are writing are demonstrating the skills listed in the Statements of Attainment. Such a record will be of use both to you and to your teacher. It may be possible to include your reading log, or extracts from it, in your coursework folder.

This brief extract from a reading journal kept by Neil during the first year of his GCSE course gives a clear indication that his reading skills are of a very high level:

> 'Howard's End' - what can I say, comment would be superfluous - definitely the best book I have ever read. Poor Leonard Bast's fate was admirably conceived and well-executed, and the tragedy of this was balanced by the joy of Helen's reconciliation with her sister, and the growth of a family relationship between her and Mr. Wilcox. One only wishes that Leonard was alive to share in their happiness and equanimity (and to father the boy of course! but then Jackie would have to be out of the way - how unfortunate!)

Now I am partaking of your counsel and resting Forster for a while before attempting the 'Passage'. [A PASSAGE TO INDIA]

I am just going to start 'The Private Memoirs and Confessions of a Justified Sinner' (James Hogg). It is said to mark a peak in English (Scottish) Literature. It is 'a peculiar blend of mockery, disturbing frisson and black humour.'

- He talks to his teacher about his independent reading and follows up suggestions made.
- He has read – and enjoyed – a very challenging novel on his own.
- He shows a sensitive response to the plot of *Howard's End*.
- At the end of the extract, he shows that he is able to comment on the approach of another author (James Hogg) to his next chosen book.
- Even in this short extract, a range of reading is obvious.

Responding to set books: English and English Literature

When you undertook any of the activities outlined in the workbench assignments above, not only were you increasing your range of reading, you were also showing how well you responded to what you had read. A discussion of your thoughts or your written answers would have allowed your teacher to compare your performance with the response statements of attainment for English (see pp. 13–17), or to consider how you measured up against the additional skills you need to demonstrate to gain a high level in English Literature.

This is why it is quite possible for you to submit some of the same coursework for both subjects, and also why the study of literature is likely to help you do better on some of the reading tasks you will be asked to undertake in your final English examination.

To demonstrate how this is true, let's take a closer look at the Assessment Objectives for Level 8 in English Literature:

Level 8

(a) read a range of literature, explaining preferences and understanding through writing and talking, with reference to detail.

(b) write and talk about literature, giving evidence of personal response and show an understanding of devices and structures used by writers, with appropriate reference to details.

(c) show clear indication of ability to read, understand and respond to a variety of language, structure and form in literature.

(d) show an understanding of the writer's themes and attitudes with reference to appropriate details.

(e) show a developing awareness of personal, social and cultural significances in the study of literature with appropriate reference to detail.

(f) demonstrate, in writing and talking about literature, that they can use a widening range of forms to convey their ideas and feelings.

8a is almost identical to the Level 8 statement of attainment which outlines the *range* of reading you should undertake for English.

8b is almost identical to the Level 8 statement of attainment which outlines the way you need to demonstrate your *response* to what you read for assessment in English.

▸ Tip box

Notice in particular that 8a talks about **personal** response: examiners will be far more interested in your own views about what you read – and how you make sense of it in terms of your previous experience of life and reading – than they will be if you sit back in class and let your teacher do all the work, then simply repeat their ideas and interpretations in your coursework, or in your final examination answers.

Notice also the reference to devices and structures: to ensure a high grade in English Literature you need to develop a vocabulary to talk about special techniques writers use to communicate their ideas. You will need to be able both to identify the techniques being used and discuss how they work.

This is especially important when you are writing about poetry, and that includes the poetry of Shakespeare's plays.

Writers' techniques

An **image** is a kind of picture, as the name suggests, but in a poem it is a picture made of words, comparing one thing with something else. You use your imagination to work out the comparison so you may share the poet's mental picture.

A **simile** is a particular kind of image, where one thing is said to be the same *as* or *like* something else. You will be told by the writer what is being compared with what so this comparison is easy to follow and work out:

They collapsed like rubber dinghies with the plugs pulled out.

(from *The Lesson* by Roger McGough)

A **metaphor** is a more complex sort of image where one thing is actually said to be something else. Metaphors are more difficult to unravel than similes because you have to work out exactly what is being compared with what – and the things they have in common:

Seagulls in a loose V-formation
Fly in squadrons…

(from *Sanctuary* by Duncan Forbes)

Alliteration is where several words in a line of poetry begin with the same sound – although not necessarily the same letter:

The stuttering rifle's rapid rattle

(from *Anthem for Doomed Youth* by Wilfred Owen)

Personification is a kind of image where an object is described as if it is alive, able to move and to change rather as the poet's view of it changes:

> I am the tree
> creaking in the wind
> outside in the night
> twisted and stubborn.

(from I am the Tree by Dennis Brutus)

Onomatopoeia is where the words reflect or create the sound they describe:

> …the air cracks
> above rooftops cracking striking
> rockets guffawing before stuttering…

(from Suddenly the Air Cracks by Gabriel Okara)

Assonance is where several words in a line, or few lines, of a poem contain the same vowel (a, e, i, o, u) sound. Often this is used to capture a particular mood.

> Voice, when it came,
> Lipstick coated, long gold–rolled
> Cigarette holder pipped.

(from Telephone Conversation by Wole Soyinka)

8c explains more precisely what you should be able to talk and write about from your wide range of reading: you will see that some of the questions on the extracts were asking you to look at differences in language between two texts, or differences and similarities in the way writers created characters or used description.

8d focuses your attention on the way in which writers of literature explore serious issues and put forward a particular point of view in their writing: the books written for an adult audience section (p. 67) and the travel writing section (p. 95) are examples of this.

8e would be shown by working through the questions on the autobiographical extracts (p. 89) and also by a good understanding of literature from other times and cultures, which helps to highlight differences between the lives and worlds of writers whose experience contrasts with your own: your ability to explain these differences would demonstrate that you had fulfilled this objective.

8f means that you are able to produce different kinds of spoken and written response to literature, from a discussion of a poem to a group staging of a scene from a play; from keeping an informal reading journal (p. 102) to writing formal essays about and adaptations of the books you have read: for example, turning a novel into a radio script, or a poem into a letter, or a play into a newspaper article.

Sections 2 and 4 of this book will give you more help with how to approach these different forms of spoken and written response and the pages below will show you examples of two types of assignment which are typical of written responses.

Tip box

Annotating texts

You will notice that a phrase repeated over and over again in the statements of attainment for English and the assessment objectives for English Literature is '…with reference to detail'.

To gain a high level for reading, you need to have read your set books and the texts set for your examination papers very thoroughly and you need to be able to pick out the bits of them which will be evidence of a real understanding of all the areas listed above.

To help you do this, you will need to learn how to annotate your texts using underlining or highlighting (to make the important details stand out) and brief marginal notes (which will remind you of the reasons why you thought that particular detail was significant).

This skill is essential if you are to make the best use of literature texts in open-book exams and it is also useful in helping you cope well with unseen texts under examination conditions.

Free verse — no patterned rhyme — natural speech rhythm.

◯ = insight into character
⬭ = linguistic techniques

My Sister Betty

My sister Betty said,
'I'm going to be a famous actress.'
Last year she was going to be a missionary.
'Famous actresses always look unhappy but beautiful,'
She said pulling her mouth sideways
And making her eyes turn upwards
So they were mostly white.
'Do I look unhappy and beautiful?'
'I want to go to bed and read,' I said
'Famous actresses suffer and have hysterics,' she said.
'I've been practising my hysterics.'
She began going very red and screaming
So that it hurt my ears.
She hit herself on the head with her fists
And rolled off my bed onto the lino.
I stood by the wardrobe where it was safer
She got up saying, 'Thank you, thank you,'
And bowed to the four corners of my bedroom.
'Would you like an encore of hysterics?' she asked.
'No,' I said from inside the wardrobe.
There was fluff all over her vest.
'If you don't clap enthusiastically,' she said,
'I'll put your light out when you're reading.'
While I clapped a bit
She bowed and shouted, 'More, more.'
My mother shouted upstairs
'Go to bed and stop teasing, Betty.'
'The best thing about being a famous actress,' Betty said,
'Is that you die a lot.'
She fell to the floor with a crash
And lay there for about an hour and a half
With her eyes staring at the ceiling.
She only went away when I said,
'You really look like a famous actress.'
When I got into bed and started reading
She came and switched off my light.
It's not much fun
Having a famous actress for a sister.

Gareth Owen

dramatic — a real show off!

Use of dialogue to help tell a story and to demonstrate character

exaggerated — adds humour

Brother not impressed!

manipulative

contrast of characters — she's an extrovert

She teases him anyway — he can't win

exaggeration?

he's quiet and serious

◯ = insight into character
⬭ = linguistic techniques
rhythm — iambic pentameters — like Shakespeare

Incendiary

simile — pale colour of face

That one small boy with a face like pallid cheese
And burnt-out little eyes could make a blaze
As brazen, fierce and huge, as red and gold
And zany yellow as the one that soiled
Three thousand guineas worth of property
And crops at Godwin's farm on Saturday
Is frightening — as fact and metaphor:
An ordinary match intended for
The lighting of a pipe or a kitchen fire
Misuses may set a whole menagerie
Of flame-fanged tigers roaring hungrily.
And frightening, too, that one small boy should set
The sky on fire and choke the stars to heat
Such skinny limbs and such a little heart
Which would have been content with one warm kiss
Had there been anyone to offer this.

Vernon Scannell

metaphor dead expression and reflects his arson attempts later.

patterned rhyme — "half-rhyme" couplets

rhyme half-rhyme — why?

exaggeration — stars are personified

metaphor — out of control fire compared with a wild animal

rhyming couplet — rounds it off

Unloved child — makes a fire to compensate for lack of emotional warmth.

from SEG specimen paper, April 1992

Writing response and English Literature assignments

There are two types of written work you are likely to be asked to do in your literary reading: you may be asked to **analyse** the text or you may be asked to **extend** it.

Analysing the text

You could write an analysis of the literary qualities of the text. This could be a character study, a description of the main themes and ideas in the text, or a review and appreciation of it. For all of these you would be looking into the text and referring to it for ideas and examples.

Extending the text

You could write something imaginative based on the text. This might well be a piece of empathic writing where you imagined that you were a character in the novel or where you set another story against a similar background. Or it could be a story set somewhere else, but with a similar plot and themes.

The first thing with both these options is that the relationship between what you write and the original must be evident. This is especially important if you are aiming for Level 8 or higher. It is also important that you show your ability to write in detail about your personal response to what you have read.

The second thing to ensure is that the you are not just retelling the story. If you write about the text's literary qualities, it is important that you write about aspects of relationships, themes and the plot in detail rather than ramble on about them in general. In an examination, take care to choose a question which will help you to show an understanding of more than just the storyline. If it is a coursework assignment where you have an opportunity to negotiate you own task, it will be worth your while to discuss this with your teacher and to get his or her approval before you begin to write.

Back up what you say

Once you have completed your reading and decided on a task then your next problem is what to write. Hopefully, all your years of English lessons will help you and you will have no problem, but it is worth underlining some fundamental principles, whether you are writing coursework, or answering an examination question.

1 Remember to refer to everything you know and have been told about planning and drafting writing. Coursework needs to be redrafted to gain the best possible marks.

2 Make sure you start with an introduction which shows you have read and understood the title. If it is based on your reading of a particular book or books, mention the titles and authors' names here. Make sure that you don't start with a conclusion which just gives your opinions: that should wait until the end.

> Whilst we were reading Laurie Lee's autobiographical account of his childhood, 'Cider With Rosie', as a class, I read several other accounts of childhood, some biographical and others autobiographical. For my assignment, I intend to compare Marjory, the child whose story is told in 'No End to Yesterday' by Shelagh Macdonald with Laurie, from 'Cider With Rosie'.

3 Once that's clear in your mind, don't be afraid to think about and state your own ideas. Examiners would rather read some fresh ideas expressed in your own words than any amount of second-hand facts and copied information.

> I thoroughly enjoyed reading 'No End to Yesterday' because at sometimes it was extremely funny and at others, very sad indeed. I felt I had much more in common with Marjory than I did with Laurie because some of the mischief she was involved in reminded me of experiences I had had myself, like the time she was, quite wrongly, accused of stealing.

4 When you want to say something, try to begin by making a point, then develop the point by making clear what you mean. Finally, give an example, if possible, to back up what you are saying.

> Marjory's friendship with her cousin, Teddy, is very close. It is probably important to her because she lives with her grandparents, so she does not have the close relationship with a parent Laurie Lee had with his mother. Marjory and Teddy do everything together. One of the most memorable parts of the book tells of the time they developed a secret plan to kill their grandmother.

5 Introduce your examples and quotations clearly and decisively. Make it clear exactly why you are using them and what you are trying to show.

> The main reason Marjory's grandmother is so strict with her is that she fears Marjory will grow up like the mother who deserted her. It is almost as if she blames Marjory for this:
> 'The child should be grateful. Naughty? Wicked! We took her from the gutter; gave her a home.' This is very typical of the way she talks to others about her granddaughter.

6 Think hard about how to order your ideas into a complete piece. The sequence of ideas and paragraphs is very important if a reader is to make sense of what you write. The writing must seem to flow almost effortlessly from point to point.

> ... thus you can see the contrast between the happiness of Laurie's earliest memories of family life and Marjory's confusion and misery.
> The contrast continues into their accounts of school life: whilst Laurie does not seem to have been particularly interested in school work, Marjory here finds the happiness lacking at home...

7 Be original. Give your own views and say 'I think this…' or 'I believe that…' but always be sure to back your opinion with evidence and detail.

8 Finish your piece with a neat conclusion. Examiners want to know where you are going and what you have achieved, found out or proved in the writing. If you are not too sure then don't expect them to be!

> Although 'Cider with Rosie' and 'No End to Yesterday' both tell of children growing up in the nineteen twenties, they offer many contrasts in the picture of childhood they present to their readers. Laurie's childhood in the country seems to have been a time of carefree innocence, whilst Marjory, growing up in London, has to come to terms with adult experiences from a very early age. Although the stories were very different, I enjoyed each in its own way.

Tip box

Show the examiner that you can read challenging and difficult texts, but relate these to others which you know and like, so that your writing stems from genuine interest and enthusiasm.

Choose a task which will show what you can do when you are working to the best of your ability. Don't make life easy for yourself by choosing the simple option.

As you write, make sure you introduce your own ideas, but back them up by reference to examples and ideas from what you have read.

Writing empathically

Empathic writing is one particular kind of writing in which the writer is expected to show empathy with what is read. Suppose a friend of your breaks up with their partner after a long relationship. You feel sorry for them but maybe you think that the break-up is best in the long run. You are kind and reassuring. In this case you are being sympathetic towards your friend, you have feelings of sympathy. On the other hand, if you cried all day with your friend and told each other that is was all the partner's fault then you would be sharing what he or she was feeling rather than responding to him or her. Your reaction would be empathic – sharing the other person's feelings, rather than having a reaction towards them. Psychologists, social workers and even teachers feel that they should sometimes empathise with the people they deal with. They imagine what it would be like to be in the patient's or in the pupil's shoes. They believe that this understanding can help them to do their jobs better.

Empathic writing works in just the same way. You show understanding of a situation, not by commenting on it from the outside but by trying to be part of it and imagining that you are in that situation yourself. Apart from English, History is a subject where empathic writing is commonly used. Imagining what it would be like to be bombed during the London Blitz may tell you more about what people had to put up with than being told that so many tons of explosives were dropped in a single night.

So, with novels, stories, plays and poems it is possible to respond empathically to what you have read. How would this work in practice on the pieces of writing you have looked at already in this section?

This poem, *The Choosing*, by Liz Lochhead, is a first person narrative poem: it is written from the poet's point of view as 'I', 'me', so it encourages the reader to feel empathy with the experience she describes.

The Choosing

We were first equal Mary and I
with the same coloured ribbons in mouse-coloured hair,
and with equal shyness
we curtseyed to the lady councillor
for copies of Collins' Children's Classics.
First equal, equally proud.

Best friends too Mary and I
a common bond in being cleverest (equal)
in our small school's small class.
I remember
the competition for top desk
or to read aloud the lesson
at school service.
And my terrible fear
of her superiority at sums.

I remember the housing scheme
where we both stayed.
The same house, different homes,
where the choices were made.

I don't know exactly why they moved, but anyway they went.
Something about a three-apartment
and a cheaper rent.
But from the top deck of the high-school bus
I'd glimpse among the others on the corner
Mary's father, mufflered, contrasting strangely
with the elegant greyhounds by his side.

He didn't believe in high-school education,
especially for girls,
or in forking out for uniforms.

Ten years later on a Saturday –
I am coming home from the library –
sitting near me on the bus,

Mary
with a husband who is tall,
curly haired, has eyes
for no one else but Mary.
Her arms are round the full–shaped vase
That is her body.
Oh, you can see where the attraction lies
in Mary's life –
not that I envy her, really.

And I am coming from the library
with my arms full of books.
I think of the prizes that were ours for the taking
and wonder when the choices got made
we don't remember making.

Suppose you decided to write a letter from Liz Lochhead to another old friend from the same primary school, but whose life was now more like the poet's. If your version of the day's events told about how she had met her old friend, Jennifer, in the supermarket and how they had had a wonderful chat about how well they had both done since they last saw each other, where they went for their holidays and how they still had so much in common, you can see that, here again, you would be showing absolutely no understanding of what you had just read. Read the letter below and see how it reflects the ideas in the poem.

Address :
invented, but
made to sound
like a student's
flat

Date :
the poem sounds
recent

Reflects the
poet's life

Facts about
Mary as a child,
taken straight
from the poem

Underline for
yourself :
Facts about
Mary now

Underline for
yourself :
how the *poet's*
feelings are
reflected

> Flat 4b
> Magnolia Buildings
> Market Street
> Glasgow
>
> 21st March 1983
>
> Dear Janet,
>   How's the college course going ? I'm really busy at the moment - such a lot of reading to do!
>   Guess who I saw this afternoon? Do you remember Mary from St John's ? She had mousy hair like mine and she always used to beat us in "sums". She lived near us on the housing scheme until they moved to those new apartments. If you don't remember her, you'll probably remember her father and his greyhounds. Do you remember how upset she was when he wouldn't let her go to the High School with us, even though she was so clever, because he thought it was a waste of money for girls ?
>   Anyway, I saw her today on the bus - and she's MARRIED. She looked pregnant too - and she's only twenty-one, like us. It made me feel really strange. Look at how different her life is from ours now - married and with a baby - and all we've got is our arms full of books! Her husband looked nice, too - tall and curly-haired - obviously totally in love with her.
>   It'd be good, in a way, the security and everything. But I'm not really jealous. I mean we've got more excitement in our lives and more choice, really. I began to think if we ever had a choice of our own, when we were eleven - or was it someone else's ? I'm sure you'll know what I mean!
>   keep in touch,
>   Liz

The poem is actually about the distance which has grown between the two girls' lives. The poet looks at the way the different attitudes of the two families towards their daughters' education has resulted in these two girls, who were so alike at primary school, ending up with hardly anything in common at all.

The title of the poem is worth thinking about, because the 'choice' was not really made by them but by their circumstances.

These thoughts are reflected in a good empathetic piece of writing, which would show how you were on the bus on the way home from the library and how it made you feel to see how Mary had changed and your opinions about the contrasts in the lives you were each leading now. This letter is responding to what was in the poem. The writer is sharing Liz Lochhead's feelings about the situation and transporting herself into it.

Look at the annotations which show how the beginning of the empathetic letter relates to the first half of the poem. Try to add your own annotations, showing where the same happens in the second half.

Good empathic writing is not difficult as long as you have a clear understanding that the writing is trying to show your response to the text in another way. Therefore, what you write must have a close relationship to the original. Think hard about the points of contact between your writing and the original text – there should be plenty between them.

Tip box

When you are faced with an empathic writing task, ask yourself these questions when you draft your work.

- Have I captured the atmosphere and feeling of the original text?

- Have I said things about the characters which reveal my understanding of them and their feelings as well as saying what they are like?

- Have I noted details from the text and used them in my writing? Have I made sure that nothing in my writing contradicts details which are in the text?

- When writing about poetry, choose a poem which interests you and a task which gives you plenty to write about.

- When writing about plays, see your task through an audience's eyes.

- When writing empathically, concentrate on making clear connections with the original piece of writing.

Chapter 4
Media texts

Study skills

At the beginning of this section, you were reminded of the skills you will already have developed as a reader before you began your GCSE English course. So far this section has mainly been concerned with the development of your intensive reading skills: your ability to read every word, to read in depth, to the extent that you can understand what's going on between the lines as well as what is actually stated on the page.

The rest of this section is concerned with a much wider variety of skills: the reading skills you adopt to extract factual information from a whole range of materials, from dictionaries and telephone directories to radio progammes and computer databases. This type of reading is not exclusively to do with words, either: the ability to use an atlas, or to understand symbols like road signs, or the washing instructions on clothes labels would also be included amongst these reading skills.

It has been said that we live in an information society. We are surrounded by facts. In our lives we will only make use of a tiny fraction of the information stored in books, in libraries, held on computer memory, etc. which surrounds us every time we walk down the high street, or which pours through our letter boxes and out of our televisions and radios every day. It is important, though, that we have the skills to find and use the fraction of that information that is necessary in our individual lives.

Workbench assignment

You will be able to see for yourself the huge variety of information skills you use in your daily life by keeping a record of every information text you come into contact with during one day.

Fill in the chart on the opposite page, using these notes to decide what to record in each column:

Text	Give the title of the book or television programme, or a brief statement of the information the text contained, e.g. a 'special offer' poster in a supermarket.
By choice?	Tick this column if you actually looked for the information on purpose. Put a cross if it was just something you happened to notice.
Approach?	Did you read in detail, or watch with your full attention? Or did you skim-read to get the gist, or simply notice it was there, but decide it didn't need your attention?
Outcome?	Did you do anything as a result of your reading? Did you use the information?

Your chart could end up looking a bit like this:

Text	By choice?	Approach?	Outcome?
Letter from time-share company	X	Skim read the beginning	Threw it in the bin
Radio weather forecast	✓	Listened carefully	Wore a coat
Poster about fleas in the vet's surgery	X	Looked at picture. Too far away to read writing	Bought flea collar for cat

You will probably find your chart fills up with an astonishing range of reading long before the day is out. Learning to read flexibly for different purposes is yet another language skill you will have developed without being particularly aware that you can do it.

But are you as good as you could be?

Do you ever miss out on useful information because you lack the skills needed to make a quick assessment of whether something may be useful to you or not? Are your 'information retrieval skills' (another name given to this aspect of study skills) good enough for the purposes of your school work? Can you use reference books to find the information you need to help you in your studies?

What do I need to know?

By Key Stage 4 you will be expected to know how to use anything arranged alphabetically. This could include:
- an index
- a dictionary
- an encyclopaedia
- a library classification system
- a phone book

you should also know how to search out the information you need in:
- an adult thesaurus
- contents pages of books
- texts that do not need reading from end to end, like this book, or the Highway Code
- pamphlets, catalogues and brochures

As with all reading, it will not be enough simply to do these things: you will need to have some proof, either spoken or written, to show what you have done with the information you found out.

To achieve Level 10 for this group of skills, you need to show that you are able to collect information from a wide variety of sources, and then use it for a specific purpose.

Workbench assignment

The project described below was undertaken by a group of twelve GCSE students. As you work through, you will be given examples of the research they undertook, and you will be able to practice some of the tasks that they carried out.

You could then put these skills to use on a local issue of your own. Use your local paper as a source of ideas.

Once you have found a topic, select from the strategies and activities described here to create a research project of your own.

Case study

A Research Project about a local issue: Nuclear Waste in Lancashire.

The original idea

The class was in the middle of an oral work topic about making persuasive speeches. They had already decided that a subject that provided plenty of arguments on each side was nuclear power. At the start, they were using an English text book for information, where the selection of materials had been done for them.

On the 19th November, Hayley brought newspaper Article 1 to the lesson and said she had videotaped the Open Eye programme mentioned in the article. These highlighted the pollution said to be caused by the Springfields reprocessing plant. Many of the class had either read the paper or watched the programme, and were interested in using this information to help them write their speeches.

Bruce and Daniel brought in two more articles from the same paper on the two nights that followed the television broadcast. These were particularly interesting because article two put forward the point of view of the BNFL managers, insisting that Springfields followed adequate safety procedures, whilst article three (which was front page headline news) followed the shock tactics of the broadcast, revealing worrying 'facts' about the safety procedures at the Springfields plant.

Article 1

CHILDREN playing on the banks of the River Ribble could be risking radioactive contamination from a nearby nuclear plant.

A report by pressure group Friends of the Earth claims youngsters playing along the river in the Penwortham area near Preston could be receiving large doses of radiation from mudflats contaminated by discharged from the British Nuclear Fuels Springfields plant, it was revealed today.

Lancashire County Council leader Louise Ellman immediately called for an in-depth investigation from the independent radiation monitoring group Radmil.

Frightened residents living within yards of the River Ribble today said they feared for their health.

The worried locals called for a wide-ranging investigation into the damning report.

The shock survey coincides with a hard-hitting Granada TV investigation due to be screened tonight into radiation safety standards at the sprawling Salwick site, which features ex-worker Joe McMaster, 69, formerly of Greystock Avenue, Fulwood, Preston, and his wife Stella.

Mr McMaster, who worked for 31 years as an analytical chemist, claims that three of his daughters died between 1958 and 1987 from illnesses linked to fatal doses of radiation.

Levels

Friends of the Earth today said tests carried out on the stretch of the Ribble through Preston

A-plant 'puts children at risk' – report

By JOHN LAWRENCE

revealed pollution levels higher than those published by BNFL and the Ministry of Agriculture Fisheries and Food.

Researchers monitored radiation levels at four points upstream of the Springfields discharge pipe including the cadet hut at Penwortham bridge, Broadgate.

Other points were Lower Penwortham park and the mainline railway bridge.

Doses of radioactive thorium particles were found to be up to six times higher than normal.

Radiation campaigner Dr Patrick Green said the muddy river bed and bank were popular with children.

The report says a child would have to spend on average around 80 minutes a day over a year along the river bank to receive the maximum tolerable radiation dose of 100 units.

The man who helped spark today's controversy was Paul Brown, 52, of Welwyn Avenue, Southport.

Scrutiny

He has been carrying out independent testing on the Ribble using Geiger-counters for the last 18 months.

He said today: "My inquiries led to Friends of the Earth commissioning their own survey."

BNFL information officer Peter Osborne said the pressure group's finding did not stand up to close scrutiny and denied that youngsters were in danger.

Mr Osborne said: "Any doses that children would be receiving from playing in those areas would only be one per cent of any radiation that could be regarded as remotely dangerous. To be honest, the Ribble is a pretty inhospitable play area for other reasons and not many children play there anyway."

A MAFF spokesman said government scientists always carried out tests in areas that would provide the highest doses and published their results on a regular basis.

Local residents said if the alleged nuclear waste dumping was true it should be stopped immediately. Mrs Susan Hunter of Riverside Road said: "If it's true, it is absolutely outrageous and everyone round here will naturally be very concerned."

Graham Hunter of Stonefield, Penwortham, said BNFL had to "clean up its act" if the Friends of the Earth report was true.

Article 2

SAFE IN OUR HANDS

By JOHN LAWRENCE

Nuclear bosses said today the environmental impact of radioactive nuclear waste discharged from the Springfields plant into the River Rubble was trivial.

BNFL health and safety manager Dr Tony Fishwick hit back at claims over contamination levels made by a Friends of the Earth investigation and the Granada TV Open Eye team. Friends of the Earth claimed that children could be at risk from radiation if they played along the bank of the river, particularly on its stretch through Penwortham, near Preston.

Dr Fishwick slammed the Friends of the Earth report as biased and claimed it used only test results taken when discharges from Springfields were higher than normal.

He said: "The group has taken a snapshot in time at the beginning of the summer when the plant was just starting up again after a six-month shutdown and discharges were higher than normal for a period of six weeks.

"Continuous monitoring by BNFL and independent groups over a period of years has shown radiation along the Ribble is either equal to or less than natural background radiation."

Dr Fishwick said it was scandalous for Friends of the Earth to suggest that BNFL was putting profits before safety when £1,250,000 had been spend on refurbishing the Springfields effluent drainage system and £1m on a new waste discharge station.

Three hundred million gallons of water are discharged into the Ribble every year from Springfields but most is rainwater and less than 10 per cent is radioactive.

Waste from uranium recovery work is sampled and monitored then treated with lime for acid neutralisation before being carried along enclosed drains, which pick up rainwater, and finally

Nuclear boss hits back in water storm

undergoing more monitoring at the discharge station before being pumped into the Ribble.

The only radioactive particles to be released from Springfields are soft non-penetrating beta particles, which Dr Fishwick described as "less intense" than other radiation.

Mr Tom Meredith, director of Preston's environmental health department, which carried out tests for the independent radiation monitoring group Radmil, said the risks along the Ribble were negligible.

Mr Meredith said: "According to our figures gathered monthly over two years, a person would have to spend 34 hours a week actually standing in the mud of the river bank – that's 1,785 hours a year – to receive any significant dose of radiation. As far as we know, no one does that."

Article 3

Exclusive: Scientist admits gap in monitoring

A-plant fails test

By DAVID CRAGG

NUCLEAR safety officials at the centre of an atom scare today admitted that for almost 45 years they have not carried out full radiation tests along the River Ribble.

Scientists at the BNFL Springfields plant at Salwick, near Preston, revealed they only began wide-ranging riverside searches for radiation hot spots this week.

The new comes just days after Friends of the Earth claimed children playing along the river at Penwortham, near Preston, could be receiving large doses of radiation from mudflats allegedly contaminated by discharges from Springfields.

The report coincided with a Granada TV investigation into the A-plant – which makes fuel for nuclear reactors – in which a former worker claimed three of his daughters died from illness linked to radiation.

Urgent

Today it was revealed that BNFL failed to carry out tests which specifically located the high beta radiation hot spots on the Ribble and a Springfields physicist admitted the tests have only been introduced in the last week. ◆

★ Ministry orders regular Geiger counter checks ★ 'Hot-spots' not fully tested for 45 years ★ Sellafield 'dominated' radiation levels

---

◆ Today Lancashire County Council leader Mrs Louise Ellman called for BNFL to stop discharges from the plant and said a special study by the council's own radiation watchdog, Radmil, was to be carried out. Local residents have also demanded urgent meetings with BNFL chiefs.

This week independent researcher Paul Brown, form Southport, revealed he found high levels of beta radioactive contamination – which can be harmful in high doses – in river mud.

Friends of the Earth has produced similar readings and claims BNFL has failed to meet a legal obligation to reduce radioactive discharge levels below newly-imposed limits.

BNFL has carried out riverside monitoring to

find gamma radioactivity and taken random samples to monitor beta levels, but without testing for beta hot spots with Geiger counters.

Comprehensive Geiger monitoring sweeps over a wide area, of the kind carried out by Mr Brown, are considered essential.

Now, BNFL has been ordered by the Ministry of Agriculture, Fisheries and Food to begin regular Geiger counter checks.

Area Health Physicist (Environmental), for Springfields, Roger Wilson, said that previously radioactive pollution from the Sellafield nuclear plant was so high that pollution from Springfields was considered negligible.

He said: "We only began measuring beta radioact-

ivity as part of the official programme last week.

"Previously, people's exposure to radiation levels was dictated by Sellafield, since their emissions were so much higher. As that plant has got a grip of discharges and the environment has adjusted, so the importance of Springfield's discharges has grown."

But he reassured the public that discharges were well below safety levels.

Mr Brown welcomed the move to monitor beta levels and said: "It is a vital part of assuring that strict safety levels of radioactivity are adhered to. The only way of locating where hot-spots might develop in the area is to take Geiger-counter readings of the mud."

Newspaper articles reproduced by permission of Lancashire Evening Post

By selecting information independently instead of just relying on the text book, these three GCSE students were showing promise of achieving a Level 7 grade. They were also able to show in their discussion of these articles the bias of the points of view put forward. Being able to explain how media texts use techniques of persuasion demonstrates another high-level statement of attainment.

Workbench assignment

Skim-read all three articles for the following information.

❶ What is said to be the problem?

❷ What is believed to be the cause of it?

❸ Name three areas said to be affected.

❹ Who has made the public aware of the problem?

❺ Find four reasons why the problem may be exaggerated. Who provided this information?

❻ Who are Paul Brown and Roger Wilson? What do they contribute to the debate?

❼ In conclusion, do you think local residents ought to feel worried, or reassured?

After reading the newspaper articles, the group watched the television broadcast and discussed how it presented a particular point of view by means of selecting specific information: shocking facts about radiation readings and information about families who had experienced illness and death linked with radiation.

Workbench assignment

Skim through all the information reproduced here, and summarise the main points onto the appropriate space on the grid.

Topics \ Texts	Newspaper article 1	Newspaper article 2	Newspaper article 3	Extracts from *Physics Matters*	NRPB pamphlet	BNFL pamphlet	*Friends of the Earth*, etc.
Natural sources of radiation				*p. 265 – rocks, the sun.*			
Diseases caused by radiation							*Leukaemia? Cancer?*
'Safe' levels of radiation					*50 millisieverts per year*		
Environmental damage	*Rivers and mudflats.*					*milk, fish, shellfish, p.19*	
'Half-life' of radiation							
Disposal of radioactive waste							
Types of radioactive waste							

PROTECTING THE PUBLIC

All of BNFL's waste management activities are strictly controlled.

As well as being subject to government legislation, the disposal of radioactive wastes is overseen by various authorising departments which include the Department of the Environment, the Scottish and Welsh Offices and the Ministry of Agriculture, Fisheries and Food.

In the UK, no radioactive waste disposal is allowed unless the authorising bodies are satisfied that the principles recommended by the International Commission on Radiological Protection (ICRP) are adhered to. The basic principles are:

Any practice involving radiation exposure must be justified in relation to its benefits.

Any necessary exposures must be kept as low as reasonably achievable, economic and social factors being taken into account.

Radiation doses must not exceed recommended dose levels.

Extensive monitoring around BNFL sites is carried out by the Company to ensure that radiation doses due to its activities remain a small fraction of recommended limits. For example, at Drigg, boreholes are used for the regular sampling of ground water, surface waters are monitored routinely and air samplers are situated around the Drigg site.

Regular monitoring of foodstuffs such as milk, fish and shellfish is also carried out around BNFL sites to ensure that they do not contain harmful amount of radioactivity as a result of BNFL's discharges to the environment. This monitoring process is also extended to other materials such as shoreline mud, vegetation and seaweed.

To put into perspective the effect of radioactive discharges from Sellafield into the Irish Sea, a person eating large quantities of Cumbrian seafood would only receive less than an additional one per cent of the radiation dose he would be exposed to if he lived in certain parts of Cornwall.

The Government departments involved in authorising radioactive discharges also have their own independent programmes of environmental monitoring. In addition, a number of independent researchers carry out measurements and publish results.

BNFL also publishes annual reports on health and safety matters covering radioactive discharges, monitoring of the environment and occupational safety.

BNFL welcomes the public debate about its waste management activities because it is vital that the public feels confident and safe in order to ensure that Britain can continue to reap the benefits of nuclear electricity generation.

from NUCLEAR WASTE What's to be done about it?   *British Nuclear Fuels plc, 1991*

RADIATION PROTECTION PRINCIPLES

These are the recommendations of the International Commission on Radiological Protection (ICRP).
This scientific organisation has published recommendations for protection against ionising radiation for over half a century.

The three central principles of the ICRP recommendations are as follows.

JUSTIFICATION

1   No practice involving radiation shall be adopted unless its introduction produces a positive net benefit.

ALARA

2   All radiation exposures shall be kept as low as reasonably achievable, economic and social factors being taken into account.

DOSE LIMITS

3   The radiation dose to individuals shall not exceed the limits recommended for the appropriate circumstances by the Commission.

Justification
Obviously, the practice should be of overall value to society. Harmful effects and alternatives should be considered. This can raise profound questions often requiring resolution by governments, e.g. on nuclear power. Even some medical uses of x-rays, generally hugely beneficial, may require strong justification and careful techniques.
Some practices are clearly not justified.

Medical uses	✓
Nuclear power	✓
Smoke detectors	✓
Luminous devices	✓
Children's toys	✗
Jewellery	✗

Keeping doses as low as reasonably achievable
Since it is assumed that all radiation doses carry some risk, complying with the limit is not enough. Doses must be further reduced. However, dose reduction meets with diminishing returns.

Dose limits
Individuals must not be exposed to an unacceptable degree of risk. However, dose limits do not mark an abrupt change in biological risk but rather the level of risk that, if received over a lifetime, would verge on the intolerable.

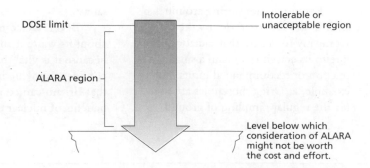

DOSE limit — Intolerable or unacceptable region

ALARA region —

Level below which consideration of ALARA might not be worth the cost and effort.

Dose limits have to be observed regardless of cost and represent a level that it is illegal to exceed. There is also a legal requirement for ALARA.
Governments put the ICRP recommendations into practice in a manner appropriate to their own countries.

RADIATION EFFECTS

There are two kinds, those that occur early and those that occur late.

Early

Whole body, high radiation dose	Death in a matter of days or weeks
Limited area exposed briefly to high dose	Reddening of skin

Late

Lower dose or same total dose over a long time	No early signs but presumed late effects – cancer and hereditary disease

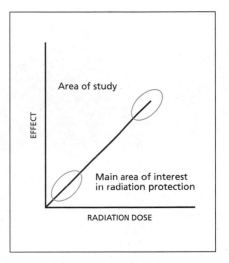

It is <u>assumed</u> that, however low the dose, there is some risk. This is derived from studies of people who were exposed to <u>high</u> doses of radiation, such as the survivors of the atomic bombing of Japan, patients exposed to radiation for treatment or diagnosis, and some groups of workers.

Information on the biological effects of radiation is reviewed periodically by the United Nations Scientific Committee on the Effects of Atomic Radiation (UNSCEAR) which was established in 1955. The Committee is made up of scientists from 21 countries round the world.

— HARM AND SENSITIVITY —

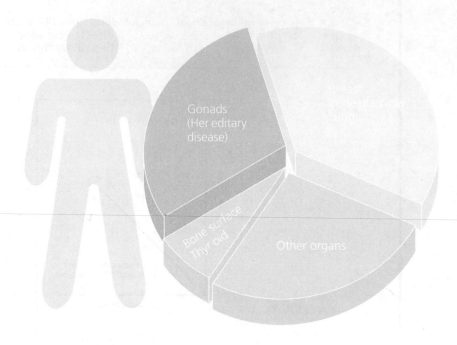

QUALITY FACTORS

```
Alpha    (α)    × 20
Beta     (β)    × 1
Gamma    (γ)    × 1
          x     × 1
```

Different types of radiation vary in the effectiveness with which they cause harm in tissue. To allow for this, absorbed doses are multiplied by quality factors, to produce the 'dose equivalent'. However, we still have the problem that some organs are more sensitive to radiation than others.

So, the dose equivalent to each organ is multiplied by a weighting factor. This give the 'effective dose equivalent', which measures the overall risk from any combination of radiation affecting any organs of the body.
*   Generally, effective dose equivalent is what is meant when the term 'dose' is used; its units are 'millisieverts'.*

HIERARCHY OF DOSE QUANTITIES

Absorbed dose
energy imparted by radiation to unit mass of tissue

▼

Dose equivalent
absorbed dose weighted for harmfulness of different radiations
(quality factors)

▼

Effective dose equivalent ('Dose')
dose equivalent weighted for susceptibility to harm of different tissues
(risk weighting factors)

▼

Collective effective dose equivalent ('Collective Dose')
effective dose equivalent to all the people exposed to a source of radiation

from National Radiation Protection Board poster, 1989

7 The Hazards of Radiation

Measuring radiation

When scientists try to work out the effect on our bodies of a dose of radiation, they need to know how much energy each part of the body has absorbed. After all, the damage done to us will depend on the amount of energy that each kilogram of body tissue absorbs. The unit used to measure a **radiation dose** is the **gray**, (symbol Gy). A dose of 1 Gy means that each kilogram of flesh absorbs 1 joule of energy.

$$1\,\text{Gy} = 1\,\text{J/kg}$$

Some radiations are more damaging than others, so scientists prefer to talk in terms of a **dose equivalent**, which is measured in **sieverts** (symbol Sv).

$$\text{dose equivalent (Sv)} = Q \times \text{dose (Gy)}$$

Q is a number that depends on the radiation, as shown in Table 1. Alpha particles are very strongly ionizing and cause far more damage than a dose of beta or gamma radiation that carries the same energy. Usually the amounts of radiation that we are exposed to are very small. Most people receive about 1/1000 sievert each year, this is a **millisievert** (symbol 1 mSv).

Q	Type of radiation
1	beta particles/gamma rays
10	protons and neutrons
20	alpha particles

Table 1

The Chernobyl nuclear reactor near Kiev in Russia. During an unauthorised experiment in 1986, the core of the number 4 reactor unit melted, causing an explosion which released a large amount of radioactive material. This will be a very serious health hazard for many years to those living close to the reactor. Winds carried some of the radioactive material to many countries in Europe

Risk estimates

On 26 April 1986 there was an explosion in the Russian nuclear reactor at Chernobyl, causing a large leakage of radiation. During May the **background count** in Britain increased causing us all to be exposed (on average) to an extra dose equivalent to 0.1 mSv. This is a small dose and no worse than going on holiday in Cornwall, where granite rock areas produce low amounts of radiation. However, estimates have been made to suggest that over the next 30 years, extra people will get cancer as a result of the Chernobyl disaster.

Research suggests that for a population of 1000, about 12 fatal cancers will be caused by a dose equivalent of 1 Sv. In Britain, the population is about 50 million, so the number of deaths expected by a dose for all of us of 1 Sv would be:

$$\frac{12}{1000} \times 50\,000\,000 = 600\,000$$

However, the dose from Chernobyl was only 0.0001 Sv, so the estimated number of deaths from the Chernobyl disaster, in Britain over the next 30 years, is about $600\,000 \times 0.0001 = 60$.

How dangerous is radiation?

Radiation affects materials by ionizing atoms and molecules. When an atom is ionized, electrons are removed or added to it. This means a chemical change has occurred. In our bodies such a chemical change could cause the production of a strong acid which will attack and destroy cells.

- **High doses** of radiation will kill you. There is only a 50 per cent chance of surviving a dose equivalent to 4 Sv. A 10 Sv dose equivalent would give you no chance of survival. Such high doses kill too many cells in the gut and bone marrow for your body to be able to work normally. You could be exposed to such doses in a nuclear war, and people certainly died in Hiroshima and Nagasaki as a result of such doses.

- **Moderate doses** of radiation below 1 Sv will not kill you. Damage will be done to cells in your body, but not enough to be fatal. The body will be able to replace the dead cells and the chances are that you would then recover totally. However, a study of the survivors from Hiroshima and Nagasaki shows that there is an increased chance of dying from cancer some years after the radiation dose. Even so, you would only have a chance of about 1 in 100 of getting cancer from such levels of radiation.

- **Low doses** of radiation, below 10 mSv, are thought to have little effect on us. However, some people think that any exposure to radiation will increase your chances of getting cancer.

There can be no doubt that radiation doses can cause cancer or leukaemia (see Table 2). Uranium miners are exposed to radon gas, and girls who painted luminous watch dials were exposed to radium.

Workers in the nuclear power industry are exposed to more radiation than the rest of the population. Special monitoring and remote control are used to keep this extra radiation exposure as small as possible.

Questions

1 In Table 1, the value of Q for alpha radiation is 20. Why is it so high?
2 What does a sievert measure?
3 Summarise the effects of high, moderate and low doses of radiation on us.
4 Many modern watches do not have luminous dials. Instead they have small lights that turn on at the press of a switch. Explain why lights are safer.
5 Use the data in Table 2 to show that exposure to alpha radiation is more likely to cause cancer than exposure to gamma radiation or X-rays.
6 In a nuclear reactor disaster about 200 workers are exposed to a radiation dose equivalent to 2 Sv. Use the data in the text to estimate the number of them likely to die from cancer some time after the accident.

Source of radiation	Type of radiation	Number of people studied	Extra number of cancer deaths caused by radiation
uranium miners	alpha	3400	60
radium luminisers	alpha	800	50
medical treatment	alpha	4500	60
medical treatment	X-rays	14000	25
Hiroshima bomb	gamma rays and neutrons	15000	100
Nagasaki	gamma rays	7000	20

Table 2. This table illustrates the connection between radiation and the increased chance of cancer.

They decided they needed to know more facts about radioactive waste and more about the danger of radiation to make up their minds who was right.

They practised their formal letter-writing skills, contacting pressure groups like Friends of the Earth, Greenpeace and British Nuclear Fuels information service for further information about both sides of the argument.

They wrote to their MPs and received all sorts of information from them.

Philip found some information about radioactivity in a Physics text book.

Next came the stage of looking at all the information they had collected and sorting out what it had to say. They made a project grid and noted down facts from the various sources.

Finally, they made use of what they had learnt by role-playing a public enquiry meeting. They split into four small groups:

• One group represented the views of the managers of BNFL;

• One group represented the views of local parents;

• One group represented the views of employees at Springfields;

• One group represented the views of Friends of the Earth.

Each of them wrote a persuasive speech, using information they had selected from what they had read to put forward the personal worries, concerns or reassurances.

Workbench assignment

Which group would you have chosen to be in? Use the information you have learnt and the advice about making a speech on p. 43 to prepare notes for the points you would make.

Finally, they acted out the meeting, using the best of the prepared speeches, and the whole class took part in a debate. The role-play was videoed so they could watch their own performances afterwards and assess their performances.

Tip Box

This case study shows how you can demonstrate reading skills it would be very difficult to test in your final examination. One of your pieces of coursework will need to show you have the ability to use study skills in this way.

If your final examination includes media texts amongst its pre-released materials, your ability to extract factual information and to recognise biased opinion will be of great use. When you are annotating your texts in preparation for the writing tasks in your exam, remember to make use of these skills.

Revision File

10% of your final GCSE marks come from your reading coursework.

Make sure there is evidence of areas you will not be able to demonstrate in the exam:

• a wide range of reading (a reading record or log);

• study skills;

• any types of reading your syllabus does not examine (e.g. Shakespeare, media texts) – check this with your teacher;

• records of any spoken response to reading you have taken part in;

• 30% of your final GCSE marks come from your English examination.

Make sure you go into the exam well prepared, with all the texts you will need to use:

• pre-release materials;

• books you have studied.

Check the information on p.106 to remind yourself of the importance of annotating texts.

Learn the names of the literary techniques listed on pp.105–6 and practise explaining how and why writers use them.

Make sure you have read (and re-read) your texts sufficiently often to be able to make use of them in the exam without wasting time.

Make sure you choose questions which allow you to demonstrate your detailed understanding of your prepared texts.

Chapter 1
Your own writing

Building on what you know

Writing is the most important skill you have to show evidence of in your English coursework and examination. You are assessed on your ability to write in different ways for different purposes and to use writing to comment on your reading. Your writing is also assessed to see that it is correctly punctuated and spelled, redrafted with care and legibly presented. That is a lot of work to cover.

You will realise from your reading of Section Two that learning about language and the dialect of English called Standard English is a major part of your English course. But it is part of writing as much a speaking and listening. When the spelling mistakes you make in a piece of writing are corrected by your teacher, he or she may well be telling you that your spelling of that word is wrong in the sense that it is not written in correct Standard English. When people first started to use writing, and even in the early days of printing, words were spelled in all sorts of different ways. The words themselves were often different, or used in a different order, or the same word had different meanings to different people, depending on where they lived.

However, as the printed word has became commonplace – in the last two hundred years

or so – Standard English has increased in importance. It has become the accepted, correct form for writing of all kinds so it is important that you are able to write it confidently and to express yourself clearly through it. It does not matter at all if you speak with an accent – in fact, we all do – or if you use dialect in your speech – nearly all of us do – but you do need to be a competent writer and that means using Standard English correctly. In this book a lot of emphasis is placed on careful re-reading and redrafting of everything you write. One of the reasons for this is that writing in Standard English does not come as naturally as talking. It takes practice, thoughtful reflection and continual correction to do it as well as you can.

The written work that you do says a lot about you. It is the written record of something which is going on inside your head! A stimulus, such as reading a story or listening to a poem, is processed inside your brain into a piece of writing. Speaking and listening help to sort out the process before you write.

One of the consequences of this is that the only record of your achievements in reading, listening and speaking may be in the form of writing. In one sense, although Reading is

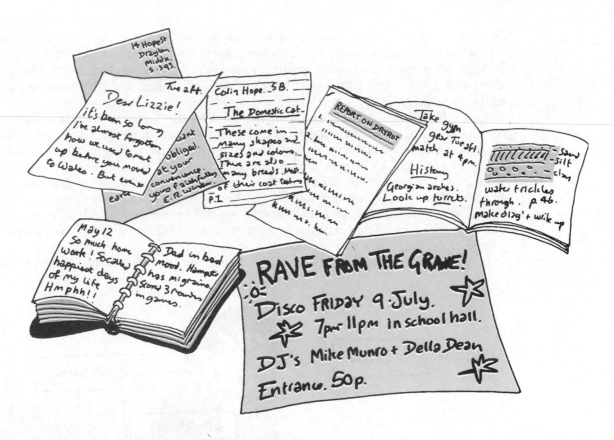

a separate Attainment Target in the National Curriculum, your achievements in reading have to be assessed through writing. Even if you talk about a book you have read, there still has to be a written record of the event before it can be assessed!

Areas of assessment

The National Curriculum and your GCSE syllabuses ask a lot from you as a writer. There are seven areas where you have to show evidence of what you can achieve. In practice, they tend to overlap so that one written task is likely to cover nearly all of them, but for assessment purposes they are likely to be separated. The areas are:

1 Writing for a range of audiences and purposes

All the writing you do has an audience, even if it is only your teacher! Other pieces of writing may have very specific audiences, like a secret note to your best friend or a story written for young children. You need to start thinking about **who** you are writing for and why you are writing, whenever you start a new piece of work.

2 Structuring and organising writing

All good writing is structured and organised. In a story, the sequence of events provides structure, but other kinds of writing may have to be structured and organised in different ways. You have to develop an awareness of how to plan your writing, so that the structure is clear to a reader. You have to organise exactly what you want to say in your writing.

3 Using Standard English

This is concerned with your ability to use different styles in your writing and to know when you are being persuasive, informative or complaining. It is also concerned with the accuracy of your writing and your use of punctuation.

4 Drafting and redrafting

You have to show that you can redraft your work. Sometimes that just means correcting if and adding some punctuation, but it may involve a wholesale reorganisation, the insertion of extra material or the addition of a conclusion.

5 Writing about language

You are expected to show that you can stand back from your own language and comment on it. You might note how you use language differently in letters and in formal essay writing, write about your dialect, or about how some kinds of language are acceptable in writing, while others are not.

6 Spelling correctly

Your spelling is assessed here. You are expected to know how to spell common words and to know how longer words are often made up from or based on combinations of shorter words.

7 Using legible handwriting and presenting work neatly

Presentation is now assessed as part of English. It means that you must write legibly, without printing. Ideas about improving the presentation of your work will also earn your credit: for example, the way you set out a poster with bold headlines, capitals and underlining.

Different syllabuses assess these seven areas in slightly different ways. Sometimes, for example, handwriting will only be assessed in coursework. Your ability to draft and redraft is unlikely to be part of a written examination, and your writing about language may actually be done through your speaking and listening work! Here we focus on each of the seven areas which make up the Writing attainment target.

Chapter 2
Audience and structure

Writing does not take place in a vacuum. It is impossible to imagine writing that does not have some communicative purpose – i.e. writing that does not say something. At the same time, the purposes and audiences for your writing are enormously varied. In your coursework alone you could be showing some of these things about yourself:

- that you appreciate literature and understand and enjoy the books, plays and poems you read;
- that you can read and enjoy a long and quite difficult book or play;
- that you can be moved or affected by someone else's personal, imaginative or descriptive writing;
- that you can understand informative and argumentative language, whether you read it or hear it.

And to show this, you might be expected to produce any of these kinds of writing clearly and accurately:

- personal writing about yourself;
- argumentative writing which gives your opinions;
- descriptive writing;
- imaginative narratives or stories of your own;
- writing which sets out instructions for others;
- writing which gives information;
- writing where you imagine that you are a character in a book or play;
- writing which describes a character in a book or play;
- commentaries or accounts of what you have read.

Audiences

What is important is that, when you start to write, you have an idea of who your audience is going to be. That knowledge will affect the style you use. You may do this without realising it. Asked to write a simple story for young children you would – almost without thinking – use short sentences and simple words.

But sometimes your audience is more complicated, and you need to think before you write.

Even with a simple subject, you might be surprised to realise how much you modify your language to suit different audiences.

Workbench assignment

Writing for different audiences

Try writing some of the following to get into the habit of thinking about your audience. Each piece of writing is started for you. Do not try to complete the task, but write enough of it to feel confident with the style required. Write:

1 The start of a story for five-year-old children about a cat called Celestine and the little girl, Jessica, who owns him.
Hints:
- Write short sentences, use simple words.

Who you are talking to

Your Audience

What you say

How you modify your language

Young people

> You just wait until September.
> You'll hate it when you see what the older kids do to the new ones!

Your friends

> I'm sick of this place.
> I just can't wait to get out.
> The theatre trip will be a laugh, though.

Your class

> School is a place where – although we become young adults – we continue to be treated as children.

Your English teacher

> I hate school... but your lessons are OK, suppose.

Your headteacher

> Dear Miss Whiplash,
> We the undersigned members of 11PJ would like to be excused from Upper School Assembly on Thursdays because...

Your parents

> I need £8.50 for a theatre trip, by yesterday. We've got to go, as it is part of the course.

Old people

> Yes, Gran, I know it was harder in your day but you didn't have ten GCSEs and a National Curriculum.

Experts

> In the last days of Kenny Dalglish, a series of errors in the transfer market rocked the confidence of the team which had dominated English football for twenty years.

Non-experts

> Liverpool FC was formed over a hundred years ago and their ground, Anfield Stadium, has become a Mecca for fans of the game.

- Repeat words from sentence to sentence, rather than referring back with words such as 'he'.
- Use only simple connecting words, like 'and' and 'then'.

> *This is Celestine the cat. Celestine is a big, black cat . This is Jessica. One day Jessica and Celestine went out to play in the park.*

2 The ending of a speech opposing deer hunting, to be given at a school debate.
Hints:
- Address the audience.
- Use emotive and persuasive language: 'bloody', 'torn apart', 'wicked'.
- Ask questions.

> *Ladies and gentlemen. Imagine the exhausted and cornered deer. Imagine its suffering as the dogs begin to tear it apart. How would you like to watch this sickening and bloody spectacle? How would you feel if your own father or mother enjoyed doing this for pleasure?*

3 The climax of a ghost story in a teenage novel.
Hints:
- Build up the suspense with short sentences.
- Use descriptive adjectives.
- Hold back surprises.

> *The wardrobe door was open. He knew he had left it shut. There was an unfamiliar odour in the air. It might have been damp earth with a hint of rotting cheese. He could feel the hairs on his neck rising with fear. If only Wayne were here. He would know what to do. Suddenly...*

4 A letter to the paper about increases in bus fares.
Hints:
- Make it clear what you are concerned about by using simple language and separating points.
- Say exactly what you would like to happen.

> *Our opposition to these fare rises is based on three points: the steepness of the increase, the lack of notice given and the withdrawal of travel cards for school pupils. In our view, the council should...*

Writing purposes

There are many purposes for writing. You could be writing to achieve all kinds of results. You may be asked to write in a particular form as well. The purpose for writing is concerned with what you want the writing to achieve and its form is the structure and style which you adopt to make it do that, In practice, that is not as complicated as it sounds. What usually happens is that you select a style of writing once you decide on the purpose or select the purpose once you are given a style. In examinations, it is likely that you will be told which form to use.

FORM OF WRITING	PURPOSE FOR WRITING
Form	*Intention*
Narrative	informing
Letter	persuading
Article	describing
Summary	narrating
Diary	explaining
Poem	instructing
Leaflet	analysing
Poster	comparing
Script	
Notes	

In your coursework, it is important to show some variety of style and purpose, but this will inevitably be limited by the number of pieces set by your examining group's syllabus. It could be argued that every writing task should be allocated a purpose, form and audience. Certainly a coursework folder would be weakened if all the work was, for example, made up of stories and narratives or consisted only of responses to short-answer questions, so that a sense of variety was lost.

The purpose of your writing is an important consideration. In the last Workbench exercise, your purposes were to entertain, to persuade, to frighten and to inform and those purposes dictated the style of your writing.

Here are some examples of how different writing purposes affect the style and content of writing.

WRITING PURPOSES	WRITING FEATURES
Informing	• Clear introduction. • Straightforward sentences and paragraph structure. • Use of subheadings. • Use of facts and figures. • Factual details.

The Kenilworth Canal is eight miles long and runs from Kenilworth Castle to Baginton, on the outskirts of Coventry. A culvert carries the canal under the A46 Warwick by-pass and there is an aqueduct where it crosses the old GMR railway line.

History: Work started on the canal in 1843 when a local employer...

Persuading	• Use of rhetorical language and questions: "Surely you would like to help... would you leave an innocent man in prison?" • Colourful and descriptive language. • A personal style, 'you', to create the reader's involvement.

The Kenilworth Canal Preservation Trust needs your help. Please give just a few hours of your time, or a small donation, to help restore this beautiful, old waterway. Don't let more of our local history be lost forever...

Describing	• Longer sentences. • Use of adjectives and comparisons – similes and metaphors. • An organisational move from overall description to the specific.

Deep in the heart of leafy Warwickshire lies the tranquil Kenilworth Canal. In the eight miles of countryside through which it slowly wanders, expect to see herons and water fowl in abundance, open fields — golden with corn in the late summer — and to hear only the sounds of nature in full flow. Sometimes the silence is disturbed by the gentle chug of a pleasure boat, brightly decked out in transfers and awash with colour...

Narrating	• A story structure. • A chronological account (events in their order of occurrence). • An introduction. • Use of adverbs and phrases to describe how things happened. • Variations in pace and sentence length to lead to a climax. • Use of direct speech (the words people say enclosed within speech marks). • Use of familiar description. • The development of characters by description.

Now it began to fit together in the detective's mind. The declining relationship, the boat trip, the sudden push, water and then darkness. "Miss Marple," he said, "I know what you did with the body. Unless I am very much mistaken, the body of your husband Eric rests at the bottom of the Kenilworth Canal!"

Explaining
- Careful structure in which each piece of information can be understood by reference back to what came before.
- Definition of technical terms and the use of technical language.
- Factual description.
- A strict and formal structure – possibly numbered in some way.

The canal locks operate in this way. Gates hold back a head of water which is released by the operation of what is known as a paddle. When rotated, this opens a sluice, allowing the level of water in the lock to rise or fall. The canal boat rises or falls with the water level and can thus ascend or descend the lock.

Instructing
- A stepped structure with a series of mini-tasks to complete on the way to a specific intention.
- Use of imperatives: "Do this...", to tell the reader what to do.
- Short, clear sentences.
- Factual description to identify information, rather than describe it.

On your arrival at a lock, you should first inform the lock-master of your presence. Do this by ringing a bell or sounding your hooter. In busy periods, moor your boat first. When invited to proceed, enter the lock very slowly and stop your boat within two metres of any other craft in the lock. Then wait for further instructions.

Analysing
- A paragraphed structure in which each paragraph deals with a particular aspect.
- References to what is being analysed, either through summary (a shortened version), quotation (the words of an original) or anecdote (your version of something in the original).
- An introduction setting out the extent of the analysis, and a conclusion which sums up its findings.
- Longer sentences to cope with the complexity of the analysis and to make points supported by reference.

While a worthy ambition, the reopening of the Kenilworth Canal poses some serious engineering problems. The culvert (see fig. 14) is in a poor state of repair and has been losing water into the surrounding ground for some time. The consultant's report suggests that it will cost £70,000 to renovate this stretch, and additional funding will be required to bring the railway crossing up to standard.

Comparing
- A two-sided structure where ideas or facts are set against one another.
- Complex sentences, using a wide range of connectives and connecting phrases: 'nevertheless', 'on the other hand', 'but', 'in contrast'.
- Reference to support a point of view, often given as quotation or anecdote.
- An introduction, stating the scope of the comparison, and an evaluative conclusion to list its findings.

While the renovation of the Kenilworth Canal is attractive, the large sum of money involved might be better spent elsewhere on the Kenilworth Steam Railway. While the canal may be used by a few boats and hikers, the railway has the potential to become a major tourist attraction. Also, the railway restoration is already established, while the canal project is starting from scratch. Finally, the railway can call on a large number of volunteers, in contrast to the rather limited committee membership engaged in the canal scheme...

Structuring and organising writing

You will have noticed how the choice of an appropriate audience and purpose actually has much to say about the way that it should be structured and organised. In fact, it is those factors which should determine the structure of a piece of writing. The punctuation is a different matter.

Any piece of writing is certain to have some structure. That is why, at the lower levels, the Statements of Attainment ask you to set work out clearly, so as to make sense to the reader. However, at Levels 7 and 8 you are expected to start to make some conscious decisions about structuring as you work.

Workbench assignment

Developing a structure

Study this map and the accompanying information about popular places for tourists to visit in the British Isles, and complete the task beneath.

See how the task expects you to be able to:
• sort out what information should go in each section;
• write in the form of a leaflet and to a specific number of words;

- write for a specified audience – tourists;
- write with a specific purpose – to inform them of what is available in a persuasive way.

What is important in completing a task like this is that you are shown to be thinking about the structure you are going to employ. Leaflets, posters and reports are all good examples of tasks where thinking about structure is vital.

① **Edinburgh** was built in an area of deep canyons. Steep winding streets look down over rooftops and up to the Edinburgh Castle battlements. Parts of the castle date from 1100. In one room Mary Queen of Scots gave birth to James I of England in 1566. Throughout the city, traces remain of such famous citizens as writers Sir Walter Scott and Robert Louis Stevenson. Exploring Edinburgh's streets, especially during the busy August festival period, is a rich experience.

② **Bamburgh Castle, Northumberland** — a scenic castle with splendid views of the coastline.

③ **The Pennine Way** — the most famous path along the backbone of England.

④ **Blackpool**, the entertainment centre of the North, is home to Pleasure Beach – a 40-acre site that's famous for its 360 degrees roller coaster, the first in Europe. Blackpool is convenient for touring the lovely Lake District and the ancient walled city of Chester.

⑤ **Jorvik Viking Centre, York** — A celebration of Viking England and a trip through a re-creation of Viking life.

⑥ **Alton Towers, Staffordshire** — Leisure park. (£8.00 inc. rides.)

⑦ **Offa's Dyke Path** — runs through the Welsh border country.

⑧ **Warwick Castle** — Superb grounds. Claims to be the best preserved castle in England (Adm. House £5.00. Grounds only £1.50. No discounts.)

⑨ **Stratford-upon-Avon** — Shakespeare's birthplace. Home of Royal Shakespeare Theatre. (Performances 1.30 and 7.30. Tickets from £8.00.)

⑩ **Bath** is the site of an ancient Roman spa built round warm mineral springs and dating from AD44. The city is an elegant showcase for Georgian architecture with magnificent examples of crescents and terraces, and some beautiful gardens.

⑪ **Ridgeway Path** — runs through the Chiltern Hills.

⑫ **Madame Tussauds, London** — world famous waxworks. (Adm. £4.00 with student card.)

⑬ **The Tower of London** — London's historic castle.

⑭ **Longleat Safari Park, Wiltshire** — the first safari park in England, famous for lions.

⑮ **London Zoo** — One of the biggest animal collections in the world. (Adm. £3.50 with student card.)

⑯ **London** is filled with history, pageantry and entertainment. Discover its rich and glorious past, visit Westminster Abbey, Buckingham Palace and the Tower of London. Take a river cruise up the Thames to Hampton Court or down the Thames to Greenwich where 'The Cutty Sark' is moored. Check out museums and galleries. Wander round Covent Garden's piazza and stroll through the City with its fine skyscrapers. Find London on foot with the Wimpy Walks Guide to local sites which is available free from the British Tourist Authority.

⑰**South West Way** — 515 miles of coastal paths around Devon and Cornwall.

⑱**Newquay** in Cornwall is Britain's main surfing centre. Its scenery features headlands and sandy beaches with plenty of nightlife for the young and young at heart.

⑲**Bournemouth** on the south coast is a year-round resort with the best sunshine record in Britain. "Bournanzas" are short breaks with full board. Available from £50 per person for two nights at The Marine Hotel, 47 Esplanade, Bournemouth, Dorset.

⑳**Brighton** is ideal for seaside weekends. If the ocean is too cold try the King Alfred Leisure Centre with tropical pools, badminton and sauna.

Your task:

A leaflet using this map and entitled B*ritish Holidays* is to be made for The British Tourist Board. It will have separate sections on these subjects:

> Historic Britain
> Sea, Sand and Surf
> Out and About

Your task is to write the copy (the writing) to go in this leaflet. The purpose of the leaflet is to give the tourist an attractive impression of the range of holiday activities that Britain has to offer. Do not write a set of lists or copy out the information. Keep each section separate and write about 150 words for each.

Chapter 3
Using Standard English

There is a definition of Standard English in Section Two. Standard English is the accepted form for writing in English. Using Standard English means that people share word meanings, construct sentences in the same way, and use the same spellings. This has not always happened. Shakespeare, for example, wrote his plays out in longhand (his own handwriting) and they were then copied by other people. His spellings vary from one copy of his plays to the next and he often spelled the same word differently. So did the people who made copies of his work. In modern terms, Shakespeare would not be classed as an excellent speller but, in those days, there was less agreement about how words should be spelled. In fact, it was not until the invention of the dictionary – about a hundred years after Shakespeare died – that anyone thought anything of correct spelling and it is only with the widespread use of printing that spelling has become a cause for concern.

However, as far as your writing is concerned, Standard English is what most people would call 'correct' English. That means the choice of words is appropriate, the way they are linked together into sentences makes sense and the punctuation and spelling is accurate. Remember that 'correct' English is not the same as 'good' English. Writing which is poorly organised or lacks any focus on the audience or the purpose for writing will not communicate anything to the reader – whether or not it is written correctly.

For example, if you were writing your leaflet for tourists and you used a lot of long words which they were unlikely to understand and used very long, complex sentences which were difficult to follow, you could well fail to communicate with your readers, even though you were writing correctly.

Improving your use of Standard English

How can you improve the way in which you write Standard English? This is a difficult question to answer. All the English teaching you have ever experienced has been directed towards doing exactly that. Speaking, listening, reading and writing Standard English over a lifetime of education will all help you to become more familiar with this kind of language and more accustomed to using it. But what can you do to improve your use of Standard English in a short time, when you have an examination to face in a few months or weeks? Below is one way to approach the problem. Look on it as a 'crash course' in Standard English.

Read Standard English The best way to take in new ways of speaking and writing is to read good examples. Start off by reading a quality newspaper each day or read some highbrow magazines. This does not mean you have to read about difficult subjects. Look for clear accounts and descriptions and study them as you read. Concentrate on how words and sentences are linked and pick out phrases which you find particularly effective and you could use in your own writing.

Speak to Standard English users Make the effort to talk to people who use Standard English themselves. What you must try to do is to have conversations with people other than your good friends or those in the same group at school. Asking people their views is a good way to start. Joining a new club or society could turn out to be excellent examination preparation!

Review your own writing style Look at how you write. You will probably find that you write Standard English with mistakes in it. These are likely to be of four kinds – tense errors, agreement errors, punctuation confusion or omission, and misspellings. Spelling is dealt with separately in the curriculum but it is helpful to think about whether your writing is as correct as it can be in the other three areas.

❶ Tense errors

The use of a tense in writing tells the reader when something happened – in the past, the present or the future. A tense is a form of a verb – an action word. The word changes to show when the action takes place. The use of tenses is more complex in writing that in speech. Young children, when they start writing for the first time, often only use the present tense:

> *My name is Amy. I go to school. I am in Mrs Wilson's class. My friend is Polly. We paint. Sometimes we play in the sand.*

But if Amy looked back on her schooldays, she might write in a more complicated way:

> *I recall the time when I was in Mrs Wilson's class. She was a kind teacher and I look back on those days with pleasure. I had a friend called Polly and we used to play together. Sometimes we painted and at others we played in the sand pit. Looking back, how I wish that we had received structured lessons in Standard English. Then I could have gone to university and I would no longer have to spend my days working behind the counter at Joe's Cafe. Taking my examinations would have helped me to achieve something in my life.*

What you should notice here is that what Amy has to say has placed a greater demand on the tenses she is using.

Workbench assignment

Dear Jackie

> Two weeks ago I went on holiday to Majorca and met this gorgeous girl called Mandy. We spent a wonderful week together going to discos and partying the night away and I thought that our relationship would last forever. Then, I found her at the disco with a man called Pedro who worked in the hotel. She said he was her brother but they were not behaving in a very brotherly way! The next day she apologised and said I was silly for being so jealous. I forgave her at once.
>   When we left, she promised to write to me but has not done so. I wrote to the address she gave me but I have had no letter from her. I am also a bit worried because I seem to have mislaid my bank card and today I had a letter from the manager saying I am £200 overdrawn although I thought I was £100 in credit. Do you think I have been taken for a ride? What should I do?
>
> Confused of
> Shepherds Bush, London W12

Using tenses

1 Read this letter sent to a magazine by Wayne. Write a reply to it answering Wayne's questions and giving some helpful advice. You

will need to use a range of tenses.

2 Think about a place you have visited on holiday. Imagine that it has been hit by a natural disaster – an earthquake or flooding, for example. Then think about how it might be restored, rebuilt or changed in the future. Write an article for a magazine about how the place was, what happened to it and what will have to be done in the future.

3 Write about what happened in a situation where you ended up feeling rather embarrassed. Make it up if you like! Then write about what you wish you had done as the situation developed. Lastly, write about what you will do if it happens again!

Doing exercises like these and practising writing will not on their own help you to use tenses more effectively. You need to think about *how* you are using them and watch out for tense use in your writing as well. This is especially important when you revise your work.

2 Agreement errors

One of the most common forms of mistake in the use of Standard English concerns mistakes where the use of a singular or plural word is not followed up later in the writing where a verb is used. Correct this piece of writing yourself. There are at least ten mistakes of agreement!

> *Trevor and me was going to the park when we come across a gang of bikers. They was obviously looking for trouble. The leader were a huge bloke about seven feet high and the all of the gang were nearly as tall. I were ready to run but Trevor stays put. The gang got off their bike and the leader walks towards me. "Is there a McDonalds near here, please?" he asked us.*

Of course, these are obvious errors and you will easily have spotted them. But watch out for other examples, where a singular word describes a number of people or things, as in the words 'range' or 'variety'.

e.g. The **range** of portable CD players available **is** quite limited.

3 Punctuation errors

The best way to improve the punctuation of your written work is to revise it carefully. One way to do this is to read it aloud in your head because most punctuation marks are just ways of showing in writing the pauses and emphases we make in speech. These are common errors to watch out for. Make sure you don't make these mistakes!

• Using commas where you should use full stops:

  I got up late, I had a shower and then went down for breakfast, my uncle was there and asked if I wanted to go fishing.

• Forgetting to use capital letters:

  We went to the river in his car. it was a long way, he told me about the biggest fish he ever caught.

• Forgetting to use commas, speech marks and apostrophes:

  I was on holiday he said and i thought it would be good to spend some time fishing as there had ben quite a lot of rain and it wasnt very warm.

• Forgetting that for each new speaker you start a new line. Omitting question marks:

  "What did you catch" I asked. "Was it a salmon" "No," he answered, "but it was nearly as big."

Workbench assignment

Using punctuation

Write out this story with the correct punctuation and then continue it for about a page of writing. Make sure there is plenty of conversation.

> *Trevor and me was going to the park when we come across a gang of bikers. They was obviously looking for trouble. The leader were a huge bloke about*

seven feet high and the all of the gang were nearly as tall. I were ready to run but Trevor stays put. The gang got off their bike and the leader walks towards me. "Is there a McDonalds near here, please?" he asked us.

If, after completing this exercise, you are confused about the rules which govern punctuation ask your teacher for help. In an examination, don't be afraid to put in more punctuation – rather than less – especially where the breaks between sentences are concerned.

Chapter 4
Revising your writing

There is extra advice on drafting and redrafting, or revising, your work in Sections Five and Six. In fact, in all your English work you should always take the time to stand back and review what you have done. Starting with notes or a plan and then redrafting allows you to change and improve what you write as you go along. In this sense, redrafting means more than correcting your mistakes. In your writing, you will probably be expected to show that you can redraft work and, for coursework, the examining group may expect you to include the rough draft of a finished piece of work in your folder.

The redrafting process

Imagine that you have been asked to write about your favourite television programme, saying what it is and explaining what you like about it.

1 **Your plan** Decide what the programme will be and make some brief notes about it. Notice how the notes should be structured to allow you to group information as you think.

2 **Reviewing your plan** Are you answering the question you have been asked? Are you saying too much about the the programme and not enough about what you like about it? You can easily modify the plan. It would be much harder if this was a piece of finished writing.

3 Writing the first draft Don't worry too much about the introduction at this stage, but try to get involved in the writing. Don't worry about minor errors either – focus on what you want to say.

> The most important family is the Fowlers. Arthur and his wife _____ and their son _____ and their daughter Michelle. They live in a small house on the square. Arthur has been secretly seeing a woman called Mrs Hewitt. They met when Pauline went to New Zealand a few months ago. Their son is H.I.V. positive...

4 Revising the first draft Look for areas of your plan which you have neglected. See if there are obvious omissions in what you have written so far. Is the balance of the writing all right? Add new sections or paragraphs and write them out on fresh paper or at the end of the draft. Work hard on your introduction and the conclusion to your writing. Ask a friend or a teacher to read your work so far and comment on it for you.

If you have made a lot of changes or the writing is beginning to look messy, you may want to make a second draft before you start revising the writing in detail.

> I like the way that the programme tackles ^social issues like unemployment ^and AIDS. It does not take sides over things but shows them as they really are. One character's business has just gone ~~bust~~ bankrupt but he is planning to start again.
>
> Another character has just got pregnant after being left by ^her boyfriend who ~~ran off to sea and~~ has joined the merchant navy. It asks the question about whether she should ~~of~~ have told him.

5 Looking closely at your writing Do **two** specific things:
1 Add extra linking words, new paragraph beginnings, descriptions or phrases to sum up where you have got to. All of these will make your writing more interesting and readable.
2 Check your use of Standard English, your punctuation and your spelling. Look closely at the names of people you have mentioned.

'Eastenders' is probably the most successful 'soap opera' ever to appear on British television. Screened twice weekly, it has overtaken 'Coronation Street' as the preferred viewing for millions of teenagers. In this essay, I intend to explore its popularity and its continuing success.

6 **Writing the final draft** Head the writing correctly with the title you have been set. Take your time and think as you write. This is not just a fair copy. While you are writing, think about the effect you want to have on the reader.

Practise redrafting in all of your coursework and don't be afraid to go to two or even three drafts if the work is unusually complex. Remember that almost all of the printed material you see around you – articles, reports, advertisements and so forth – is the product of many drafting sessions and long discussions between the writers, editors and clients.

Writing about language

The ability to write about language is an important part of the National Curriculum and the GCSE course. In your examination, you could be asked to comment on the language used in a news story, a poster or an advertising leaflet. This is a slightly different skill from using language when you write. It asks you to stand back and look both at the **way** people write and **why** they write as they do. Doing this makes use of your knowledge about language – sometimes known as KAL by teachers.

Showing that you can do this is not difficult if you have followed the advice given about writing earlier in this section. When you are asked to comment on language first ask yourself these key questions:
• For what purpose is the language being used?
• Who is it written for?
• Who is the intended audience for the writing?
Then make use of your ideas as you look at the **features** of the writing. You will notice that effective writing is that which meets the requirements of a particular purpose and audience. Ask yourself these questions:
• How has the writer's style been changed by the needs of this purpose and audience?
• Where has the writer used specific words to meet the chosen purpose and audience?
• How is the writing organised or structured to serve its purpose and communicate with its audience? How does the layout of the writing on the page help with this?
• How are images – photographs, cartoons – used to make the writing more effective?
• How is colour used – if it is – for effect? If colour is not used, does the use of black and white have its own message for the reader?
• How does the size of the print on the page, or the range of typefaces used, or the relationship between the amount of print and white space make the writing effective?
• How are titles and sub-headings used on the page? Are they effective in terms of layout and/or content?
As you write your analysis, you might also remember that almost all writing is intended for a purpose and an audience but sometimes the purposes can be quite varied. The audience can be very broad or very limited. Imagine a range of leaflets designed to sell burglar alarms to old age pensioners, well-off working couples and small businesses. Think of the slightly different things they would say about the same product.

Purposes for writing can be quite complex. Imagine a simple little book called *Welcome to the Chunnel!* which is written to be given to young children when they arrive at the entrance to the Channel Tunnel. It would look as if its purpose was to inform and its audience was young children but it could be written to serve other purposes as well.

- It would REASSURE young children and make them feel happy about travelling under the sea.
- It would KEEP THEM QUIET during the trip and make their parents feel more contented and, therefore, likely to use the tunnel again.
- It would REPEAT BASIC SAFETY INFORMATION which parents would note as they skipped through its pages.
- It would ADVERTISE what an engineering achievement the tunnel was and make the parents feel that the cost was worthwhile.

Your detailed analysis of the features might bring these concealed purposes out.

Almost all writing – and especially advertising, newspaper and magazine articles, posters and leaflets – has a message for the reader apart from what it actually says on the page. Sometimes, as in cigarette advertising, the message – smoke these cigarettes – is concealed under glossy images. Sometimes, startling images are used to make the message as forceful as possible – don't play with fireworks. More subtly, a news story may be written in such a way as to make people think that one particular group of people are responsible for something. A good analysis of language goes beneath the surface of the words on the page.

Workbench assignment

Knowledge about language

1. Buy three daily newspapers on the day when a big story breaks and compare the way that they treat it. Do they look at the drama or the issues? Do they focus on the people involved or the consequences? How does their treatment of the story relate to the readers of the newspaper?
2. Pick up a selection of leaflets from your public library on as varied a range of topics as possible. Then analyse and compare three of them using the questions discussed in this section to help you.

Spelling correctly

There is advice on what to do about your spelling if you have problems throughout this book. The advice on Standard English applies here as well. As you read, focus on the spelling of words. Where your writing is concerned, remember these basic tips to help you.

When you write coursework, if you are not sure about a spelling, look it up in a dictionary. If your teacher advises you to check work, make sure that you do. Always check as you redraft. Get used to knowing when a word 'looks' right.

In an examination, it is worth avoiding words which you know you always get wrong! If you always write 'recieve' when you mean 'receive', get used to writing another word or phrase instead. If you know that you have problems with spelling words like these, look out for them when you revise and check your writing.

Keep a spelling book containing words you find difficult and new words. Look at it regularly when you write. This will help you with your vocabulary building as well.

Learn spelling rhymes and memory tips. Remember 'I before E except after C' and that the difference between 'practice' and 'practise' is the same as between 'advice' and 'advise' (the first is a noun and the second a verb in each case).

Learn about word-roots and words from other languages to help improve your word-building skills.

Never misspell words you have been given as part of an examination paper or the names of characters in books you have in front of you.

Don't scrawl over words in an examination and hope that the examiner will think you had the answer. An illegible spelling is a wrong spelling and you could lose marks for untidy presentation.

Using legible handwriting and presenting work neatly

One of the requirements of the national curriculum is that you show that you can write in a joined up way. Some syllabuses ask you to show this in one piece of coursework; others will just mark you down for the folder as a whole if it is hard to read. The marks involved are unlikely to make a significant difference to your final grade but there are plenty of other good reasons for writing neatly, so practise neat handwriting as a habit.

If you don't usually join your letters it would be a good idea to put a piece of work in your coursework folder where you show that you can. Perhaps you could copy out a poem you had written or use joined up writing for effect somewhere.

If your handwriting is generally untidy and hard to read, think about modifying your style. Look at other people's handwriting and copy styles you like. If it is really bad, get a book to help you form letters from scratch, but only do that in a crisis situation! You will be surprised what a few weeks of concentration can achieve, especially if you are prepared to buy a new pen and to write a little more slowly.

Your folder can also be given credit for its presentation. Try to include one piece of work where presentation is a feature. If you write a report, use subheadings and diagrams. If you write a children's story, a poster, a leaflet or a playscript set it out like one with different sizes of writing and make sure that it is appropriately spaced on the page.

Summary

- This section should have raised your awareness about some very important, and widely misunderstood points about written English language:
- There is no 'bad' English, there is not 'right' and 'wrong' English. But there is English which is appropriate or inappropriate for different circumstances.
- Being good at English means being flexible: being able to choose from a variety of styles to suit particular circumstances.
- Some purposes, forms and styles are more difficult to sustain than others. Your final level will reflect how well you handle the 'difficult' styles.
- Being able to recognise and discuss the styles of your own and other people's writing in a conscious way will improve your final level.

Chapter 1

Preparing your coursework

So far, this book has concentrated on the content of your English course and the kinds of skills you must acquire to be successful. In this section and the next, the focus is different and looks at the ways in which you will be assessed through a mixture of coursework and terminal examination papers. You should remember from Section One that the coursework assessment is less important than the examination in determining your final result. Nonetheless, a good coursework performance could certainly raise your level for the subject as a whole.

The good news about coursework is that you will have the time to ensure that the work you do for English and English Literature reflects your best efforts. You will be able to rewrite pieces of work which were not too good in the first place and you will only have to submit the best of your work to the examining group at the end of the course. In other words, the ball is in your court!

The bad news is that you will have to work consistently throughout your course. You will not be able to leave it to the last minute and then redeem yourself by working hard for the exam. If you do not mind doing exams and are not generally a well-organised person, you may see grave disadvantages in coursework!

It is important as you do your coursework to bear in mind what you are trying to show your assessor. Much of the help this section will give you is concerned with making certain that the coursework you do reflects your abilities and capacities to the full so that you do not sell yourself short in any way. Remember that your coursework says things about your intelligence, your sensitivity to what goes on around you, your ability to communicate with other people and your willingness to learn new skills.

Also, coursework should show you at your best. If you did badly in an examination, you could say you were nervous or that you answered the wrong questions. But coursework allows you the time to make the right choices and to show your best abilities. If you are prepared to work through this section and follow its advice, then you can improve your coursework performance and learn about being a better reader, writer, listener and speaker as well. This section sets out some general steps you might take to do any piece of written coursework well. It applies equally to English and English Literature coursework.

Getting organised

Being well organised is the starting point for any piece of coursework. Good organisation involves careful planning of three things: your time, your equipment and the space where you work, as well as a distinctive attitude towards your writing. Do not ignore the first three of these. Many excellent students fail to get the grades they deserve because, although their writing is basically very good, the preparation of their work is hurried and its presentation is scrappy.

Managing time

A problem you are likely to encounter as soon as you start doing coursework is that you will be taking a number of other subjects at GCSE as well as English. These will make demands on your time, with even more coursework. You need to organise your time and you will need a lot of self-discipline to make sure work is not left to the last minute.

You will have to get used to working to deadlines. This is the most important change your GCSE coursework will make to the way you approach classwork and homework. Before you started your GCSE course, if you did not complete your homework you might have ended up in detention, but it probably would not have caused major problems with your school work. English coursework is different! Some deadlines for the handing in of assignments will be set by your teacher. These are not intended to ensure that you die of overwork: they are set to help you to progress through your coursework at a steady rate.

If you fail to stick to deadlines, you will find yourself frantically trying to complete work at the end of the course. If you do not manage to complete enough, then you will not gain a level for the subject. It really is worth sticking to the deadlines your teacher sets, or, better still, planning ahead and getting a piece of work in early if you can see another subject about to demand other coursework from you.

Some more important deadlines are set by the examination group. Sometimes, certain pieces of work have to be completed by certain dates during the course. All GCSE courses give a final date for coursework to be with your teacher for assessment at the end of the course. If you miss that deadline, there are no second chances.

Managing equipment

It is vitally important to make sure that your work is well presented. Not only is good presentation now part of the formal requirement for the assessment of AT4/5, but there is little doubt that assessors look more kindly upon work which is neatly written. It is worth investing in a few basic pieces of equipment to help you look after your coursework properly before you start the course. Even if you have picked up this guide in the middle of the course, now could be the time to get rid of that dog-eared, coffee-stained old folder which lets the edges of your pages get grubby and torn. One of the biggest differences between English and coursework in other subjects is that in English you will do a larger number of short pieces of work. These take more looking after than a couple of long projects.

If you have just moved up from Year 9 into Year 10, you may be used to doing your English work in an exercise book. Working on loose-leaf, A4-sized paper can cause problems, particularly if you are not the world's neatest person, or you are the type who loses things! One of the things to learn about coursework is that you can make your task, and your teacher's job, a lot easier if you are organised and methodical. Being organised and methodical when you are scatty and untidy by nature may not be easy, but there is some educational research which shows that teachers and assessors, in all subjects, give higher grades to written work which is neat and legible. Exactly the same work, when untidy and hard to read, was found by the researchers to receive lower grades. That is why this guide encourages you to be tidy and organised in the presentation of your writing – it really is a simple way to improve your marks.

Looking after coursework while you are writing it is not as simple as it might seem. Pieces of paper easily can easily be lost, screwed up, or even destroyed if they are not looked after. You will need the following items. Your school may provide some of them, others you may already have at home.

- **A notebook** for rough notes and early attempts at written work. This is easier to handle than file paper and also gives you a record of your work in case the worst happens and you lose an assignment.
- **A4 punched file paper.** Don't use very thin paper, or notebooks where the top of every sheet in your folder is an ugly tear. Don't use narrow feint (the distance between each line which dictates the number of lines on the page) because, even if your writing is small, there will not be space for teacher comments and corrections. If you can find paper with a printed margin (the line which runs down the left-hand side), so much the better.
- **A strong waterproof file** for carrying assignments to and from school or college is vital. It protects work from rain as well as leakages! It does not have to be fancy – a strong polythene bag and a piece of cardboard to stop your work getting crushed is perfectly adequate. Don't buy the biggest file in the shop, either. Remember you have to carry it around with you.
- **Your own file for storing finished assignments.** Make sure that it has plenty of space in it and that is a true A4 size with overlapping edges to protect your work.
- **A small stapler and a hole punch.** Most of the paper you use will already be punched, but you may want to include working notes or materials which you collected for an assignment – like work on leaflets, for example.
- **An efficient pen with blue or black ink.** The best pens for writing lengthy pieces of work are ink pens with either roller balls or nibs. Fibre-tips are all right but, as soon as they start to age, the ink begins to dry up and they become harder to write with and scratch the surface of the paper. Do not use very cheap ballpoints, felt-tip pens or coloured ink for written work. It may look snazzy at the time, but you will probably feel different about it twelve months later when you are submitting your finished folder.

You may be lucky and find that, once your work is finished and marked, your teacher will keep it safe until the end of the course. This may be disappointing if you want to take a good piece of work home to show around but, in the long run, it does stop work getting lost. A whole set of folders locked up in a school is less likely to disappear than an individual assignment in your bedroom! On the other hand, if the folders are left in an insecure cupboard in a classroom where anyone can rummage through them, you may feel that your work will be safer at home. It is up to you to negotiate this with your English teacher and, once you have agreed on a system, stick to it. So do not say you will keep your work at home and then start leaving it in the cupboard – that is where things can go seriously wrong!

Remember that if you do not have the correct number of pieces of coursework, or include the right types of writing, you will run the risk of not being entered for the exam at the end of the course. If you *are* entered, and then do not have the right work, you may end up having to pay the exam entry fee if it is your fault that work has gone astray – so be careful.

Most examining groups now allow almost all coursework to be completed using a word processor, although some require evidence of your abilities to write using script to be included somewhere in the folder. If you use a word processor, remember to save each draft. Choose a clear font and leave a double space between paragraphs. Leave good-sized margins on the left and right of your writing, and use no more than 80 characters to each line.

Managing space

One other piece of equipment is space. Try to find a reasonable space in which to work at home, so that your coursework is not buried under books and other writing. If you are to do your best you need to give some thought to where and when you will work. For a start, you will need a place at home where you can read. Most of the time, the only requirements for this are a comfortable chair (or a piece of floor, or a bed) and peace and quiet to get on with it. The furniture should not cause too many problems.

Getting the right kind of atmosphere for concentration might be more difficult in some households, though. Wearing headphones to a personal stereo (without music) is a good

way of blocking out unwanted interference and noise.

When it comes to written assignments, or even making notes on your reading, you may have more difficulty finding a good place to work. You will certainly need a desk or table where you can spread out your books and papers. Working on the floor, or with your book on your knee in front of the television, will not help you to do your best work. On the other hand, if you do find a good place to work you should find that your best work is written in your own time, when you are in the right mood, away from the distractions of the classroom.

If you are looking after your own coursework, you will need a drawer or cupboard to keep it in, where you are sure nobody and nothing will be able to interfere with or damage it.

Finally, if you can already see that any of this will cause you problems, do discuss possible solutions with your teacher. Most schools are open long after you leave at night: it may be possible for you to stay behind to work, and arrange somewhere to keep your work there, too, if you feel that it may not be safe at home. The public library is also a good place to find some peace and a big table.

If you are lucky, you will have a room of your own at home where you can organise and keep your work, but do not despair if you have not: plenty of people get good GCSE grades by using their ingenuity to create the right working conditions. You can, too, if you are determined enough.

Chapter 2

Approaching a coursework task

You have been in an English lesson. Your group has read a story and done some discussion about it in small groups. Towards the end of the lesson, the teacher tells you you are to do a piece of writing, using some of the ideas from the story. There is a choice between writing another story, a diary entry or a piece about the characters in the story. You are given a sheet of written guidelines and your teacher leads a brief discussion about good ways to start, warns you of problems you might encounter in the work and discusses ways to deal with them.

Then you are told you have tonight's homework, the next English lesson in school and another homework to complete the task. It is to be handed in a week on Friday.

Now you have sorted out your equipment and divided up the time you have been allowed, it is time to think about the subject of your writing. This is the kind of approach you should adopt.

The first homework

If you are the type of person who can think better at home (or in the place you have chosen for out-of-school work), use this homework time to get some rough ideas for the assignment down on paper. The last thing you should be worrying about at this stage is how long it is meant to be. Concentrate on what needs to be included: this is much more important.

There are a number of ways of approaching a piece of written work, depending partly on the kind of writing it is, but also depending on how your mind works, too.

Some people like to begin with a preparatory activity like brainstorming, where you write down any and every idea that occurs to you, or collect linked ideas together on a spider-plan.

If your mind works better in straight lines, then you might start off by making a list of a sequence of connected ideas.

You could re-read the original story quite quickly and jot down ideas as they come to you.

Some tasks lend themselves to one of these approaches in particular, but you should try them out and decide which one suits you best. You will notice that in all these alternatives you have been asked to write something and not just to think. That is because, as you write, you are taking the first steps towards organising your thoughts on paper. Next, you could:

Go on to decide what will go into each paragraph. You could number the random ideas from your spider-plan into a sensible order for writing.

'Scan' read the story (this is where you read quickly in order to find particular information, like looking for a character's name) and write down brief passages which you might be able to incorporate in your work.

You could have several attempts at good opening and closing paragraphs. These will not necessarily be the ones at the beginning or the end of your notes! Starting a piece of writing is often the hardest part of the whole process. Doing it this way, you have not wasted a whole hour trying, and failing, to get started!

Remember that even this work is best done on A4 paper. Scraps of paper are too easily lost: you may even screw up and throw away the beginnings of a good idea if you do preparatory work on smaller sheets. Also, all of this work is valuable. You do not know yet which parts of it you will be able to use or improve later, so keep it all.

Tip box

Making notes

- Notes are NOT the same as scribble and they should never be done in an untidy scrawl. They need to be easy to read, so write them neatly.
- Space your notes clearly. DON'T cramp your notes on the page, because you will have to add to them as you go on. You will need space for this.
- DON'T copy out large chunks of writing. When you write notes about something, use your own words where possible to show that you are making sense of what you read.
- By the end of the time allocated to your homework, you will have something concrete down on paper and your mind will be applying itself to the assignment. Notice that there is a big difference between worrying and planning! If a good idea strikes you before the next lesson, make sure that it is added to your notes.

The lesson

Here is a chance to start writing your first draft when you will have help available if you need it.

First, turn your notes into a first draft of your assignment. Do a bit of thinking first. Have you got your ideas into the right order to commit them to paper?

Think about the type of writing you are about to undertake and decide what would be an appropriate style to suit the task and your intended reader. Is this a story which, like an essay or composition, needs to be written in a very formal style? Or is it something more like a diary entry, where a more colloquial (conversational) style would be appropriate?

- Begin with a suitable and interesting introduction. Try to get your reader's attention by being slightly unusual.
- Organise your ideas into well-formed paragraphs, each of which links logically and smoothly with the next one.
- Try to end with a suitable conclusion. Be careful not to let your writing fade out into a weak ending.

At this stage, do not worry if you need to cross out and correct details, or even begin a short section again if you are unhappy with the first attempt. However, do make sure that this version could be read and made sense of by someone else. It goes without saying that you need to take care with spelling and punctuation. No matter how brilliant the quality of your ideas, you will lower your final grade if your writing skills are weak technically.

Read through what you have written at the end of the lesson, correct spelling and punctuation errors and rephrase ideas which are clumsily expressed. Identify words which do not feel quite right for the style you have adopted, or places where your sentence structures seem awkward. Mark any words that you ought to check in a dictionary. If you cannot think of ways to improve the writing yourself, make a pencil note in the margin that it needs further thought and perhaps discussion with your teacher.

Getting help from your teacher

Towards the end of the lesson – not when the bell has gone – is a good time to ask your teacher to read the draft through and give you some guidance about the things you need to improve. However, the examination groups have strict rules about the amount of help you may be given with some coursework, by teachers or by anyone else. This is necessary in order to be fair to everyone and to ensure that the work you are assessed on really reflects your ability.

Your teacher is not supposed to:
- correct spelling;
- correct punctuation;
- rephrase sentences for you;
- tell you what to include when you rewrite.

But your teacher is allowed to:
- discuss your work with you;
- give you guidance;
- suggest briefly other ideas you might include in the final draft;
- point out repeated errors and factual slips;
- give you an idea of the grade the work is worth in its present draft and how much you could realistically hope to improve it by a redraft.

So, for example, your teacher could say, 'The style of your introduction is too colloquial and the spelling is shaky in the final paragraph' but not, 'deceive has the "e" before the "i" ' or, 'say that the book is "entertaining", not "loadsa fun"'.

Essentially, your teacher must not add to the quality of the work, but he or she can tell you where, and generally how, you might improve it. Examination groups allow general comments of this sort to be written on pupils' rough drafts. Now that drafting is a highlighted aspect of the writing course, it is essential that your teacher sees your work and comments on it – however briefly – before you continue.

Tip box

Writing the final draft

- Like this guide, most examination groups recommend the use of A4 paper. Use it unless you have a particular reason for using another size to suit a particular type of writing.
- Unless you have a really good reason not to, write on both sides of the paper. Don't be wasteful: you will use a lot of paper on this course.
- Remember that several people will have to read the assignment, not just your own teacher, who is used to your usual scrawl! So keep your handwriting neat. It can affect your results!
- Use black or blue ink, unless you have a particular reason for working in pencil or some other colour.
- Remember that bad word processing – big gaps, poor punctuation, faint print – is as hard to read as poor handwriting and that the word processor shows up spelling mistakes and an absence of punctuation very clearly. Typographical slips may count as much against you as spelling mistakes.

- Avoid the use of correcting fluid: it can look as if you have altered work after marking, and writing on top of it often fades over a period of time.

The second homework

By now, you should see where you are going. Your first draft has been looked at by your teacher. Only if you, or your teacher, feel that the first draft was absolutely disastrous should you need to do a second draft. At this point, your writing 'goes public', so you need to bear a few more points in mind as you begin the final draft.

To begin with, always head assignment pages carefully. This should become a habit and

▶ 20/11/90   ▶ 9a

▶ Mary Farrel's Secret Diary
(based on the short story "Their Mother's Purse")

▶   Sharon Wright

ENGLISH COURSEWORK FOLDER

▶ Diary writing, based on a literary text.

▶ Story read and discussed in class. 2 homeworks and one double lesson in school for writing.

be the first thing you do when you begin a final draft. If you do not do it properly each time you write, it will take you hours to sort all your work out at the end of the course.

The front page should have your **name**, the **date** (including the year because this is a two-year course) and the **full title** plus an assignment number, if required. You must include details of any titles and authors' names if your assignment is based on literature you have read. Writing out the title might seem a waste of time but it will help you to fix your mind on the exact task you are to undertake, as well as making your work easier for other people to assess. It makes sense to put your tutor group and the name of your school, too.

Because you have to show coverage of varied aspects of writing for the National Curriculum, it is important to make sure that the nature of the task you have been set is clearly noted. Writing down 'Work based on *Lord of the Flies*' is not enough. You must say whether you are writing a character study, a story, an empathic account, or whatever.

Each page should have at the top the date (including the year, as this is a two-year course) your name and the assignment number. Not all the examination groups ask for these, and if your syllabus wants anything more, your teacher will tell you. Of course, it also makes sense to number your pages.

Some schools develop their own cover sheets for assignments. These are duplicated forms which are used as the top page for an assignment and include spaces for all the details mentioned above. An example of one is shown below. You could adapt and use this to make sure that you include all these details on the front sheet every time.

Tip box

Reviewing your work

As you write, check the following:
- Your opening paragraph should have clear links with the title and should set the tone and style for what follows.
- Ensure that the paragraphing you checked in your first draft is maintained, or improved.
- If you were dissatisfied with any parts of your work, uncertain about the style or you need to add sections to make the final draft more complete, you should experiment with these sentences or paragraphs in a notebook before committing them to paper.
- Make sure your conclusion still has a connection with the title. Do not let your work wander off the point.
- When you think that you have finished, have a last read-through to check for careless errors. Remember the warning about correcting fluid. A tidy crossing-out and correction may well be better.
- Number your pages, staple them together and take your completed assignment to your teacher, clean and tidy in your waterproof folder.

Chapter 3

Organising your folder

Whether your work is stored at school or kept at home, it will help you to ensure you are working towards the grade you want if you keep an index of the assignments you have completed and the marks you get for each piece of work your teacher assesses.

After reading Section One carefully, you will know that the examination groups are quite precise in stating not only **how many** but also **what kind** of coursework assignments you need to do to gain a grade.

It is true that only your best work is assessed at the end of the course, but it is also true that your folder must contain examples of a wide variety of types of written work to meet these syllabus demands. So, you may be a brilliant writer of imaginative stories, Level 9 or 10 every time, but if you find close-reading assignments or media work difficult, your hopes of a high level may be dashed if your syllabus states that you must include one or two pieces of work done in this way.

It is the same with work on literature: you may gain high marks for your work on Shakespeare's plays, but find that the marks you get for wider reading assignments on books you have chosen and read for yourself are much lower. If your syllabus says you have to include one of each, then you will have to work hard to raise your grades in the weaker areas of your work.

The lesson to learn is that you certainly cannot avoid having to do work you find difficult: if you do, you run the risk of not being entered for the exam at all. Careful indexing and organisation will help you to see the gaps and identify which aspects of your coursework will repay extra effort.

Your index should be divided into sections which reflect the kinds of writing your syllabus requires you to be assessed in. A good index does three things:

❶ It highlights those sections where you are very short of work.

② It highlights those sections where your grades are low, so you will know where improvement is needed.

③ At the end of your course it will help you to sort out which piece, or pieces, of work from each section will be the best to submit for your final assessment to ensure the highest level possible.

When you are looking after your own folder, you may find it useful to separate different types of writing, using cardboard dividing pages. You may well have difficulty telling which kind of writing is which. Don't worry that you find this difficult. It is complicated, and some pieces could go in more than one section. Ask your teacher for help if you are not sure because, if you don't know this, you will have no way of telling where you are going wrong or which areas of your English work are weak and need some extra effort. Once you have identified your weak points, then you can pay special attention to those particular types of assignment.

Chapter 1
Preparing for the examination

Before the introduction of National Curriculum assessment, it was possible to get a GCSE in English or in English Literature without taking an examination paper. But things have changed. Now, not only must you take two examination papers, but how well you do will have a considerable effect on your final result. However good your teacher's assessment of Speaking and Listening is, and however well you have done on your coursework, the examination is a hurdle you have to cross.

Even if you dislike examinations, it is important to remember that everyone else feels the same. Also, the new GCSE examinations have to show what you can do in relation to the National Curriculum. That means they should contain few unexpected and unpleasant surprises. The purpose of this section is to help you to take the examinations in your stride.

There are three things to concentrate on if you want to do well in examinations:

1 Preparation
2 Organisation
3 Practice

1 Preparation

You should be preparing for your examination almost from the first day of your course. As you learn something, it is important to store that information in a form which you can draw on later, when you are revising for the final examination. As you work, you need to get used to answering the types of questions at the kinds of speed that will be required in the final examination. There are also some basic things which you need to find out about early in the course.

What does the terminal examination consist of? How many papers are there? How long are they? Do they ask many short-answer questions, or fewer questions which require longer answers? Do they give stimulus material for you to work from on the paper, or in an anthology which is sent to schools in advance of the examination date? Examination papers are usually given titles and these give you an indication of what they test as well as which attainment targets they cover. All of this information is in your examination syllabus, but it is something you need to be familiar with from the start.

What special requirements are there? Some examination papers are now based on an anthology of material. This is issued to schools before the date of the examination and some of the questions asked in the examination are based on it. Others use less material but it is still **pre-released** – given out in advance of the examination. For English Literature exams, there are **set texts** – book titles which are usually chosen from a list but whose study is compulsory. You may also have to decide on an **area of study** – a linking theme which connects some of the books you read during the course.

2 Organisation

As you go through your course, it is vital to make sure that you know what you have done and what remains to be done. This is as important for the examination as it is for your coursework, because you must make sure that you have rehearsed all the skills that you are likely to be asked to show in the examination. Collect sets of sample papers and start to plan your revision timetable early – especially where the re-reading of your set texts is concerned. Aim to get your coursework out of the way by the spring half-term (the end of February) in the year you are taking the examination. That will allow you enough time to revise and prepare for the examination papers.

3 Practice

There is a real difference between the techniques you have to use in writing coursework answers and those used in sitting examination papers. Most people would agree that it is easier to do your best in coursework than in the examination. Some advantages of coursework over examinations are listed below:

Coursework	Examination papers
Time to think and plan	Exact time limits make you feel hurried
A chance to revise your writing	Time for only one draft plus corrections
Familiar material	Unseen material
The opportunity to revise spellings and word meanings	No dictionaries are allowed
A chance to consult your teacher	You are on your own
You don't have to submit a weak piece for assessment	You only have one chance

What matters is to make sure that you feel relaxed when you have to work within the constraints of the examination. The way to make sure of this is to practice reading and writing under the kinds of pressures you will have to face in the examination room. In class, that may be difficult to achieve. Even if you try to treat a writing task as a test, other people will be asking questions, looking for reference materials or consulting the teacher. So it is important to take every chance you get to work under what are called examination conditions.

Sometimes in the classroom you will be asked to complete an assignment under controlled conditions. This kind of work is a half-way stage between classwork and examination conditions. Unlike an examination set externally, controlled tasks are set by your teacher. He or she chooses the time, the place and the work you are to do. Sometimes all the teachers in an English department may decide to give the whole year group the same task to do at the same time, but they still decide what it should be and also mark the work themselves, so they will be able to give you advice about how to do better next time, which is useful.

You can do controlled work in a manner very like a traditional exam: a time limit on the session and all work to be finished by the end of that time. Some people respond well to that pressure and produce better work under those circumstances. Others, of course, do not. The important thing, however, is that you are not allowed any help from or discussion with the teacher or class before or during the work: the work must be completed while the teacher is supervising you, to ensure there is no discussion or copying. That is why your teacher will have to collect and keep all your work and any stimulus material at the end of each session of work.

You may be allowed to use reference works: a dictionary, a thesaurus, the book you are studying for your literature work and even notes you have prepared out of school. The assignment you are set will frequently be a piece of work which provides a test of your close-reading skills (like questions designed to test your understanding) and a test of your extended-writing skills (like writing a story or giving an opinion).

Very often, you will be given a fairly lengthy piece of factual writing to read before you begin to write. This could be anything, from a letter to the press, to a newspaper or magazine article (possibly including diagrams or charts adding further information to that in the written part of the article) about a topical issue. You may even be asked to read something persuasive, like the copy of an advertisement or the descriptions of seaside resorts from a holiday brochure.

The tasks will vary a great deal, too, because of the variety of possible things you could be asked to read but there may be a set of questions, either to test that you understood the details of the writing or to focus your attention on some details which you will need to concentrate on in the longer piece of writing, you will be asked to do later on. They will tend to be similar to the kinds of tasks you will be set in your final examination.

The tasks you are set can be of several types. Those which ask a set of questions or expect you to write a formal letter are known as **closed assignments**, because you have little choice about what or how you write. In answering them, you will be writing about a certain subject, using a particular type of writing for a specified audience. An **open assignment** asks you to extend the situation or to add to information you have been given. For example, if you had read some holiday brochures you might be asked how you would write something similar to promote the good points about the place where you live.

For your English Literature course, or to test your reading achievement, you may well be set a **literary closed assignment**. For this, the stimulus material will be a passage from a novel, or a whole short story, or maybe an extract from a play, or a poem. The task may be a comparison of any two of these, where a similar subject is discussed from different viewpoints. It may be what is called an 'unseen' passage. That is something you have never seen before: you may not even be told the title or who wrote it, so all you have to go on are the words on the page. On the other hand, it could be a passage from a book you are studying in class, provided your teacher has not told you exactly which passage it is in advance and you have not at any time discussed the task you are set.

For the task itself, you may be asked a number of questions on the passage, either in the way of a traditional comprehension to test your in-depth understanding of the passage, or as preparation for a longer piece of writing to follow. You may be asked to write **empathically**.

As you become familiar with writing under controlled conditions, you will be getting ready to face the problems set by an examination paper, where the limitations on time and the unfamiliarity of the material will make your work that much harder.

The next stage is **examination practice** or **rehearsal**. It is absolutely essential that, towards the end of your course, you take advantage of every opportunity to write under examination conditions. That means working on a number of problems against the clock, in silence and without the help of reference books or your teacher.

Some people believe the old story that you cannot revise for English. It may be true that there are no actual facts to learn, but there are ways of preparing, and things to check up on, which might help to raise your grade.

Doing your best in the examination

There are plenty of things which you can do to make sure that an examination shows you at your best. Look on the examination papers as a message to the examiner, saying 'In these few pages I am going to show you all the things in the syllabus which I can do well.' Don't make any of the silly mistakes that your teacher will have warned you about!

The obvious mistakes

DON'T try to revise all of the night before	DO arrive fresh and relaxed
DON'T leave too little time to get to the examination – especially when its starting time is different from the time you normally arrive at school	DO sit back and read the paper through
	DO make sure that your pens work
DON'T forget your equipment	
DON'T start writing as soon as you turn over the paper	

Countdown to the examination

The final countdown to the examination should begin as soon as you have completed your coursework folder. Then is the time to work out a clear timetable for yourself.

❶ **When you complete your coursework folder**
Photocopy any work which it will be useful for you to have to reread before the examination. For example, you may well have writing in your folder on the texts which you are studying for the examination.

Find out exactly when any pre-released materials or anthologies are scheduled to arrive. Make certain – even if you have practical examinations in other subjects, or college interviews – that you will be at any lessons in which your teacher discusses them.

Get hold of as many sample examination papers and tasks as you can. Your teacher may have these, but they can also be obtained direct from the examining groups for a small charge.

2 In the next few weeks

Make sure you have detailed revision notes on any set texts and pre-released materials you have been given. Keep this work together.

Take every opportunity you can get for examination practice. Do homework under examination conditions, for example. Set yourself some work from your sample papers.

Assess how well you are doing by looking at the Statements of Attainment and comparing your performance with what they ask for. Ask your teacher to look through your work.

3 In the weeks before the examination

Start to learn your notes. If your examination is open-text and you can take copies of the book in with you, then make sure that the permitted annotations are clear to you. Ask your teacher to set you additional work on set texts and other materials.

Make sure that you understand how the papers are structured and, if necessary, which sections you should answer questions from.

Practise writing examination answers in – at least – one hour blocks.

4 On the night before

Do a quick last-minute check on any notes you have made.

Check your equipment: take two pens. Don't forget any books that you are allowed to use in the exam.

When you have done your preparation, go out and enjoy yourself, get to bed at a decent time and have a good night's sleep.

5 On the day

Read through all of the paper, identifying what you have to do. If something about the rubric (the instructions) is unclear, ask the invigilator for help.

Re-read the details of the tasks first, even if they are printed after the written stimulus, so you can think about the tasks as you read the stimulus material. As you read, jot down notes as you read of ideas which you might use when you write. If you are allowed to write on the stimulus materials, underline useful parts.

Don't rush: read the whole thing through, twice if you need to, before you start work on the task. Decide roughly how long to spend on each task or part of a task. Leave time to amend and correct your work. Make sure you stick to this schedule during the exam. An incomplete paper where questions have not been attempted is much more likely to lower your grade than the odd piece of unfinished work.

Start your answer with a very rough draft or a plan. Think hard about the task at this point. Check that you are producing the sort of writing it asks for. Make sure that your plan can be read by the assessor, if necessary.

Allow at least ten minutes or so at the end to check your work. Marks for examination work are usually lower than for normal classwork, simply because of bad organisation, lack of time and carelessness. Make clear, neat corrections. If you want to insert extra material, use an asterisk at the point in the writing where you want the insert to begin and write it neatly at the end of your answers.

Chapter 2
Examination practice

By now it should be clear that there is no substitute for examination practice, especially in the last few weeks leading up to the big day. If your teacher can mark your work for you then so much the better, but even if that is not possible the practice is still vitally important. This is because writing under examination conditions is so different from writing coursework in class. This section starts in the examination room but – this time – there is a guiding voice at your shoulder showing you how to think your way through the examination.

It's June. Although it is only nine o'clock it is already quite warm in the sports hall and the sun is beating through the windows behind the wall bars, making regular shadows on the rows of examination desks set out all around you. The examination paper is face down in front of you. This is it. Your day of reckoning. You've prepared as well as you can for this paper by practising on sample papers. Your coursework was all right as well. Now, it is down to this...

ENGLISH

PAPER ONE: READING AND WRITING NON-LITERARY AND MEDIA TEXTS
(2 HOURS)

Candidates will be required to answer all the questions in Section A and **one** question from Section B.

SECTION A

Save our youth clubs!

Below are a number of news items and extracts relating to the closing of the city's youth service. Read them carefully and use your reading to help you answer all the questions below.

> ### *Radio WRMB News Bulletin – January 12th*
> Walton City Council today recommended the shutting down of the City's Youth Service with the loss of over 200 jobs. Twelve youth centres will close from April 1st and some part-time workers will be made redundant before then. The cuts – part of a package involving educational administration and school meals – will save almost £2 million of the £8 million savings which the council has been told to make in the coming financial year.

Walton Observer – 18th January

ACTION TO SAVE YOUTH SERVICE

YOUTH workers have launched a massive protest campaign to fight plans to scrap the City's Youth Service. The plan, part of the City Council's attempt to keep within government spending limits, is intended to save £1.7 million.

The workers and their supporters packed into one of the City's teacher centres on Saturday to draw up battle plans. At the meeting, the Council's principal youth worker, Alison Hubbard, described the situation as unthinkable. "The service has been going on for over half a century. Families, teachers, the police and social services all rely on us to keep almost a thousand youngsters off the streets on any weekday night. I want us to make as firm a stand as possible," she said.

And she warned that once the service had gone, it would be impossible to get it back.

Lobbying

Youth workers will now be lobbying local councillors, MPs, the Prime Minister and even the Royal family in a bid to save their already heavily cut service.

In a highly organised campaign which will culminate in a massive rally in Market Street, the workers plan to bring the message home both nationally and locally.

Kevin Grimley, one of the organisers, said: "The youth service provides an essential safety net for some youngsters who might otherwise be involved in all sorts of trouble. It gives them a regular meeting place apart from parks and bus shelters and keeps them away from pubs and alcohol. What's more, it provides excellent returns when you see what it does and realise that schools are spending over £100 million a year".

The cuts that kill

The Observer speaks...

IT IS HARD not to feel a degree of sympathy for those who have campaigned so tirelessly on behalf of the city's youth service over the past few weeks. They have made clear to all that the Youth Service is popular, well-used and excellent value for money.

At the same time, one has to recognise that, when savings must be made, the non-essential services are likely to be the first to go. Our city is obliged by law to provide access to education, to clear refuse from the streets and to help fund the police force. It is not compelled to open halls and community centres for young people in the evenings, to provide coffee bars, table tennis tables and programmes of social events and entertainment.

It is necessary, therefore, to judge the Youth Service provision alongside the provision of bus passes and home helps for pensioners or of 'meals on wheels' for the housebound. Then, the issue becomes one of financial priorities for the community as a whole.

When such priorities are determined, one must appreciate that young people have the spark and energy to fight their own battles. The young people of Walton have shown in the past few weeks that, even without financial assistance, their effort and determination can bring an issue to the forefront of debate.

Perhaps that same dynamism can be focused on the continued voluntary youth provision which now offers the best hope for the future.

Walton Observer – 10th February

30,000 strong protest fails to stop the unkindest cut of all

WALTON City Youth Service will be killed off despite bitter protests from thousands of people. The City Council pushed ahead with the cuts at its meeting yesterday after receiving a 33,756-signature petition on the steps of City Hall, the Council's headquarters in Market Street.

CHARLES WATTS, Chairman of the Education Committee, told the meeting: "It is not our proposal to abandon the youth of Walton or abandon our responsibility for youth provision, but we cannot conjure up resources out of thin air.

"We had to make a hard choice and we had to protect our schools and the children in them from further financial cuts. The Youth Service is well used and popular, but it is the icing on the cake of our educational provision. We have asked schools to take over the running of the Youth Service and we are prepared to keep one officer on to co-ordinate the new arrangements."

But other members of the council claimed young people would be forced on to the streets where they could be enticed into taking drugs and alcohol or rioting. Councillor Ronald Wood said: "There will be fewer leisure opportunities for teenagers and no support, advice or

guidance for these young people when things go wrong. Then sparks will fly and somebody will have to pick up the pieces. The police, social services or Alcoholics Anonymous?"

Councillor Mary Faithful argued: "The impact on the Youth Service will be disastrous. The professional workers are the core of the Youth Service and hold it together."

Other council members defended the cuts, saying tough choices had to be made to try and protect schools, but opponents claimed that schools would be indirectly affected, especially those community schools which currently offered youth services on site. Councillor Jack Bruce said: "These proposals are indirectly impoverishing the whole of the quality of life for thousands of families – not just the teenagers – in this community".

The recommendation that the cuts be made still has to be finally approved by the City Council's Policy and Resources

Committee but that is usually just a formality.

Youth workers face redundancy

Unions representing youth workers have been told to expect large-scale redundancies, the City Council announced yesterday. Redundancy notices will be issued almost immediately in order to give the required three months' notice for permanent staff. Keith Relf, Branch Secretarial for the Community and Youth Workers Union, said: "It looks like large-scale redundancies but it is still not clear what the new proposed Youth Service will look like, or whether it will need any staff at all".

There are currently 25 full-time and 183 part-time youth workers in the city and, with unemployment figures already high, their prospects of finding other work are considered slim.

Walton Observer – 25th January

Dear Editor,

Of course no one wants to see the City Youth Service disbanded for the sake of it but people must recognise that money does not grow on trees and that local government has to make choices.

At the end of the day, someone has to pay the bill and, as a regular contributor to the City Council funds, I think that this saving is a sensible one.

It is the school's job to educate these young children and they should be at home doing their homework on weekday evenings not wandering the streets and hanging round at these clubs or getting into trouble with the police.

Maybe, if things improve, the Youth Service could start up again or perhaps it could be included in what the schools provide and they could stay open in the evenings?

Yours faithfully,
Katie Warren (Mrs)
12 Elizabeth Street, Strawton.

1 What are the main reasons put forward for keeping the Youth Service? Summarise them in a series of short paragraphs.

2 Set out and write a leaflet which can be printed and handed out on the day of the proposed demonstration. It should have three sections with these headings:

What's happening to our youth clubs

Why we are fighting

How can you help

Make each section about 100 words in length and give your leaflet an eye-catching slogan. Make your writing both informative and persuasive.

3 Look closely at the newspaper editorial and the letter from Mrs Warren. Write a fully argued reply to be published in the newspaper. Refer to the points they make, as well as giving your own opinion.

Set your letter out formally, including your address and that of the newspaper. The newspaper's address is:

City Centre House,
36 Avignon Boulevard,
Walton,
WA31 8PQ

SECTION B

4 Imagine that the *Walton Observer* has asked you to write a feature article presenting the views of young people about the proposal to cut the Youth Service. Write the article, including some background information about the plans and the opposition to them and the views of some of your friends, teachers and adults. Give the article a headline.

5 Imagine that you became closely involved with the campaign to save Walton's youth service. Write some diary entries describing two or three significant days of events in the campaign, including the day of the demonstration. Write about your feelings and reactions, as well as describing what happened.

"Turn over your papers and begin. You have two hours."

9:31 All this writing. All these questions. Oh no, not youth clubs. Never been to one.
Now wait, take a deep breath and relax. Look carefully at what you have to do. What have you been given?

9:35 Right, I'll try to calm down. There's a page of questions – tasks, I mean. There are five. No, wait a minute. I only have to answer one from Section B, so that makes four in all. That's about half an hour each. No, wait. There's the same number of marks available for each section, so I need to spend an hour on each section – well, maybe 50 minutes' writing time.
What else is there?

9:36 Um. A sheet with all the details on. There's some newspaper stories and a letter.
Good. What are you going to do now?

9:37 Get stuck into question one? Start scribbling down reasons as I read these newspaper stories? No, I remember. First look at the tasks, then the material. So, what have I got to do? Write a list of reasons, then a leaflet and then a letter. That's not so bad. Right. Let's read the material.
Read it slowly and carefully. Think about what you are reading. Notice that you have got two newspaper articles and one editorial. That will give somebody's opinion. Then, there is a news story from a radio bulletin and a letter – that will be opinion as well. As you read, underline the reasons you notice and highlight things that ought to be in your leaflet. Take your time.

9:45 Right. I've done that. But that's a quarter of an hour gone, and I haven't written anything. Ben is scribbling fast, Amy is staring into space holding her pen and Louise has already got the correcting fluid out.
Don't worry. There is plenty of time. Now look at Question One. What have you got to do?

9:46 Write the main reasons... well, here goes. I'll just write 1–10 down the page and fill them in as I find them.
Hold on. Look at the task again. What sort of writing does it want from you? It doesn't ask for a list but a summary in a number of short paragraphs.
Oh, yes.
So what should you do?

9:48 Read through, make notes, then write them into a summary. Put the most important reasons first?
Exactly.

9:49 But there isn't time for that! Oh, well. Here goes. What's this? 200 jobs lost. Is that a reason? Yes, it could be. Think REASONS WHY. Think that 'because' is going to be the start of every reason. 'The youth service should be kept because 200 valuable jobs and the skills of the youth workers will be lost forever.' Yes, that's a reason but not a very important one. Make a note, '200 jobs'.
Here's another. It has gone on for half a century – that's 50 years. Make a note, 'well established'.

9:50 Everyone relies on the service... so what? Ah, here's the reason why. The youth service keeps youngsters off the street. Make a note, 'many clients'. Once it's gone it can't come back. That's a reason which links with the 200 jobs note. Link them together!

9:52 Keeps kids out of trouble... away from pubs... these reasons link to the 'many clients' point and keeping youngsters off the street. What's this? There could be trouble ahead. Tie that in as well. Let's start writing these down into an answer.
Hold on. Try to structure them more.
What do you mean? I see. Group them in some way?
Yes. How many groups of reasons are there?

9:54 Er..., three. Reasons to do with the youth workers losing their jobs, to do with the effects

on the young people, the effect on society as a whole. Wait, there's another one. The amount of money involved is relatively small.
Anything else to think about?

9:55 No. Wait, yes. Putting them in order. Young people, effects on society, consequences for youth workers and then a last point about money. Let's get writing.
And remember, short, separate paragraphs.
Thanks.

10:05 Right, that's done. All the information down neat and tidy. Single line through the notes and then Question 2, here I come. I feel better already!
Question 2…, a leaflet. That's like a poster. Big headline, STUFF THE COUNCIL. That'll be good. Big picture of a riot going on as well. Border it in red – to show blood will be spilled if they go ahead!
Hold on. Look again. Put your pen down and think. It is a leaflet, not a poster. It has to have three sections, each about 100 words long. It needs a slogan and has to be both persuasive and informative. Imagine who it is for. Mrs Bhamra is out shopping and she sees these young people outside City Hall. Someone gives her a sheet of paper. What does she need to know?

10:06 What's happening? Why is there a demo? What she can do to help the young people if she wants to?
Precisely. Now you can see why the leaflet is structured like it is. The first bit is information, the second explanation, and the third persuasion. Remember that you have to show the examiner what you can do well and here is a chance to show you can cope with three different sorts of writing. Get on with those in note form. Leave the slogan until you have finished, rather than spend a long time now.

10:15 Done that. And I've thought of a slogan, 'The young are the adults of tomorrow – look after them well.'
Good, now write your final version. Check you are being informative – using facts and numbers and avoiding comment in the first part. Check that you are explaining in the second part – could the word 'because' go in front of what you say? Check that you are being persuasive in the third part – using phrases like, 'you should help', 'we need your help' and 'support us now!'

10:25 That's done. I've shortened the slogan, as well – 'Youth today, voters tomorrow' and I've underlined the word 'because' three times in the middle section to make it more eye-catching. The last section was a bit long – about 120 words – so I neatly crossed out one sentence. I think I'm a bit behind time, though.
Don't worry. Now you know the material, things won't take as long.
Question 3. Write a letter. Can I just bang this off and say what a daft old trout she is?
No. Look at what you have to show here. That you can argue against her points as well as giving your opinion and the letter must be formally set out – that means writing both your address and the newspaper's address at the top. Start with a rough draft of the points she makes and your responses to them.

10:30 That's done. She only really makes three points – about the money, about it being the school's job and about how the service could be restarted and I can answer all of them with arguments of my own.
Carry on. Remember to be polite in what you say and remember that you are writing to the Editor, not Mrs Warren. Start the letter, 'Dear Sir,' and end with 'Yours faithfully,' because you have not written to a named person. Write in separate paragraphs as you deal with Mrs Warren's points.

10:40 Thanks. I almost forgot the paragraphs! Now, Section B. I like writing imaginatively, so I think I'll do Question 5. Do you think that's a fair choice?
Certainly. Where you are given a choice, choose the task you will do best. But, again, think hard about what you are being asked for: not just to write a story but to weave in the events of the campaign and your feelings. AND you have to write in a diary format, with entries covering a couple of days.

10:45 Right, and I'll make my feelings change from hope to disappointment as it goes on. That'll be good. First I'll jot down some of the things I want to put in, from the material.

Sorry to interrupt, but it's 11.15. You ought to be winding it up by now.

Yes, I was getting carried away. It's fine as it is. So what next?
Read through all your answers. This is a check that you have covered all the relevant points and that you have not made mistakes in spelling and punctuation. In particular, check words which have been given to you in the passage and always expect to add some punctuation!

That's done. On the leaflet I'd left out about the Youth Service cut only saving £1.7 million, but I was able to slot it in neatly. I'd also called Mrs Warren, Miss Waren in one place in the letter! I spelled demonstration wrong as well and had to add quite a bit of punctuation towards the end of Question 5 where I got involved in the writing. It's fine now.
Well done!

"Please put your pens down. Don't speak until the papers have been collected..."

Of course, in reality you will not have a chance to talk over the questions with anyone else once you are in the examination room. But this is the kind of conversation you need to practise having with yourself.

The next paper is a slightly different one, based on reading. It uses a **pre-released extract** (sent to schools in advance) and an unseen passage (printed with the examination paper) to test your ability to read in detail and to respond to what you have read. With some examining groups all the material is unseen and with others the pre-released material comes in a larger anthology on which more of the examination is based.

As you read through this paper, note down exactly what you think the examiner wants you to do. If you do this while looking at the Statements of Attainment for Reading (given below), you can begin to see how the questions are covering these statements at a range of levels. Next, work through the paper for practice and compare your writing with the highlighted statements. What are you showing that you can do?

Statements of attainment for Attainment Target 2: Reading

Level 7

(a) read a range of fiction, poetry, literary nonfiction and drama, including pre-twentieth century literature, explaining their preferences through talking and writing, with reference to detail.

(b) **talk and write about literature and other texts, giving evidence of personal response and showing an understanding of the author's approach.**

(c) show in discussion that they can recognise features of presentation which are used to inform, to regulate, to reassure or to persuade, in non-literary and media texts.

(d) **select, retrieve and combine information independently from a wide range of reference materials.**

(e) **show in discussion or in writing an awareness of writers' use of sound patterns and some other literary devices and the effect on the reader.**

Level 8

(a) read a range of fiction, poetry, literary nonfiction and drama, including pre-twentieth century literature.

(b) **talk and write about literature and other texts, giving evidence of personal response and showing an understanding of the devices and structures used by the writers, with appropriate reference to details.**

(c) show in discussion and writing an ability to form a considered opinion about features of presentation which are used to inform, regulate, reassure or persuade, in non-literary and media texts.

(d) **select, retrieve, evaluate and combine information independently and with discrimination, from a comprehensive range of reference materials.**

(e) discuss and write about changes in the grammar of English over time, encountered in the course of their reading.

Level 9

(a) read a range of fiction, poetry, literary nonfiction and drama, including pre-twentieth century literature.

(b) **talk and write clearly about literature and other texts, giving sustained evidence of personal response and showing an understanding of the devices and structures used by the writer, making comparisons within texts and between different texts.**

(c) show in discussion and in writing an ability to recognise techniques and conventions of presentation in non-literary and media texts, and judge the effectiveness of their use.

(d) **select, retrieve, evaluate and combine information independently and with discrimination, from a comprehensive range of reference materials, making effective use of the information.**

(e) **demonstrate some understanding of the use of lexical and grammatical effects in the language of literature.**

Level 10

(a) read a range of fiction, poetry, literary nonfiction and drama, including pre-twentieth century literature.

(b) **talk and write cogently and knowledgeably about literature and other texts, giving sustained evidence of personal response and showing an understanding of the devices and structures used by the writer, making comparisons within texts and between different texts.**

(c) show in discussion and in writing an ability to evaluate techniques and conventions of presentation in non-literary and media texts, and judge the effectiveness of their use.

(d) **select, retrieve, evaluate and combine information independently and with discrimination, from a comprehensive range of reference materials, making effective and sustained use of the information.**

(e) **demonstrate in discussion and in writing some understanding of attitudes in society towards language change and of ideas about appropriateness and correctness in language use.**

ENGLISH

PAPER TWO: READING AND WRITING LITERATURE
2 HOURS

Candidates will be required to answer **all** the questions in Section A and **one** question from Section B.

SECTION A

Refer to this extract from A *Breath of French Air* and answer Questions 1–3.

A Breath of French Air, H E Bates (Michael Joseph, 1959)

This passage is taken from *A Breath of French Air* by H E Bates. It describes how the Larkin family go on holiday to France. In the extract, Pop Larkin, Ma, their seven children and Charley (otherwise known as Mr Charlton and their daughter Mariette's husband) have their first meal at the Hotel Beau Rivage, somewhere in Northern France.

Nearly an hour later, when Ma brought the children downstairs for dinner, closely followed by Charley and Mariette, Pop was already sitting moodily in a corner of the *salle à manger,* a room of varnished, ginger-coloured matchboard and glass built like a greenhouse shrouded with yellowing lace curtains against the westward side of the hotel. Some squares of glass were coloured blue or ruby. A few, broken altogether, had been patched up with squares of treacle-brown paper and it seemed generally that the whole ramshackle structure, battered by the Atlantic storm, might at any moment fall down, disintegrate, and blow away.

Driven by ravenous hunger and thirst to the bar, Pop had found it furnished with a solitary stool, a yard of dusty counter, a dozing grey cat, and a vase of last year's heather. The stool had two legs instead of three and all about the place was that curious pungent odour that Ma had been so quick to notice earlier in the day: as if a drain had been left open or a gas-tap on.

In the *salle à manger*, in contrast to the silent half-darkness of the bar, a noisy, eager battle was being waged by seven or eight French families against the howl of wind and rain, the tossing lace curtains, and more particularly against what appeared to be dishes of large unpleasant pink spiders, in reality *langoustines*. A mad cracking of claws filled the air and one plump Frenchman sat eating, wearing his cap, a large white one: as if for protection against something, perhaps flying claws or bread or rain.

Three feet from Pop's table a harassed French waitress with a marked limp and loose peroxide hair came to operate, every desperate two minutes or so, a large patent wooden-handled bread-slicer about the size of an old-fashioned sewing machine; a cross somewhere between a guillotine and a chaff-cutter.

This instrument made crude groaning noises, like an old tram trying to start. Slices of bread, savagely chopped from yard-long loaves, flew about in all directions, dropping all over the place until harassed waiters and waitresses bore them hurriedly off to eager, waiting guests. These, Pop noticed, at once crammed them ravenously into their mouths and even gluttonously mopped their plates with them.

Presently the rest of the family arrived: Mariette immaculate and perfumed in a beautiful sleeveless low-cut dress of emerald green that made her shoulders and upper breast glow a warm olive colour, Ma in a mauve woollen dress and a royal blue jumper on top to keep out the cold. Ma had plenty of Chanel No. 5 on, still convinced that the hotel smelled not only of mice but a lot of other things besides.

As the family walked in all the French families suddenly stopped eating. The French, Charley had once told Pop, were the elite of Europe. Now they stopped ramming bread into their mouths like famished prisoners and gaped at the bare, astral shoulders of Mariette, Ma's great mauve and blue balloon of a body, and the retinue of children behind it.

Most of the older French women, Pop thought, seemed to be wearing discoloured woollen sacks. The younger ones, who were nearly all tallow-coloured, bruise-eyed, and flat-chested, wore jeans. It was hard to tell any of them from boys and in consequence Pop felt more than usually proud of Mariette, who looked so fleshily, elegantly, and provocatively a girl.

Presently the waitress with the limp brought the menu and then with not a moment to spare hopped off to work the bread machine.

'Well, what's to eat, Charley-boy?' Pop said, rubbing his hands. 'Somethink good I hope, old man, I'm starving.'

Mr Charlton consulted the menu with a certain musing, studious air of English calm.

'By the way, Charley,' Pop said, 'what's "eat" in French? Haven't learned any words today.'

It was Pop's honest resolve to learn, if possible, a few new French words every day.

'*Manger*,' Charley said. 'Same word as the thing in the stable – manger.'

Pop sat mute and astounded. Manger – a simple thing like that. Perfickly wonderful.

Unbelievable. Manger. He sat back and prepared to listen to Charley reading out the menu with the awe he deserved.

'Well, to begin with there are *langoustines*. They're a kind of small lobster. Speciality of the Atlantic coast. Then there's *saucisson à la mode d'ici* – that's a sort of sausage they do here. *Spécialité de la maison*, I shouldn't wonder. Hot, I expect. Probably awfully good. Then *pigeons à la Gautier* – I expect that's pigeons in some sort of wine sauce. And afterwards fruit and cheese.'

'Sounds jolly *bon*,' Pop said.

Charley said he thought it ought to satisfy and Ma at once started remonstrating with Montgomery, Primrose, Victoria, and the twins about eating so much bread. She said they'd never want their dinners if they went on stuffing bread down.

'What shall we drink?' Charley said.

'Port,' Pop said. He too was stuffing down large quantities of bread, trying to stave off increasing stabs and rumbles of hunger. Ma agreed about the port. It would warm them all up, she said.

'I doubt if they'll have port.'

'Good God,' Pop said. '*What*? I thought you said the Froggies lived on wine?'

'Well, they do. But it's their own. Port isn't. I suggest we drink *vin rosé*. That'll go well with the fish and the pigeon.'

The harassed waitress with the limp, freed momentarily of bread-cutting, arrived a moment later to tell Charley, in French, that there were, after all, no *langoustines*.

'Sorry, no more *langoustines*,' Mr Charlton said. 'They've got *friture* instead.'

'What's *friture*?'

'Fried sardines.'

Ma choked; she felt she wanted to be suddenly and violently sick.

'Oh! Fresh ones of course,' Charley said. 'Probably caught this afternoon.'

'In that lot?' Pop said and waved a disbelieving hand in the general direction of the howling, blackening gale that threatened increasingly to blow away the *salle à manger*.

A second later a vast flash of lightning seemed to sizzle down the entire length of roof glass like a celestial diamond-cutter. A Frenchwoman rose hysterically and rushed from the room.

The chaff-cutter guillotine attacked yet another loaf with louder and louder groans and a long black burst of thunder struck the hotel to the depth of its foundations.

Alarmed too, the children ate more bread. Pop ate more bread and was in fact still eating bread when the *friture* arrived.

'They're only tiddlers!' the twins said. 'They're only tiddlers!'

'Sardines never grow any bigger,' Charley said, 'otherwise they wouldn't be sardines.'

'About time they did then,' Ma said, peering dubiously at piled scraps of fish, 'that's all.'

'*Bon appétit!*' Mr Charlton said, and proceeded enthusiastically to attack the *friture*.

Pop, turning to the attack too, found himself facing a large plateful of shrivelled dark brown objects which immediately fell to pieces at the touch of a fork. Scorched fragments of fish flew flakily about in all directions. The few crumbs that he was able to capture, impale on his fork and at last transfer to his mouth tasted, he thought, exactly like the unwanted scraps left over at the bottom of a bag of fish-and-chips.

'Shan't get very fat on these,' Ma said.

In a low depressed voice Pop agreed. Ma's great bulk, which filled half the side of one length of the table, now and then quivered in irritation and presently she was eating the *friture* with her fingers, urging the children to do likewise.

The children, in silent despair, ate more bread. Savagely the guillotine bread-cutter worked overtime, drowning conversation. And presently the limping waitress brought the *vin rosé*, which Charley tasted.

'Delicious,' he said with mounting enthusiasm. 'Quite delicious.'

At last the multitudinous remains of the *friture* were taken away, plates piled high with brown wreckage, and Ma said it looked like the feeding of the five thousand. Pop drank deep of *vin rosé*, raised his glass to everybody, and unable to think of very much to say remarked mournfully:

'Well, cheers, everybody. Well, here we are.'

'We certainly are,' Ma said. 'You never spoke a truer word.'

After a short interval the *saucisson à la mode d'ici* arrived. This consisted of a strange object looking like a large pregnant sausage-roll, rather scorched on top. Slight puffs of steam seemed to be issuing from the exhausts at either end.

Ma remarked that at least it was hot and Pop, appetite now whetted to the full by another sharp draught or two of *vin rosé*, prepared to attack the object on his plate by cutting it directly through the middle.

To his complete dismay the force of the cut, meeting hard resistance from the surface of scorched crust, sent the two pieces hurtling in the air. Both fell with a low thud to the floor.

'Don't touch it! Don't touch it!' Ma said. 'Mice everywhere.'

I'll order another,' Charley said. '*Ma'moiselle!*'

In silent patience Pop waited, but by the time a waitress could be spared from the bondage of bread-cutting the rest of the family had finished the battle with the *saucisson à la mode d'ici*.

With gloom, drinking more *vin rosé* to fortify himself, Pop waited while Charley explained to the waitress the situation about the unfortunate disappearance of his second course.

The waitress seemed dubious, even unimpressed. She simply stared coldly at Pop's empty plate as if knowing perfectly well he had eaten what had been on there and crushingly uttered the single word 'Supplement'.

'She says if you have another you'll have to pay extra,' Charley said.

'Better order another bottle of vin rosy instead, Charley,' Pop said.

Weakly he started to eat more bread. He had, he thought, never eaten so much bread in his life. He no longer wondered why the guillotine worked overtime.

Suddenly thunder roared again, faintly echoed by the rumblings of his own belly, and presently the little man in pince-nez appeared, making his furtive mole-like way from table to table.

When he saw the Larkins, however, he stood some distance off, in partly obsequious retreat, an uneasy grimace on his face, his hands held together.

Once he bowed. Mr Charlton bowed too and Ma grinned faintly in reply.

'Nice to see that,' Mr Charlton said. 'Typical French. He's come to see if everything's all right.'

'Why don't we tell him?' Ma said.

'What do we have next?' the twins said. 'What do we have next?'

'Pigeons,' Pop said. The thought of stewed pigeons made his mouth water. In wine sauce too. 'Pigeons.'

'We want baked beans on toast!' the twins said. 'And cocoa.'

'Quiet!' Pop thundered. 'I'll have order.'

A moment later a waitress, arriving with a fourth plate of bread, proceeded to announce to Mr Charlton a fresh and disturbing piece of news. There were, after all, no pigeons.

Pop felt too weak to utter any kind of exclamation about this second, deeper disappointment.

'There's rabbit,' Charley told him, 'instead.'

Instantly Pop recoiled in pale, fastidious horror.

'Not after myxo!' he said. 'No! Charley, I couldn't. I can't touch 'em after myxo!'

Myxomatosis, the scourge of the rabbit tribe, had affected Pop very deeply. No one else in the family had been so moved by the plague and its results. But to Pop the thought of eating rabbits was now as great a nausea as the thought of eating nightingales.

'It started here in France too,' he said. 'The Froggies were the ones who first started it.'

'Have an omelette,' Charley said cheerfully.

'They don't suit him,' Ma said. 'They always give him heartburn.'

Pop could only murmur in a low, dispassionate voice that he had to have something, somehow, soon. Heartburn or no heartburn. Even an omelette.

'A steak then,' Charley said. 'With chips.'

At this Pop cheered up a little, saying that a steak would suit him.

'Alors, *un filet bifteck* pour monsieur,' Charley said, 'avec *pommes frites.*'

'Biff-teck! Biff-teck!' the twins started shouting, punching each other, laughing loudly. 'Biff-teck! Biff-you! Biff-you! Biff-teck!'

Pop was too weak to cry 'Quiet!' this time and from a distance the man in pince-nez stared in disapproval at the scene, so that Ma said:

'Ssh! Mr Dupont's looking.'

'That isn't Mr Dupont,' Charley said. 'He's only the manager. Mr Dupont's dead.'

'Die of over-eating?' Ma said.

Pop laughed faintly.

'The hotel is run by a Miss Dupont—Mademoiselle Dupont,' Charley explained. 'But it seems she's away in Brest for the day.'

'When the cat's away,' Ma said.

'Well,' Charley said, 'I wouldn't be at all surprised if that didn't explain a slight lack of liaison.'

Pop, too low in spirits even to admire Charley's turn of phrase, drank deeply of *vin rosé*.

'Better order some more of the juice, Charley old man,' he said. 'Got to keep going somehow.'

'Biff-teck! Biff-teck! Biff-you! Biff-teck!'

'Quiet!' Pop said sharply and from across the *salle à manger* several French mammas looked quickly round at him with full sudden glances, clearly electrified.

Half an hour later he had masticated his way through a bloody piece of beef roughly the shape of a boot's sole, the same thickness, and about as interesting. He ate the chips that accompanied it down to the last frizzled crumb and even dipped his bread in the half-cold blood.

Ma said she hoped he felt better for it but Pop could hardly do more than nod, drinking again of *vin rosé*.

'Don't even have ketchup,' he said, as if this serious gastronomic omission were the final straw.

1 What impression does the passage give of the hotel and the French guests who are also eating there?

2 (a) In a few words, how would you describe Pop's reaction to the holiday so far? How does this reaction contrast with Charley's and Ma's?

   (b) What impression do you get of Pop's character and personality? How is this brought out strongly in the way in which he speaks, contrasted with the language Charley uses?

3 Did you enjoy reading this extract? Discuss in some detail your reasons for answering yes or no.

Now read the following extract which is taken from another book about the Larkin family. Two neighbours, the Brigadier and Angela Snow, stay for dinner.

Soon the delicious unbearable fragrance of roasting pheasant was filling the house. Every few minutes the Brigadier sniffed openly at it like a dog. It seemed as if a long night, a grey mixture of solitude, sandwich lunches, bone-hard apple pies and cold bacon, was at last breaking and passing him by. He hardly noticed the arrival of a fourth and then a fifth whisky and it was from the remotest ends of a waking dream that he heard Pop calling with ebullient cheerfulness to Mr Charlton:

'Shall we have pink tonight, Charley boy? Why not? Get three or four bottles on the ice quick. Ought to go well with the pheasants, I think, don't you?'

'Darling, if that was champagne you were referring to I shall remain faithful to you for ever,' Angela Snow said. 'I adore the pink. It's absolutely me. Quite my favourite tipple.'

The Brigadier might well have wept again except that now, by some miracle, there was nothing to weep for. Had there ever been? He simply couldn't believe there ever had. He was beginning to feel alive again, terrifically alive. Pink champagne? By God, that took him back a thousand aching years. He was again a crazy subaltern on Indian hill-stations, lean and active as a panther: dances and parties everywhere, polo and pig-sticking, affairs with two married women running at the same time, servants everywhere as plentiful as beetles. He was the gay dog having champagne for breakfast, with a certain madness in the air, and nobody giving a damn.

'Glad to see you're perking up, General,' Ma said as she passed him with two deep glass dishes of strawberries, each containing half a dozen pounds. 'Got your glass topped up?' 'Splendid,' the Brigadier said. 'Splendid. Absolutely splendid.'

'Don't spoil your appetite, though, will you?' she said. 'Supper'll only be ten minutes or so.'

The Brigadier found it suddenly impossible to believe how swiftly the evening had gone. The time had whipped along like prairie fire. He took his watch out of his breast pocket and discovered it to be already eight o'clock. Spoil his appetite? He could have eaten horses.

Ma had cooked two brace of pheasants, together with chipolata sausages, thin game chips, potatoes creamed with fresh cream and the first Brussels sprouts with chestnuts. Brimming boats of gravy and bread sauce came to table as Pop started to carve the birds, the breasts of which crumbled under the knife as softly as fresh-baked bread.

'Tot the champagne out, Charley boy,' Pop said. 'And what about you, General? Which part of the bird for you? Leg or bosom?'

The Brigadier immediately confessed to a preference for bosom and a moment later found, his eye roving warmly across the table, in the direction of Angela Snow, who met the gaze full-faced and unflushed, though with not quite the elegant composure she always wore. This started his juices flowing again and with a brief peremptory bark he found himself suddenly on his feet, champagne glass waving.

'To our hostess. I give you a blessing, madam. And honour. And glory. And long, long health –'

The unaccustomed extravagance of the Brigadier's words trailed off, unfinished. Everybody rose and drank to Ma. The Brigadier then declared that the pink champagne was terrific and immediately crouched with eager reverence over his plate, the edges of which were only barely visible, a thin embroidered line of white enclosing a whole rich field of game, vegetables, sauce, and gravy.

Later, strawberries lay on the Brigadier's plate like fat fresh red rose-buds, dewed white with sugar. The visionary sherry-coloured figure of Angela Snow came to pour the thickest yellow cream on them, her voluptuous bare forearm brushing his hand. Then as she went away to take her place at the table a sudden spasm of double vision made him see two of her: a pair of tall golden twins of disturbing elegance who actually waved hands at him and said:

'You're doing fine, Brigadier, my Sweet. Does my heart good to see you. This afternoon I thought you were for the coal-hole.'

What on earth she meant by the coal-hole he didn't know and cared even less. He only knew he was doing fine. The strawberries were simply magnificent; they came straight from the lap of the gods. Only the gods could send strawberries like that, in October, to be washed down by champagne, and soon he was eating a second dishful, then a third.

'The General's away,' Ma kept saying with cheerful peals of laughter, 'the General's away.'

4 Compare and contrast this meal with the previous one. As you plan your answer, think about:

   the meal and the way it is described;

   the moods of the Larkins and their guests;

   how the writer uses language.

SECTION B

5 On the days after their disastrous meal the Larkins visit other restaurants. One specialises in seafood, while another claims to offer 'traditional' English food. Write your account of what happens on either occasion.

6 Imagine that you are a member of one of the French families eating in the hotel. Write your account of the evening.

Chapter 3
Assessing your progress

As you practice for the examination, you may often find it useful to compare what you do with the Statements of Attainment for Reading and Writing (see pp. 14–17). Asking your teacher to look over your work will also be valuable. Sometimes you can obtain mark schemes as well as sample questions from the examining groups but these, because they are designed for teachers to use, may not be that much help. The next section looks at how to use self-assessment to improve your level.

Making the level

What makes someone buy and read a book like this? Well, the fact that you are reading it at all shows a number of positive things about you and your attitude to your work. You must be a committed student with a strong desire to succeed. You also recognise that by following advice you will be able to improve your chances of doing well.

You may have very particular reasons for reading this book. Many of you will need a particular grade in English in order to secure a place in further or higher education, or to be considered for a job you have set your sights on.

Some people in this group will need a better grade in English than in any other subject: if that Grade B in English materialises, they will be happy with Grade C for the other subjects.

There will also be some people who are very much better at other subjects than at English (often maths and science subjects) but who have frustrating problems with English: they know they are heading for Grade A in every other subject, but just cannot get on with the kind of work English requires, even though they know they will need a Grade B or C for a place in higher education.

Another group of readers will always have been 'good at' English, and love reading and writing. This group wants to continue their study of the subject after GCSE. They will do everything they can to ensure the best possible result.

If you recognise yourself as belonging to one of these groups you will want to know the same thing: is there anything more you can do, besides working hard, to get the grade you have set your sights on?

That is what this section of the book is about. While there is certainly no simple 'trick' which guarantees examination success every time, there are things you can do to find out more about how levels are awarded. One very easy thing to start with is to look closely at your examination syllabus – you should have done that by now after reading Section One. The other place to look is in the Statements of Attainment. These show you what qualities teachers will be looking for in your work when they award levels.

One consequence is that different types of work allow you to demonstrate different skills. You will also notice that the skills are cumulative. This means that each level builds something else on what you were expected to do for the level below. So, for Level 7 you must do more than for Level 6 but if you gain a C grade, you will also be able to do everything described in Levels 4–6 as well. At the higher levels, some skills appear which are not mentioned at all lower down, while some skills just become more sophisticated.

If you are to make much practical use of this knowledge to improve your grading, it is obvious that you will have to become skilled in the art of assessing your own work.

The skills you have to show

The place to begin is with the Statements of Attainment. This the 'mark scheme' against which the examiner and your teacher will measure your progress. There are some important boundaries here, but the most crucial is between Level 6 and Level 7. What do you have to do, in coursework or examination, to justify the higher level? Below are printed the Statements of Attainment for Reading and Writing at Level 7. The bold print shows what you have to do – over and above the Level 6 requirement – to obtain Level 7.

Statement of attainment for Attainment Target 2 Reading
Level 7

(a) read a range of fiction, poetry, **literary nonfiction and drama, including pre-twentieth century literature**, explaining their preferences through talking and writing, with reference to detail.

   To make Level 7, you will have to have read some pre-twentieth century writing, as well as some Shakespeare. You might do some coursework on famous poetry (poems by Wordsworth or Coleridge, for example) or read a novel by a writer like Thomas Hardy.

(b) talk and write about literature and other texts, giving evidence of personal response and **showing an understanding of the author's approach**.

   Many of the Level 7 statements want you to be able to stand back from your subject. If you read *Animal Farm*, to achieve this statement you would have to write about what George Orwell was trying to tell his readers about people by writing a story in which animals took charge of their farm. You would have to write about why *Lord of the Flies* is more than just an adventure story about a stranded group of boys on a desert island. Whatever you have read, pick a coursework task for yourself which focuses on what the writer is trying to achieve. Watch out for an examination question that targets this kind of understanding as well.

(c) show in discussion that they can **recognise features of presentation** which are used to inform, to regulate, to reassure or to persuade, in non-literary and media texts.

   The same kind of skill is asked for. You have to be able to write about how an advertisement uses graphic illustrations, different sizes of print, slogans and emotive language to make its point. You could analyse the way a newspaper front page covered an important story, for example, showing how the headline, the sub-headings, the page layout and the language of the story worked together to create an effect. See how this is a more advanced skill than explaining what you like about the advertisement.

(d) select, retrieve and **combine information independently** from a wide range of reference materials.

   Retrieving and combining information are what is rewarded here. In coursework, make sure you have a task which draws on two or three sources of information. For example, you could write an essay on global warming, based on a newspaper report, some statistics and some scientific information. You could write a report on child abuse, based on eye-witness stories, social workers' views and government statements. Again, watch out in the examination for tasks which involve more than one piece of stimulus material, and make sure you draw your information from all the material you are given.

(e) show in discussion or in writing an **awareness of writers' use of sound patterns and some other literary devices and the effect on the reader**.

   This is a fancy way of saying you need to have some work which reveals a close reading of literature. That is the kind of commentary which mentions devices like similes, metaphors and the way that poets use rhyme for effect. Again, watch out for this question in an examination paper, and prepare for it by studying the anthology or pre-released materials.

Statement of attainment for Attainment Targets 3–5 Writing (including Presentation)
Level 7

(a) write in a wider variety of forms, with commitment and a **clear sense of purpose and awareness of audience, demonstrating an ability to anticipate the reader's response**.

   Much of what is new at Level 7 in writing is concerned with your attitude to writing and the way that you select a style to match an audience and to achieve an effect. Do this by making sure that your coursework tasks have a clear sense of purpose – a letter of explanation, a report, a detailed account; and an audience – a newspaper, the local council, someone else in school, younger children. For example, your writing on global warming could be written as a talk to a group of junior school pupils.

(b) **produce well-structured pieces of writing**, some of which handle **more demanding subject matter**; punctuate their writing so that meaning and structure are clear to the reader.

Here, you are being asked to go beyond a simple story structure. Your report on child abuse with sub-headings would show that you were thinking about the structure of your writing. If you wrote on a poem by dealing with different aspects of it in turn, that would have the same result. The punctuation does not have to be absolutely accurate but every sentence would need to have a capital letter and full stop.

(c) **make a more assured and selective use of a wider range of grammatical and lexical features**, characteristic of different styles, that are appropriate for topic, purpose and audience; use Standard English (except in contexts where non-standard forms are needed for literary purposes).

This is asking for variety – especially in your coursework. Show that you can write an exciting story, a clear leaflet, and a persuasive speech in Standard English. In the examination, watch out for places where you are challenged to go beyond your usual style by certain questions.

(d) demonstrate an **increased awareness** that a first draft may be changed, amended and re-ordered in a variety of ways.

This is a coursework skill. Show it emphatically by presenting a brief commentary on the changes made to a redrafted piece of work, explaining why you made the changes you did.

(e) **show in discussion and in writing an awareness of what is appropriate and inappropriate language use in written texts**.

You could show this in your speaking and listening record, perhaps by a discussion of slang and swearing in books which relates their use to the purpose of the writing and its audience.

Presentation
Level 7

(a) spell (and understand the meaning of) common roots which have been borrowed from other languages and which play an important role in word-building; recognise that **where words have been borrowed in the last 400 years, there are some characteristic sound-symbol relationships which reflect the word's origin**.

(b) check final drafts of writing for misspelling and other errors of presentation.

(c) write fluently and legibly.

(d) show an increased ability to present finished work appropriately, clearly and attractively.

Spelling needs to be largely accurate and there should not be any repetitive mistakes. So check coursework carefully and revise work done in the examination. In at least one piece of coursework, consciously focus on the presentation of a leaflet or a poster or produce your report neatly using a word processor.

The importance of choosing the right task

One thing you will have noticed is that moving up a level often involves doing a different sort of task, rather than doing the same thing better. This applies at all levels and it is also important in making sure that your coursework covers a reasonable variety of the Statements of Attainment. Whenever you are set or choose a coursework task, think hard about:

Your purpose for writing: Why are you doing this writing – apart from the fact that the teacher has told you to! Is it to inform, to persuade, to explain, or for another purpose?

Your audience: Who is the writing for? Anyone, your peers, your teacher, old people, young people? Giving a writing task an audience can often make it easier than working in a vacuum.

The form of the writing: Are you writing a story, a letter, a report, a commentary? If it is a poster or a leaflet, the form affects how you write, as well as what you have to say.

In examinations, you will often be told what form to use, or who your audience is. Think about what this tells you about the kind of writing you should be producing.

There is an enormous range of writing choice when you mix purpose, audience and form together. In general, when you have a prescribed purpose, audience and form, you are likely to be targeting the higher levels for reading and writing.

Workbench assignment

Purposes for writing

Study these alternative titles for some work on the character of Lady Macbeth in Shakespeare's play. What is the purpose and audience for each one? What form would you write in? Also, consider how different titles might meet the statements of attainment at different levels.

• Write Lady Macbeth's last letter to her husband.
• Imagine that Macbeth's plot succeeds and Lady Macbeth lives on. Write about how Banquo's heirs plot to seize the throne.
• Analyse the character of Lady Macbeth and the way it changes and develops throughout the play.
• Is there anything you like about Lady Macbeth?
• Use a series of private diary entries to trace the downfall of Lady Macbeth.
• Imagine that you are a courtier to Lady Macbeth. Write your account of the events of the play from the arrival of Macbeth's letter.
• Write Lady Macbeth's obituary as it might appear in two newspapers – one which supports Macbeth and one which is opposed to his rule.
• Pick two contemporary film actresses and say how you think they could portray Lady Macbeth in exciting new ways. If you were given the chance to play the part, what emotions and feelings would you try to convey? How would you want to dress and move around the stage?
• Imagine that Lady Macbeth lives and is put on trial for treason. Write two speeches, one defending her and the other on behalf of the prosecution.
• Analyse and compare three speeches by Lady Macbeth, identifying their key features.

The unwritten basics of good English

While it is possible to target and work towards levels in the ways outlined above, there are still some basic rules of good writing which, though not precisely covered by the levels and the statements of attainment, can still make a big difference to your eventual result. So in all of your writing, be prepared to:

• Change your style to suit your task (what you are asked to do) and your audience (the intended reader or listener).
   This means: you will need to demonstrate that you can write in a **formal** style for writing to, or for, people you don't know, and a **literary** style for writing about books, plays and poetry you have read. Of course, this is in addition to handling with confidence more everyday styles of writing, like stories or letters.
• Vary your vocabulary (the words you choose to use) enough to reflect the style you have chosen to use.
   This means: make yourself think about the words you use to **label** and **describe**. It is hard to describe what using a wider range of words means in practice but basically it is a matter of finding the best word for the job. Referring to a thesaurus as you write and reading widely are ways of increasing your word power. Other ways are using extra **adjectives** and **adverbs** (the describing words which go with nouns and verbs), or by putting **comparisons** (sometimes called **similes**, they use the words 'like' or 'as') into your work.
• Spell most common words correctly and also words which appear in the stimulus material, like the names of characters in a story or play or technical terms.
   This means: that you should not be confusing 'there' and 'their', that you should know the difference between words like 'practise' and 'practice' and that the letter 'i' normally comes before the letter 'e', except where they follow the letter 'c' in

words like 'receive'. If you are writing about a character like Lenny in *Of Mice and Men,* don't write 'Lennie', or say that the book is by 'Jon Stienbock'!

- Punctuate your work appropriately.

  This means: that you should clearly show where sentences begin and end, using capital letters and full stops or question marks, and you should punctuate direct speech so that even if it is not perfect, it is clear who is talking when.

- Structure complex sentences in a variety of ways.

  This means: that you should write in longer sentences, which are made up of sections joined by words called **connectors**. The most common connector is 'and' and a good tip is to look at where you use 'and' to see if another connector might be better.

- Write work which demonstrates all these qualities at length.

  This means: that some of your pieces must be more than 400 words long – that is not always stated, but it is what most experts think of as extended writing. A few should be up to 600 words or so in length. Anything longer will not earn you extra credit, because to write even 400 words you have to be able to think ahead, plan, and organise your writing.

- Organise ideas into a logical sequence of well-formed paragraphs.

  This means: that you should always write in paragraphs. A paragraph is a group of sentences (more than one) which have something in common. Not paragraphing makes writing hard to read, follow or understand – no wonder examiners think it is important!

- Be sensitive to tone and atmosphere when you write about books.

  This means: that you have to be able to do more than re-tell the story. You have to make comments about what happens in the book, and consider what events show about characters, not just say what characters do.

- Recognise an author's purposes in using language and to write about these in detail with examples.

  This means: that you have to comment on a writer's use of language: not only recognise that he or she uses it in a particular way, but be able to say *why* and for *what effect.*

Going for grade A

If you have ambitions in this direction, you probably realise that everything said above about getting a Grade C applies equally to raising your grade to an A, only more so! Remember that the grades are cumulative and that each higher grade adds something more to the one beneath.

Remember, as well, that you will have to demonstrate a uniformly high standard of achievement in all your work, no matter what it is. Your use of language will need to be consistently fluent and flexible enough to tackle almost any written task you are given. It should be obvious that you will have to achieve an extremely high standard of accuracy in technical skills like spelling and punctuation. If you have difficulty in either area, then you must do everything in your power to remedy your weaker points.

Your English Literature level may survive a particular weakness in spelling or punctuation, because you can see from Section One that literature work is assessed primarily on the content of what you have to say. But your English level will undoubtedly be lowered by such a problem.

There are also certain reading and writing tasks which will offer you the greatest possibilities to show off those skills which top-level candidates have, and which other candidates lack. The Statements of Attainment help you to identify what these are. It is important that you make sure that the work you submit for assessment at the end of the course does reflect that you have these particular skills. You will probably find that some pieces of work, by the nature of the task set, limit the number of skills you are able to demonstrate. For example, the script of a play set in a youth club would probably only allow you to demonstrate your ability to write in a very colloquial (chatty) manner.

Some creative assignments based on the literature you are reading will tend to focus your attention on the content of the book, rather than more complex matters like the language it is expressed in, or the issues which the book investigates. For example, assignments based on newspaper articles will do this, unless you are aware enough to show that you see more in what you have read than just a good story.

Also, if you base a wider reading assignment on a 'best seller', or something specifically aimed at the teenage market, you would have to look much harder to find Level 10 insight into the reading than if you tackled a recognised work of literary merit. If all of your coursework was like this, it would be hard to judge whether or not you had shown evidence of Level 10 performance. You need to be careful that you do not limit your own level by falling into a trap like this. On the other hand, there are some tasks which encourage you to display Level 10 qualities. These are the ones where you pull out all the stops!

One way to think of reading and writing at Level 10 is that it not only reports, or even comments, but it also analyses an issue, a piece of writing or something you have read. **Analysis** means taking something apart into the parts which make it up, describing each one of them and its purpose. Good analytical writing does exactly that. It is the kind of writing you might need if you were discussing how a play is structured by the author to hold your attention. You would need to consider what was going on in each scene in order to keep the tension of the drama going.

Sometimes the analysis is accompanied by your comments, to sum up what you have discovered. Then the writing can be described as evaluation, especially where you put two possible views or solutions to a problem alongside one another. The opposite of analysis is **synthesis**, which basically means putting the bits you have analysed back together again or comparing two things to see, as you analyse them, what they have in common. It is another kind of writing where you can really show a wide range of writing skills. You might do this when you look at another play by the same author and see whether the same kind of structure is found there.

Comparing and contrasting is a form of writing which requires both analysis and synthesis. It is not too difficult to say how the heroes of two plays do similar things but it is much harder to analyse features about each of them and compare their use by the author – with detailed examples, of course.

So, firstly, if you want to go for Level 10 then you need to think about the material you are reading and the kinds of writing task you are being set. Both have to be sufficiently demanding for you to show what you can do. Then, in producing writing at Levels 9 or 10, you will have to show that you are prepared to:

- Select an appropriate formal or literary style, knowing how your choice of style will affect your reader's response to your writing. You will be able to construct plots which are not just based on a simple chronology of events (saying what happened in the order in which it took place).

  This means: that you will be choosing the right style for writing, as well as showing that you can use it. If you write stories, for example, they must be structured in unexpected ways – using flashbacks, or writing as if you are a character in the story, or coming to an unexpected climax, etc.

- Use description as part of a narrative, for purposes like creating an atmosphere, or to reflect the mood of a character. You will also have to be able to use techniques like imagery and use the sound of words in a sophisticated manner.

  This means: that you will be using description self-consciously, knowing what effect you want to achieve. If you are writing about Dracula you may want to create the effect of a storm in the background: the crash of thunder should come through in the words you choose and the way you write.

- Write fluent formal prose where its use is appropriate.

    This means: that you will know when it is important to write formally and be able to do it accurately. In general, this is when you haven't met the person or people you are writing for, when you are writing objectively, rather than giving your own views, and when you are writing something like a report, a public letter, a set of instructions or explanations.

- Construct writing which argues a case or persuades your reader to agree with your point of view.

    This means: that you will be equally at home in tackling a controversial social issue as in arguing about the literature texts you have studied. You will be able to make a series of points, in a sensible order, and to back up each one by reference to examples and/or quotations.

- Discuss and illustrate, with evidence, the features of style and language-use belonging to something you have read.

    This means: that you will be doing the analysing and evaluating referred to earlier in this section. You will write about the particular characteristics of a piece of writing and say what their importance is.

- Understand implicit meanings in your reading.

    This means: that you will notice things which are hinted at, or referred to indirectly, or suggested in your reading which are significant to the author. 'Implicit' means concealed or hidden within. It is the opposite of 'explicit', which means obvious or on the surface.

Beating your problems

Essentially, all the skills covered in this section are the ones which separate the different levels. But remember, being able to do these things is no good at all if the work you submit for coursework assessment or your writing in the examination does not actually show evidence of your ability. You may have one problem that carries right through your work and seems to reduce all of your assessments. Problems with English can be very hard to overcome, but there are some useful strategies you can learn.

Are you a poor speller?

The Problem

Spelling mistakes can make any piece of work look worse than it really is! The spelling of English is tricky because it does not follow straightforward rules. If your general command of English is good and this is one area that really lowers your standards, then it is something you will have to cope with, not only for GCSE, but for the rest of your life. At least with national curriculum assessment, the penalty for poor spelling will be limited to the presentational aspects of your writing. In other words, you will get credit for what you can do.

The Solutions

1️⃣ There are some rules to learn which will solve a number of common spelling errors. There are plenty of books which you can buy to help you learn these and your teacher may be able to supply one. Otherwise, buy one and read it. Make lists of words of the type you know you have problems with, and learn them.

2️⃣ Always use a dictionary when you are producing a final draft of a piece of work. If you are not sure of the correct spelling of a word, look it up. You can buy special spelling dictionaries which contain only words, not definitions.

3️⃣ As you do this, compile a vocabulary book for yourself where you can keep lists of words you habitually misspell. Put into it any words your teacher marks or corrects in your writing, words you learn in school or while you are reading, and words you have checked in the dictionary. One word of warning. Do make sure they are spelled correctly. Find someone who will read through and check them from time to time. Get a friend to test you on the spellings. A trendy way to save this list is on a word processor because it can organise the words into alphabetical order for you and keep printing out updated lists.

4️⃣ In the case of really problematic (the ones you can never get right!) words, there is no substitute for looking at the correct spelling to fix it in your head, then writing it out from memory so many times that you will never forget it.

Is your punctuation terrible?

The Problem

This is another difficult area. True, there are rules about where punctuation marks should be used, but knowing the rules is not quite the same as being able to apply them in your own writing. The more complex your sentences become, the more difficult they are to punctuate. Commas and apostrophes can be very slippery creatures when you are pushing your language abilities to full stretch! The first thing to decide is whether your problem is not knowing the rules or whether you just forget them when you are working through a piece of writing.

The Solutions

1️⃣ If your basic problem is that you do not know the rules, then, again, a self-help book will be useful. Going through a piece of writing in detail with your teacher should help you to see what you do wrong. After that, it is simply a matter of practice.

2️⃣ Concentrate on your punctuation at the redrafting stage. Reading your own writing through and correcting (which usually means adding) punctuation is the best way to make accurate punctuation a habit. If you find sentence breaks (where a sentence starts or stops) difficult, and are not sure about using commas, try reading your writing aloud with exaggerated expression, as if you are on a stage or talking to a dimwitted eight-year-old! The pauses should then be obvious if your writing makes sense.

3️⃣ Take an interest in the way punctuation is used in the things you read. Compare the way different publishers punctuate direct speech (the words actually spoken) in teenage reading books. Look out for mistakes in your local newspaper.

Is your vocabulary limited?

The Problem

This is a common weakness which lowers the grade of otherwise fluent writers. The issue of choosing words appropriate to the task is bound up with the style you choose for different types of writing. If you tend to use the same basic, everyday words for every piece of writing you undertake, you are unlikely to reach a C grade. You will also run into problems when you read anything which is in any way complex. You are unlikely to be able to discuss a writer's choice of words if you don't even know what the words mean. Using a dictionary to look up the meaning of a word will be of only limited help if you are not familiar with that word in other contexts.

The Solutions

1 The only real remedy for this is a lifetime of reading. The greater your exposure to a wide variety of written language, the wider will be your understanding and use of vocabulary. Read widely from a range of books and magazines – not just those intended for a teenage audience.

2 Take an interest in unusual words. If you hear a word you are not familiar with in conversation or whilst watching television, look it up to find out how it is spelled, as well as its meaning. While you are doing that, why not have a browse through the dictionary? You may be surprised at how much this sort of interest in words can increase your vocabulary.

3 Use a thesaurus and a co-build dictionary. The thesaurus will introduce you to a whole world of words which you never knew existed and the co-build dictionary will show you how to use them.

4 When you redraft a narrative, consciously do the following:

(a) Look at each noun (the names or labels for objects and feelings). Try to change each of these for a more precise or interesting alternative. Don't use the same noun more than once in the piece of writing.

(b) See if you can change pronouns (words like 'she' and 'they') back into nouns with adjectives (the 'exotic model', the 'stumbling, exhausted animals').

(c) Make sure that each noun has at least one adjective to describe it. Add an interesting and descriptive adverb to each verb (the words which describe actions).

(d) Add a comparison to every paragraph.

Your writing will look a bit strange at first, but at the final draft stage you should edit it by cutting words to achieve the best effect. Use your thesaurus to give you ideas.

Only practice will teach you to use your new-found word power better, though. As with any new skill, you will not always get it right first time. Your teacher will always be the best person to advise about appropriate uses of new words which you are learning how to use in your writing.

Make a list here of any other areas of your English work which you think need more attention.

Your questions answered

Q Is it all right for me to use my Mum's word processor to do my coursework on? Can I use the spell checker as I work?

A Different groups have different regulations about the use of word processors and they keep updating them – generally to allow more use rather than less. It is better to check with the small print of your syllabus and to tell your teacher exactly what you want to do, but here is the essence of what is permitted.

Yes, it is fine to use the word processor for most of the pieces, but not for all of them. This is because you have to show in your coursework that you can write legibly and spell correctly, and a word processor could conceal this. For some examining groups this evidence will be supplied by your examination papers but even then it is a good idea to make sure that at least one piece is handwritten. Also, remember that you may need to show the drafts of at least one piece, so make sure that you have copies of these.

Two words of warning. Firstly, remember that the word processor will show any weaknesses in punctuation and spelling, and don't get the spacing confused so that your paragraphing is lost. Secondly, it is the quality of your writing that counts, not its attractiveness, so don't waste time messing about with a computer when you could be writing.

Q I'm certain that my teacher does not like me and he always gives me lower marks than my friends. I'm afraid that this will lower my level at the end of the course. What can I do?

A Firstly, stop worrying. Every student feels like this at some time during a two-year course. It is the teacher's job to criticise your work and there is never enough time to talk it through. Secondly, if there is a real problem, remember that your teacher is not going to be the only person to assess your coursework. The rest of the English department has to agree on the grades for the school as a whole and then the external assessor has to see a sample of folders as well. If you still feel anxious, it would be best to talk to the Head of the English Department and if he or she is the teacher in question then speak to the school Examinations Secretary, or your class tutor. Also remember that, whatever happens elsewhere, the examination is down to you!

Q I have a pronounced regional accent. Will this lead to me being awarded a lower level for Speaking and Listening?

A No. The important thing about using Standard English is that you are able to speak it when necessary. And you can speak Standard English with a local accent. For example, if some foreigners asked you for directions, could you tell them so that they would understand you? There is some argument about whether you need to be able to speak Standard English in formal situations, such as giving a speech. Doing this, you would have to avoid dialect constructions (changing the words themselves, or the word order), but it would be perfectly acceptable to speak with an accent (changing the sound of words).

Q If I am unhappy about my level, can I appeal and have my work re-marked?

A This is quite a grey area because, yes, you are entitled to appeal if you think your work has been severely marked, either as a whole or for a specific Attainment Target. This has always been allowed with examinations and, if you pay a fee, you can have your papers re-marked. But with coursework, the whole centre has to be re-marked because your grade relates to all the other grades awarded. So, if you really feel hard done by over coursework, then your best strategy is to find other students who feel the same and try to persuade the school to have all the folders checked. If everyone else is happy with their grades it is unlikely, because of how the assessment is done, that yours will be the odd one out.

Q   I am finding one of my set texts really difficult. I don't like it and that makes it hard to study. What can I do?

A   Quite a lot, but it may involve you in a lot of extra work! There is a choice of texts on every syllabus, but you would have to accept that if you change books, your teacher may not be able to give you the individual attention you might need with your new title. You could always study an extra book, which would give you more choice in the examination.

Q   I thought you could read anything for the wider reading work in my folder so I wanted to write about a book called *The Liquidator* – but my teacher said it was not suitable. What does she mean?

A   Basically, you can read what you like. Maybe your teacher did not think the book was offensive or anything like that, but was concerned that writing about it would not show your skills to the full. It is also true that if you are going for the higher grades it is worth writing about the kinds of books which are accepted as having literary value and which schools are encouraged to use. However, if you like horror stories, stand up for your rights. Read some Roald Dahl, some Edgar Allen Poe and the latest Stephen King – there'll be plenty of work to do in comparing them!

Q   My teacher says I can use the same work in my English and in my English Literature folders but my elder brother says that is not allowed. Who is right?

A   Your teacher. The regulations have changed and you can now use the same piece of work for more than one subject. So, you could photocopy a piece of writing based on a book you have read and include it for assessment both for English and for English Literature. What is more, if you have written an interesting case study in Geography or some work on primary sources in History you could include those in your English folder as well. All you have to do is to photocopy them (don't expect your school to pay for this, by the way, and make certain that the copies are clear), and they will then be marked on the standard of English in them and the way you have used language, rather than on your response to reading or your geographical knowledge.

Q   Who decides which work is chosen for assessment: me or my teacher?

A   Both of you. This is a negotiated decision and it should not be left until the last moment. By Christmas in Year 11 you should have talked about this with your teacher and you should be starting to agree about what pieces to include and what still needs to be done. If you have not done that by then, you should make it a priority. And remember that your teacher probably has a lot more experience of what the assessor will be looking for than you have, so listen hard to her advice. You may be surprised by how much your teacher wants to leave out, but remember that it is not necessary to show the same skills over and over and it is important to show the range of your reading and writing in coursework. Because coursework has to show you at your best, you may find that most of the work has been completed in Year 11.

Q   I'm proud of my coursework and I want it back. When can I have it?

A   Once the results have been published in mid-August there is normally a period when appeals can be submitted, which runs until the end of September. After that, your school should be willing to return your work and, if it has been sent to the examining group for assessment, they should ask for its return on your behalf. One or two of the groups, however, do reserve the right to retain work for various purposes.

Q   What are my parents allowed to do to help me with my coursework?

A   Just as much as your teachers are. If they nag you into turning off the television at home and being a bit neater as well, it might be no bad thing. Some people have suggested that, because parents give varying amounts of help to their children, coursework is unfair, but really that has always been the case with homework.

Q If I get a lower grade than I had hoped for, can I re-take a Key Stage 4 examination in the autumn or in the following year?

A Yes and no! Your assessment in Year 11, when you are sixteen, is a compulsory national assessment and you cannot change that. But you can take any GCSE again and get a better grade for yourself. That involves some changes to your coursework and sitting a new set of examination papers. Different groups have different regulations about exactly how much or how little of your coursework you will have to change, and there may be special forms to fill in.

Q I know that someone in my group is cheating by copying work from someone in another group. What should I do?

A Tell your parents, your English teacher or your form tutor. If this person is found out, and the chances are that they will be, then all the school's grades could be delayed or questioned and the assessor might be told to be especially strict with all of them. This is a situation which could really affect your chances and you must do something about it.

Appendix
GCSE/Key Stage 4 English Syllabuses

Exam group	Syllabus ref.	Tiering	Written coursework (20%)
SEG	English	Foundation Levels 4–5 Higher Levels 6–10	A selection to include: ● personal writing; ● response to literature (at Levels 7–10, this must include pre-twentieth century literature). The work should show evidence of these skills but they do not need to be demonstrated as separate pieces of work: ● research and information retrieval; ● drafting, redrafting, revising and proofreading; ● knowledge about language.
NEAB	English	Levels 4–5 Levels 6–10	Two, three or four pieces of written coursework giving adequate assessment of Reading and Writing. Must give emphasis to Statements of Attainment not tested in the terminal examination.
WJEC	English A similar course with a different choice of materials for mature students is now available.	Levels 4–5 Levels 6–10	Reading: Two pieces of work: ● one a study of a whole work of literature; ● one based either on a literary or on a non-literary or media text. (Above Level 7, at least one piece of work must be written, and evidence of a study of Shakespeare is expected.)

Oral coursework (20%)	Terminal examination (60%)
A record of work covering a range of oral activities is required. This must include an assessment of reading and it can include self-assessment.	Version 1 (2400P/2400M). This uses a pre-released thematic anthology sent to schools 4–8 weeks before exam. Part 1 Reading (1 hour) – unseen passage on same theme as pre-released material. Part 2 Writing (1 hour for Foundation Tier, 1 hour 30 minutes for Higher Tier) – directed writing questions on pre-released material which test reading, writing and presentation. Version 2 (2400T/2400X). This uses no pre-released material. Part 1 Reading (1 hour) – reading and response to unseen passage(s). Part 2 Writing (1 hour 15 minutes for Foundation Tier, 1 hour 45 minutes for Higher Tier) – directed writing questions on unseen material which may or may not be related to Part 1.
Teachers will assess and record oral evidence for Speaking and Listening, and Reading at suitable points in the course.	Paper 1 (2 hours) This paper assesses Reading (30%) ● Section A – an anthology of prepared texts covering a range of genres, including Shakespeare, and relating to a theme will be sent to schools for the second half of the spring term. Tiered questions will be set. ● Section B – response to unseen texts. Paper 2 (2 hours) This paper assesses Writing and Presentation (30%) ● Section A – Requires presentation of facts, ideas and opinions based on stimulus materials. ● Section B – imaginative writing in response to stimulus materials.
Must include work in: ● pairs; ● small groups; ● larger groups. Must provide evidence of achievement in: ● communicating to an audience; ● interacting with others; ● developing understanding through talk.	Tier 1: Two papers, 1 hour 30 minutes each. Tier 2: Two papers, 2 hours each. Paper 1 ● Section A (15%) Structured questions about unseen literary material, in the form of prose, poetry or drama. ● Section B (10%) Two writing tasks – one linked to reading material in Section A and one based on a wide choice of stimuli. Presentation (5%) assessed on Paper 1 as a whole.

Exam group	Syllabus ref.	Tiering	Written coursework (20%)
WJEC (cont.)			Writing: Two pieces of work in different forms, e.g. narrative or poem **and** formal letter or article or leaflet. ● Evidence of planning, drafting and editing is required.
ULEAC	English 1202 English 5202 is a similar course with a different choice of materials for mature students.	Foundation Levels 4–6 Higher Levels 6–10	The coursework is known as Paper 1. Three pieces of work are required: ● Language Unit – exploring written and spoken language. ● Literature Unit – study covers a range of genres, periods and cultures and must include pre-twentieth century works and Shakespeare. Can include personal, creative responses and candidate's own writing. ● Negotiated Unit – this must relate to Statements of Attainment and draw on individual interests and skills. Can include self-evaluation of activities.
MEG	English 1510	Standard Levels 4–6 Higher Levels 5–10	Coursework must include up to five pieces of work, at least one handwritten by the candidate, and a written record of texts studied (e.g. a reading log or diary). The folder must contain evidence of the candidate's: ● range of reading; ● study of language; ● study of whole works of literature; ● achievements in Speaking and Listening; ● redrafting and revision of writing.

Oral coursework (20%)	Terminal examination (60%)
A form showing each pupil's assessment and activities has to be available for the external moderator.	**Paper 2** ● Section A (15%) Structured questions on unseen non-literary materials (visual material may be used). ● Section B (10%) Two writing tasks – one linked to material in Section A, and in at least one of the two tasks candidates are required to write for a clearly defined audience and purpose. Presentation (5%) is assessed on Paper 2 as a whole.
Must show effective expression in a variety of oral activities. A summary of activities has to be recorded on the folder frontsheet.	Paper 2 (2 hours) Reading and Response The paper assesses Reading 20%, Writing and Presentation 10%. One or more passages will be presented, in varied styles. There will be two tasks, with the same number of marks available for each. ● Task 1 showing response/understanding of material; ● Task 2 showing a personal response. Paper 3 (2 hours) Writing This paper assesses Reading 10%, Writing and Presentation 20%. One or more passages will be presented, in a range of styles. There will be two tasks, with the same number of marks available for each: ● Task 1 personal/imaginative/expressive/poetic writing; ● Task 2 factual/transactional/informative writing.
A written record of oral activities and the teacher's assessment of them must be included in the coursework folder.	Standard Tier Paper 1 Non-literary and Media texts (2 hours) ● Section A – response to texts; ● Section B – broader response to same texts requiring sustained writing. Paper 2 Literature (2 hours) Based on pre-released material. ● Section A – questions on pre-released and unseen texts; ● Section B – imaginative and creative response to the same material. Higher Tier Paper 3 Non-literary and Media texts (2 hours) ● Section A – questions on and evaluation of texts; ● Section B – broader response to same texts requiring sustained writing. Paper 4 Literature (2 hours) Based on pre-released material. ● Section A – questions on pre-released and unseen texts; ● Section B – imaginative and creative response to the same material.

Exam group	Syllabus ref.	Tiering	Written coursework (20%)
NISEAC	English	Tier S Levels 4–8 Tier T Levels 5–10	Coursework must include two pieces of work on Reading and two pieces on Writing. One piece may combine Reading and Writing to give a total of three or four pieces of work in the folder as a whole. Work can include critical and creative responses to literature, empathic writing based on literature, personal writing and creative writing. One piece of work must be completed under teacher supervision.
SEB (Scottish Certificate of Education)	English	Foundation General Credit	The five best pieces of work produced by the candidate in Writing and Reading must be included. Drafts are not required. The work should include examples of transactional and expressive writing and two evaluations of literary texts. The work on literary texts can be provided as evidence for either reading or writing.

Note: The Scottish system of assessment at Key Stage 4 is different from that used in England, Wales and Northern Ireland. Although the same areas – Talking, Reading and Writing – are assessed, the way in which the assessment is organised is slightly different. If you are using this book in Scotland, check the details with your teacher.

Oral coursework (20%)	Terminal examination (60%)
A written record of the candidates four best performances in speaking and listening should be prepared and submitted with the folder as part of the candidate record sheet.	Tier S and Tier T Paper 1 30% (2 hours) ● Section A – 4–6 questions on a literary text. Assesses AT2 only ● Section B – Imaginative response to task, based on Section A material. Assesses AT3 only. Paper 2 30% (2 hours) ● Section A – Choice of questions on the reading and interpretation of non-literary material. One question to be answered. Assesses AT2 only. ● Section B – Choice of questions requiring functional or practical writing in response. One question to be answered. Assesses AT3 only.
Talking is assessed as either Discussion or Individual Talk. Grades are presented for an external moderator to assess. Three is no formal record.	Close Reading (50 minutes) ● A mixture of one word and short-answer questions are set for each of the three levels of assessment. At Foundation Level, there will be more one word answer questions. Writing (1 hour 15 minutes) ● The same test is set for all levels. Candidates choose one question from pictures or written titles.

GCSE/Key Stage 4 English Literature Syllabuse

Exam group	Syllabus ref.	Tiering	Written coursework (30%)
NEAB	English Literature (Revised 1992)	Levels 4–5 Levels 6–10	Three pieces of work based on Areas of Study. One piece may be an oral record. All three pieces are equally weighted. They must cover a range of texts and satisfy a range of Assessment Objectives.
MEG	English Literature 1512 and 1513 Syllabus 1512 requires the study of three set texts for the examination, while syllabus 1513 requires the study of only one.	Standard Levels 4–6 Higher	Three pieces of work must be included, based on one of the prescribed Areas of Study and relating to at least three texts. At Level 7 and above, an additional pre 20th-century work (apart from the work of Shakespeare) must be studied in either the coursework or for the examination. 1512 – One piece on poetry must be included. 1513 – Drama and poetry, including a response to the works of Shakespeare, must be included.

Areas of Study	Terminal examination (70%)

Terminal examination and coursework:
- Images of war
- People and environments
- Heroines and heroes
- Myth and symbolism
- The experience of school

A choice of ten other titles is offered for coursework only study.

Paper 1 (2 hours) 30% This is a common paper with Paper 1 of the English syllabus.
- Section A (15% – an anthology of prepared texts covering a range of genres, including Shakespeare, and relating to an Area of Study and theme will be sent to schools for the second half of the spring term. Tiered questions will be set.
- Section B (15%) – response to unseen texts.

Paper 2 (2 hours) 40% The paper contains five sections, each relating to one Area of Study. Candidates choose between two approaches:
- Alternative A (set texts) – where they answer questions on two set texts;
- Alternative B (open choice) – where they answer generic questions on two texts of their own choice.

Candidates may choose which alternative to offer on the day of the examination, and may also choose to answer generic questions on set texts.

Annotated copies of texts may be taken into the examination room.

1512
Coursework:
- Heroes, heroines and villains
- Love
- Other people, other lands

Examination:
- A – The experience of growing up
- B – Conflict

1512 Paper 1 and 2 (Standard and Higher Tiers) (2 hours 30 minutes)
- Set texts (70%). Three questions on each text – one on a selected passage, two of a more general nature. Candidates must answer three questions, one of which must be passage-based.

Annotated copies of texts may be taken into the examination room.

1513
Coursework:
- Home and abroad
- Ancient and modern
- Men and women
- Humour and horror

Examination:
- Prose fiction is compulsory for all candidates. A choice of ten book titles is offered.

1513 Paper 1 and 2 (Standard and Higher Tiers) (2 hours 30 minutes)
- Section A – Set texts (50%). Three questions on each text. Candidates must answer two questions, one of which must be passage based.
- Section B – Unseen (20%). One question on passage(s) of prose fiction.

Annotated copies of texts may be taken into the examination room.

Exam group	Syllabus ref.	Tiering	Written coursework (30%)
WJEC	English Literature	Levels 6–10 Tier 1 Levels 4–5 Tier 2 Levels 6–10	Four assignments, one of which may be oral. • Two assignments must be an appreciation of poetry (one requiring links or comparisons between poems). • One assignment must be an appreciation of prose. • One assignment must be an appreciation of drama (can include plays, television and films).
SEG	English Literature	Foundation Levels 4–5 Higher Levels 6–10	Up to three Areas of Study should be represented in the work selected, which should have a minimum length of 1500 words for the folder as a whole. Some coursework should be produced under supervision. The coursework can include some oral work, but the majority of work should be written.
ULEAC	English Literature	Levels 4–6 Levels 6–10	The coursework is known as Paper One. Based on Area of Study 1: Comparative work on texts. • Section A: Open Study – must include the related study of two whole texts and involve some independent work. • Section B: Shakespeare – work on a single play or theme, or a comparison between plays and approaches to them. Total number of words should be between 1500 and 2000.

Areas of Study	Terminal examination (70%)
Coursework ● Prose ● Drama ● Poetry Examination ● A choice of prose and drama prescribed texts	Tier 1 Paper 1 (2 hours) Tier 2 Paper 1 (2 hours 30 minutes) Assessment of prose (25%), drama (25%), poetry (20%) ● Section A and B – Candidate must answer one question on prose and one question on drama texts from a choice of two questions on each; ● Section C – Candidates must respond to unseen poetry (for Tier 2, an element of comparison is required). Candidates must take copies of the texts studied into the examination room.
There are five areas of study: ❶ Characterisation ❷ Plot and structure ❸ Setting/atmosphere ❹ Style ❺ Viewpoint Two or three Areas of Study must be covered during the course and at least two must be covered in the terminal examination.	Version 1 (2 hours 45 minutes) A paper without set texts (2495R). ● Part 1 Reading (45 minutes) – candidates read an anthology of material (common to both tiers), then questions are distributed. ● Part 2 Writing (2 hours) – candidates must answer three questions, at least one from Section A, and at least one from Section B. ● Section A – candidates write a comparison between text studied and pieces read in Part 1. ● Section B – candidates answer open-ended questions referring to course texts. Version 2 (2 hours) A paper with set texts (2495T/2495X). ● Candidates must answer three questions, one from each section (drama, poetry, prose). Copies of each text can be taken into the examination room.
There are three Areas of Study: ❶ Comparative work on texts ❷ Poetry ❸ Option A: writers and their culture; *or* Option B: a thematic study.	Paper 2 20% (1 hour 15 minutes) ● One question on unseen poetry Paper 3 50% (2 hours) Area of Study 3 ● Candidates answer two questions on either Option A or Option B. One question on specified text, one on related reading. Copies of each text can be taken into the examination room.

Exam group	Syllabus ref.	Tiering	Written coursework (30%)
NISEAC	English Literature	Tier S Levels 4–8 Tier T Levels 5–10	Three pieces of work showing evidence of the study of prose, poetry and drama and the work of Shakespeare. A teacher record of reading should show how the following areas are covered by either coursework or examination: ● literary texts including prose, poetry and drama ● media texts ● texts not specifically written for children ● texts from other cultures ● pre-twentieth century texts
SEB (The Scottish Certificate of Education)	Note: There is no separate English Literature certification available in Scotland although it might be possible for students to be entered for one of the GCSE certifications available in the rest of Great Britain.		

Areas of Study

Terminal examination (70%)

There are three areas of study: prose, poetry and drama. For prose and drama. For prose and drama there is a list of set texts, one of which must be chosen from each area. For poetry, there is a general choice of writers, or a specific focus on either Women Poets or Themes in Modern Verse.

Tier S Paper 1 20% (1 hour 45 minutes)
- Section A – unseen response to one poem.
- Section B – Two unseen texts in prose or drama. The question may focus on both of these or on only one.

Tier T Paper 1 20% (1 hour 45 minutes)
- Section A – unseen response to two poems.
- Section B – Two unseen texts in prose or drama. The question may focus on both of these or on only one.

Tier S and T Paper 2 50% (2 hours 15 minutes)
- Section A – Prose: one question from a choice of two on each set text.
- Section B – Drama: one question from a choice of two on each set text.
- Section C – Poetry: One question from a choice of five open questions, related to the writers and themes set for study.

Index